D1350915

TOLSTOY

TOLSTOY

by GEORGE RAPALL NOYES

Dover Publications, Inc., New York

B TOL
109316

G 20018762

Library of Congress Catalog Card Number: 68-17399

Manufactured in the United States of America
Dover Publications, Inc.
180 Varick Street
New York, N. Y. 10014

CONTENTS

PREFACE

The purpose of this book is to give a connected view of Tolstoy's many-sided literary work, with such facts as to his life as may serve to shed light on that work and on the personality of the man who produced it. The book does not attempt to chronicle in detail the events of Tolstoy's life, or to furnish information as to each of his minor bits of writing; it avoids digressions on the members of his family and other persons associated with him.

The materials for the volume are primarily Tolstoy's published writings, letters, and diaries. In particular, I have made much use of his correspondence with the Countess Alexandra Andréyevna Tolstoy, and of his letters to his wife, both of which books have appeared in print since the lives of Tolstoy by Biryukóv, Maude, Dole, and Rolland. For the events of Tolstoy's life I have relied mainly on Biryukóv and, for his later years, on Maude. Despite the fact that I have been at work on this volume, at irregular intervals, for a dozen years, I cannot profess to have made use of all the accessible materials. Most important, the diary of Tolstoy's early years, 1847–52, reached me too late to be of service. I do not think, however, that the materials with which I am unacquainted would modify my opinions on any vital questions. The main course of Tolstoy's life, and the development of his artistic genius and of his thought, are clear and plain; new reading supplies for the most part only fresh illustrations of what was already known.

The system of transliterating Russian names that I have adopted is, with very small variations, that recommended for "popular" use by the School of Russian Studies in the University of Liverpool. The accent of Russian names is most frequently, though by no means regularly, on the next to the last syllable; it has been indicated in this book whenever it does not fall on that syllable. In this matter I have followed the excellent precedent set by Mr. Dole. The name *Tolstoy*, however, has been left unmarked: in Russian it is accented on the last syllable; whether it should be so accented in English is a question of taste.

The translations from Tolstoy and other Russian writers given in the text are my own, with the exception of occasional passages of which the Russian originals were not accessible to me. In these cases the source of the translation is duly indicated.

Dates are given in new style, that used in all English-speaking countries. For the nineteenth century this is twelve days and for the twentieth thirteen days in advance of the Russian calendar. Thus, August 28 (Russian style), the birthday of Tolstoy, corresponds to September 9 (new style) in the nineteenth century and to September 10 in the twentieth.

My work has been made far easier by the use of Professor Wiener's wonderfully complete and accurate translation of Tolstoy's works, with its indexes and bibliographic material. For the right to use numerous quotations from copyright works I am indebted to the courtesy and kindness of the following publishers: The Century Company (*Reminiscences of Tolstoy*, by his son Count Ilyá Tolstoy); Dodd, Mead and Company (*The Life of Tolstoy*, by Aylmer Maude); Alfred A. Knopf (*The Journal of Leo Tolstoi, 1895–1899*); G. P. Putnam's Sons (*The Stewardship of Faith*, by Kirsopp Lake).

Some paragraphs of this book reproduce in essentials portions of my own articles on *Tolstoy as a Man of Letters* (in the *University of California Chronicle*, April, 1911) and *The Essential Elements in Tolstoy's Ethical System* (in *Anniversary Papers by Colleagues and Pupils of George Lyman Kittredge*, Boston, 1913). My treatment of Tolstoy's *What is Art?* is founded on suggestions from Mr. Ian Ozolin, to whom I gratefully acknowledge my debt. To my colleague, Professor G. P. Adams, and to Mr. F. A. Póstnikov I owe some suggestions as to the analysis of Tolstoy's ethical system. The footnotes acknowledge some further obligations to critics of Tolstoy.

My colleagues, Professor W. M. Hart and Mr. A. S. Kaun, have read this book in manuscript and have given me many helpful suggestions, for which I am heartily grateful to them. My greatest debt of gratitude, however, is due to my wife, who has given me invaluable aid in revising the text of the work, which without her cooperation would be far more imperfect than it is. She also assumed the very serious task of preparing the index to the volume.

TOLSTOY

TOLSTOY

CHAPTER I

INTRODUCTION

COUNT LEO TOLSTOY is the greatest and
the most many-sided figure in the literature of
Russia, and he is the representative of that
country who has been the most powerful force
in the literature of the world. Other Russian writers,
such as Pushkin and Turgenev before him, and Dostoyevsky and Gorky since his day, have won international
fame, but their popularity has been restricted, for the
most part, to professed lovers of literature. Tolstoy
was the first and only Russian to reach the great reading
public of other countries, and to become known and
loved by the average man as well as by literary experts.
During the last twenty years of his life he was the
best-known citizen of the world of thought; his portrait
and the general type of his personality were as familiar
as those of his antithesis, Prince Bismarck. When he
died in 1910 no writer remained whose fame could even
distantly be compared with his own. Works by him had

been translated into almost all civilized languages and
had been read by millions of men and women, from
academicians to peasants and factory laborers. It is
safe to say that no other author has ever attained during
his own lifetime such universal fame as Tolstoy.

Yet Tolstoy was intensely Russian in his temperament and in the most striking qualities of his genius.
His unflinching realism, the unpoetic form and the un-
romantic tone of all his work, his habitual neglect of
conventional literary technique, his hatred of all compromise, his enthusiastic adoption of a revolutionary religious and social philosophy, the spirit of universal
brotherly love that fills his works, are all qualities that,
though far from peculiar to Russia, may justly be called
national, Russian traits.

Russian by temperament, Tolstoy described in his
writings, with insignificant exceptions, only Russian
life, and furthermore those sides of Russian life with
which he was familiar by personal experience. Fortunately that experience included the classes most typical
of Russia. His works will preserve for all time a pano-
rama of Russian life from the time of the conflict of the
peasant empire with Napoleon at the beginning of the
nineteenth century to the beginnings of the industrial
revolution within it at the close of that century. His
religious and social works are quite as Russian in topic
as his novels; they derive their strength and their
weakness from the intensely personal character of the
observation of life on which they are based.

This Russian temperament was Tolstoy's rightful inheritance. His father and his mother both belonged to the highest Russian nobility. The Tolstoy family, to be sure, are said to have been descended from a German who came to Russia in the fourteenth century, but the tradition, even if true, is of no moment; the whole line has been Russian to the core. The first member of the family to attain distinction was Peter Tolstoy, a favorite of Peter the Great, who, in reward for services more brilliant than honorable, conferred on him the title of count. His great-grandson, Count Ilyá Tolstoy, was the grandfather of the novelist, who used him as a model for the elder Count Rostóv in *War and Peace.* When Count Ilyá died, leaving an estate encumbered by debt, his son Nikoláy, in order to be able to support his widowed mother, his sister, and a distant relative, Tatyana Ergolsky, who was a dependent in the family, married the wealthy but unprepossessing Princess Marya Volkonsky. The situation, naturally with some changes of detail, is reproduced in *War and Peace.* In contrast to the family of Tolstoy's father, who seem to have been plain, simple-hearted country squires, the Volkonskys were distinguished for intellectual brilliancy. Their family is descended from Rurik, the founder of the Russian empire, through the princes of Chernigov; it has been constantly prominent in Russian state affairs and in Russian court society. Of all the great Russian authors, Pushkin alone was of a social station comparable to that of Tolstoy. Nor was Tolstoy indifferent to his

origin. Aristocratic traditions and pride of race shine
forth through all his works, even through those of his
latest years, in which he preaches absolute humility and
the rejection of all social distinctions. His accents are
not those of a parvenu or a peasant prophet. One may
repeat of him what has been well said of Lucretius, that
his work "shows all the courage and energy, the power
of command, the sense of superiority and the direct
simplicity of manner emanating from it, which are the
inheritance of a great governing class."*

Leo (Lev Nikoláyevich) Tolstoy was born on September 9 (August 28, old style), 1828, at Yásnaya Polyána,
a family estate of the Volkonskys, in the province of
Tula, near the center of European Russia. He had
three brothers older than himself, Nikoláy, Sergéy, and
Dmitry, and a younger sister Marya. The Countess
Tolstoy died in 1830, in giving birth to her daughter.
Seven years later the children lost their father as
well, and were left to the care of guardians and
tutors.

Thus Leo Tolstoy grew up in a family of Russian gentry
of the purest type. Among such people could be found
whatever was good in Russian traditions and culture.
The society of which they formed a part was not unlike
that of the aristocratic families in the southern states
of our own country before the Civil War. A class of
wealthy landowners was supported by the labor of

---

* Sellar:—*The Roman Poets of the Augustan Age: Virgil* (Oxford,
1877), p. 203.

serfs, who cultivated the broad acres extending around the ancestral manor, and with whom their relations were on the whole kindly and patriarchal. In the manor the owners led a life of free, open-handed hospitality. For them country life consisted partly of work, in the superintendence of their estates, partly of sport, in hunting game with hounds. Those of them who were at all prosperous spent only the summer at their manors; the winter they passed at their city residences in St. Petersburg or Moscow, leading a society life of parties, theaters, and dinners such as is the common portion of the dwellers in all European capitals. Since no gentleman could engage in commerce or industry without a certain loss of caste, and since even professional life was not in favor, these nobles could choose no occupation except service under the government, and a career in the army was reckoned more honorable than one in the civil service. In either case, through his social connections, each man of fair talent was assured of a prosperous career.

Such is the society that Tolstoy describes in his novels, not departing from it until his religious conversion gave him new interests and new points of view. The world of *Childhood, Boyhood, and Youth; War and Peace;* and *Anna Karenin,* is composed of wealthy, idle aristocrats and toiling peasants. The city is a great amusement park, in which the only workers, if we except coachmen and domestic servants, are the holders of government positions. Other laborers there may be, but they have not yet attracted Tolstoy's attention. In *Anna Karenin* he shows his distinct dislike of the whole merchant class. In the country, on the other hand, the humbler folk come to their own; the huntsmen with whom Nikoláy Rostóv lies in wait for wolves, the reapers beside whom Levin toils in the hay field, are beings with a definite character, men whom Tolstoy has known and loved.

Such a social order will in every country produce the same results. On the one hand are courtesy, kindliness, refinement of the truest sort, coupled with an abiding faith in the excellence of the conditions that have fostered this same refinement and high breeding. On the reverse of the medal are drunkenness, lechery, and a callous indifference to the sufferings of persons less fortunate by birth. In such an environment individuality may develop unchecked; there is no dull gray level of democratic uniformity. Many men may degenerate into rakes or servile courtiers; a few may become thinkers, originators of new ideas, preachers of new moral doctrines.

In the case of Tolstoy the checks upon the development of individuality were even fewer than with most young Russian nobles. Until the age of sixteen he was educated at home by private tutors, and was thus free from that constant contact with comrades of his own age and station which in an English or American school trims away personal eccentricities and accustoms a boy to cooperation with his fellows. His personality was molded only by association with his relatives and with their aristocratic friends.

Tolstoy's temperament in boyhood was passionate, jealous, vain, but affectionate, impressionable, aspiring, and truth-seeking; truth-telling also, to himself if not always to others. He worked intermittently, as the fit came upon him; neither then nor at any later time would he persevere in a task that proved uncongenial. From his tutors he acquired little systematic book-learning; but from them, and from practice in society, he gained a fine command of French and German. He prided himself particularly on the elegance of his French, the mark in Russia of a polished gentleman. Later in life he became well acquainted with English.

Tolstoy's youthful years were outwardly neither striking nor edifying. In 1844 he entered the University of Kazán, being enrolled first in the Division of Arabo-Turkish Literature and later in the Faculty of Law. He did no studying of consequence and became filled with an intense and lasting disgust for the formal requirements of the university, its methods of instruction, and its influence on the students. These ideas he sets forth in an article on *Education and Culture*, published in 1862. The following quotation will show its general tone:

Almost always, from the point of view of the students, the lectures are a mere formality, indispensable only in view of the examination. The majority of the students during their stay at the university, do not study the prescribed subjects, but others, the program of which is determined by some club that they happen to join . . . . . Here all is prescribed not in accordance with its real value, but in proportion to the severity with which it is forbidden by the authorities. I have seen in students' rooms heaps of manuscript volumes beyond comparison larger than the entire requirements of the four years' course, and among them thick copybooks of the most disgusting poems of Pushkin and the most stupid and colorless poems of Ryleyev. Another favorite occupation consists of meetings and discussions about the most various and important topics; such as the restoration of the independence of Little Russia, the spread of literacy among the peasantry, or the playing of some cooperative trick on a professor or inspector . . . . . All this is sometimes ridiculous, but is often attractive, touching, and poetic, as idle young men often are.

Tolstoy did become interested, however, in a dissertation upon the influence of Montesquieu on the legislation of Catherine II. Of this he writes: "It opened to me a new field of independent intellectual work, but the University with its requirements not only did not contribute to such work, but hindered it."* Thus his newly awakened intellectual enthusiasm was one cause of his abandoning the University of Kazán in 1847, without completing his course.

In the year after leaving Kazán, Tolstoy went to St. Petersburg, where, after wavering betwéen an impulse to enter the army and a desire to complete his university course, he attempted to take the graduation examinations at the University of St. Petersburg. After a

* Biryukóv: I, 131.

week's cramming, he passed in civil and criminal law.
"Then all my good resolutions went to pieces. Spring
came, and the charm of country life drew me back to
my estate."* The next three years were perhaps the
least admirable in his life. They were spent partly at
Yásnaya Polyána, where he started a school for the
peasants and made futile efforts to organize his estate
on philanthropic principles such as he later described in
A Morning of a Landed Proprietor (1856), partly in society life in Moscow. Despite ideal aspirations and
an attempt to do good to his peasants, his outward
existence was much the same as that of other wealthy
young Russians; he drank, was loose in his conduct
with women, gambled and involved himself in debt.
But he was ill at ease, and eager to escape from the
temptations of a purposeless life. When, in April, 1851,
his brother Nikoláy, who had been serving as an officer
in the Caucasus, returned home on a furlough, he seized
the opportunity to accompany him on his return to the
army. There he was presented to Prince Baryátinsky,
the commander in chief, who, observing his conduct
during an expedition against the mountaineers, com-
plimented him on his bravery and urged him to join the
service. Accordingly, early in 1852 he became a yunker,
or volunteer officer. The next two years, up to the
outbreak of the war between Russia and Turkey, he
spent mainly in the Cossack villages of Starogládkovskaya
and Stary Yurt, leading a life such as he described

* Biryukóv: I, 152.

later in *The Cossacks*. The Russians were engaged in guerilla warfare with tribes of mountaineers who had never submitted to the imperial authority. They were slowly pressing upon them, destroying their villages and above all felling the forests that shielded them from attack. Between these expeditions the officers had ample time for hunting and for sport of all sorts with the Cossack borderers among whom they were quartered.

The real biography of Tolstoy in these years that led up to his first literary work is found in his intellectual and spiritual life, which is revealed to us with sufficient clearness in his letters and in his diary. Here we see the moral aspirations that were to give depth to his fiction and to find full expression in the didactic works of his later years. Of this period he later wrote in his *Confession:*

My only real faith at that time was faith in self-perfection. But in what self-perfection consisted and what was the aim of it I could not have said. I tried to perfect myself intellectually —I studied everything that I could and everything with which life brought me in contact; I tried to perfect my will—I composed rules for myself that I tried to follow; I perfected myself physically, developing my strength and agility by all sorts of exercises and training myself to endurance and patience by all sorts of privations. And all this I regarded as self-perfection. The beginning of all was, of course, moral perfection, but that was soon replaced by perfection in general, that is, by the desire to be better not with regard to myself or with regard to God, but by the desire to be better with regard to other men. And very soon this striving to be better with regard to men was replaced by a desire to be stronger than other men; that is,

more famous, more important, richer than others.—[Ch. 1.
Compare pp. 205-8, 158, below.]

Quite in accord with this is the following passage from
his diary, written at about the time of his leaving the
University of Kazán:

The aim of life is a conscious striving for the development on
all sides of everything that exists.

The aim of my life in the country for the next two years is:
(1) To master the whole course of the legal sciences necessary for the final examinations at the University. (2) To
master practical medicine and a portion of theoretic medicine.
(3) To master the French, Russian, German, English, Italian,
and Latin languages. (4) To learn agriculture, both theoreti-
cally and practically. (5) To learn history, geography, and
statistics. (6) To learn mathematics, the gymnasium course.
(7) To write a dissertation. (8) To reach a higher degree
of perfection in music and painting. (9) To write rules for
myself. (10) To gain some knowledge of the natural sciences.
(11) To write treatises on all the subjects that I shall study.—
[Biryukóv: I, 145.]

Milton himself was not more ambitious in his plans
for self-improvement! Tolstoy was ultimately to rise
on stepping-stones of his dead self to higher things,
but for a time his movement seemed downward rather
than upward. The unregenerate animal often prevailed.
Only a year later, after his fiasco at St. Petersburg, he
wrote to his brother:

Serezha, I think that you are already saying that I am "an
absolutely worthless fellow," and you are telling the truth.

Lord knows what things I have done! I went to St. Petersburg without any reason whatever, and I did nothing useful there; merely squandered heaps of money and got into debt.—[Biryukóv: I, 154.]

This union of high aspiration with an irregular and sordid outward existence is of course peculiar to no age or nation, but it is certainly more common among the dreamy and emotional Russians than among our own well-disciplined and practical folk. Life in America tends towards a consistent dead level of Philistine respectability, above which it is dangerous to aspire. One must be as moral as society demands and as outwardly successful as is possible within the limits of that morality. Standards in Russia are more elastic, granting to all classes of society an easy charity such as we extend only to Bohemian artists. So long as a man is an agreeable companion and observes a conventional code of honor, his private life is his own concern. The looseness of standards that results from this point of view shocks a traveler of Puritan antecedents. On the other hand fine impulses of kindliness and unselfishness, generous enthusiasms of all sorts, play a larger part in the Russian nature than in our own.

In his serious groping after a moral law by which to guide his life Leo Tolstoy was not alone in his family. His sister Marya became a nun in her later years. His brother Dmitry, after leading almost an ascetic life, suddenly degenerated into debauchery; then, in a characteristic access of nobility, he ransomed from a brothel the first woman he had known and kept her with him until his death. His career is reflected in that of Nikoláy Levin in *Anna Karenin*.

Tolstoy's struggles with himself at this period were not religious in the narrower sense. In his *Confession* he writes:

After the age of sixteen I ceased to kneel in prayer and of my own accord ceased to go to church and to prepare for the sacrament. I did not believe in what had been taught me from my childhood, but I did believe in something. In what I believed I should have been absolutely unable to say. I even believed in God, or rather I did not deny God—but in what God I should not have been able to say. Neither did I deny Christ and his teaching, but in what his teaching consisted I should also have been unable to say.— [Ch. 1.]

This agrees with what is known of him from other sources. In a letter to his "Aunt Tatyana," written January 18, 1852, he told her, with no apparent sense of incongruity, how he had made a fervent prayer to God to extricate him from a gambling debt—a prayer heard and answered by a benevolent deity. His kinswoman the Countess Alexandra Tolstoy remarks of him as he appeared in 1857: "At that time he was by no means an opponent of the church; and, seeing us all preparing for confession, he started to do so himself—in which, however, he did not succeed."* As to the future

* *Correspondence with the Countess A. A. Tolstoy*, p. 6.

life he wrote to this same kinswoman in 1859, referring to his stay in the Caucasus:

That was both a torturing and a good period of my life . . . . All that I discovered then will forever remain my conviction . . . . . From two years of mental toil I found out a simple, old thing, but one which I know as no one else does—I found out that immortality exists, that love exists, and that one must live for others in order to be eternally happy.*

Yet in the next year, writing to the same correspondent, he denies any faith in immortality: "It seems to me that it is impossible to believe in that sincerely; it would be too good!" † In general, not even the most fundamental dogmas ever occupied Tolstoy's mind so much as questions of practical morality.

Tolstoy's choice of reading during this formative period gives clear indications of his personal character, of his intellectual convictions, and of certain features of his artistic genius. The books which he states had "immense" influence on him were: the Sermon on the Mount in the Gospel of Matthew, Rousseau's *Confessions* and *Émile*, and Dickens's *David Copperfield;* those that had "very great" influence were Sterne's *Sentimental Journey*, Rousseau's *Nouvelle Héloïse*, Pushkin's *Eugene Onegin*, Schiller's *Robbers*, Gogol's *Dead Souls*, Turgenev's *Sportsman's Sketches*, Grigorovich's *Antón Goremyka*, and Lérmontov's *Hero of our Time;* while some of Gogol's short stories and Prescott's

---

* *Correspondence with the Countess A. A. Tolstoy,* p. 131.
† *Ibid.*, p. 142.

Conquest of Mexico had "great" influence. It is noteworthy that in this list the Sermon on the Mount stands
at the very top. The precepts of brotherly love, of universal forgiveness, of non-resistance to evil, were already
dear to Tolstoy's heart. They constituted his ideal
all through his life, however much his conduct may have
fallen short of them.

Next to the Gospel Tolstoy places the work of Rousseau, which was perhaps even more potent in molding
his ideas. Of Rousseau he once said:

Men have been unjust to Rousseau, the grandeur of his
thought has not been recognized, he has been slandered in all
sorts of ways. I have read all Rousseau, all the twenty volumes,
including the *Dictionary of Music.* I was more than delighted
with him; I adored him. At the age of fifteen I wore around my
neck, instead of the customary cross, a medallion with his
portrait. Many of his pages are so near to me that it seems to
me that I wrote them myself.—[Biryukóv: I, 269, 270.]

This statement is fundamental for any understanding
of Tolstoy. One must then inquire what were the aspects
of Rousseau's genius that most appealed to him. One may
place first of all Rousseau's hatred of artificiality, pretence, and convention; his praise of whatever is natural.
With this doctrine Tolstoy was sympathetic by temperament; it underlies every page of his own writing
from the very beginning of his work. To it he was not
always true in practice: vanity was a sin against which

he constantly struggled, and in *Youth* he satirizes his own eagerness to comply with the most petty conventions of society dress. Not less in accord with his mode of thought was Rousseau's praise of the country and his hatred of the city. For Tolstoy the country was the place of wholesome work and pure enjoyment, the city was that of perverted pleasure. Finally, Rousseau's panegyric on home life in *La Nouvelle Héloïse* appealed to Tolstoy's deepest convictions; delight in home life breathes from every page of *Childhood*, and is the ruling passion of *War and Peace* and *Anna Karenin*.

The fact that the *Confessions* and *Émile* are singled out as having been of "immense" influence is significant. The absolute frankness of the *Confessions* (whether real or apparent need not be discussed here) harmonized with Tolstoy's aspirations and doubtless affected his own literary methods. Unlike other narrators of their own development, Rousseau does not confine himself to the nobler sides of his own character or to his winning and attractive human failings; to his sins he lends no air of romance; he tells candidly of base, ignoble deeds, of cowardice, ingratitude, and deceit. This method of self-revelation Tolstoy brought to perfection in his novels. We like his heroes despite their creator's frankness rather than because of it.

In *Émile*, his treatise on education, Rousseau makes his guiding principle the unfolding and developing of the natural powers, free from the corrupting influence of society. "A truly natural man desires to do only

what is within his power, and does what is pleasing to
him." Books are set aside until a comparatively late
period; true education is derived from experience and
from intercourse with one's fellows. Furthermore, a
democratic ideal pervades the book; the rich young
aristocrat Émile is made to associate familiarly with his
peasant neighbors, and has to learn a trade, as a pre-
caution against possible loss of wealth. To each of these
principles Tolstoy eagerly responded. That he had an
early interest in the problems of education is shown by
his abortive experiment of 1849; when he later took up
in earnest the trade of schoolmaster he worked in the
spirit of Rousseau.

With Rousseau's attack on civilization as the cause
of more evil than good Tolstoy came to have ever greater
sympathy as his years advanced. A long list could be
made of minor doctrines of Rousseau with which he
was in agreement, such for example as his dislike of
medicine and doctors and his abhorrence of the evils
worked on peasants by taxation. Most important,
Tolstoy, brought up on Rousseau, remained an intui-
tionist and an emotionalist all his life. He never acquired any admiration for the methods of experimental
science as applied to the study of human society. In
this respect he was a man of the eighteenth century.

Even Rousseau's sentimentality was at this period of
his life not uncongenial to Tolstoy, as is shown sufficiently
by the fact that he coupled Sterne's *Sentimental Journey*
with *La Nouvelle Héloïse* at the head of the books that

had "very great" influence on him. The fact is at first surprising. Rousseau was half an invalid, dreamy, morbid, a recluse and a hypochondriac; Tolstoy was strong, healthy, fond of society, a lover of energetic physical life. His doctrine that "calm is spiritual baseness"* is at the other pole from the sentimental languor of Rousseau. He had, however, a constant tendency to self-analysis, and a keen delight in the minute record of his own sensations, traits which are prominent throughout his work, though they never lead to the sickly, hot-house sentimentality that makes *La Nouvelle Héloïse* so unpalatable to modern readers. At times he was prone to tears. To this weakness he refers when in a letter of 1852 he calls himself "Cry-baby Leo."† But his sobs were bursts of grief interspersed amid active play or work, very unlike the plaintive wail of Rousseau. This side of his nature he seems to have partially suppressed with advancing years; his son Ilyá speaks of his aversion for outward manifestations of feeling.‡ Yet the same witness tells how his father once sobbed with emotion during a talk with him.§

In this list of reading works of fiction have rather a subordinate place, and those actually mentioned apparently interested Tolstoy by their undying ideas rather than by their excellence of style and literary form. In *David Copperfield*, if one may hazard a con-

---

* *Correspondence with Countess A. A. Tolstoy*, p. 94.
† Biryukóv: I, 189.   ‡ See p. 138, below.
§ Count Ilyá Tolstoy: *Reminiscences of Tolstoy*, p. 319.

jecture, he was attracted by the touching picture of child life in the earlier chapters and by the adulation of the home that runs through the novel, rather than by the melodramatic plot.   Tolstoy never ceased to regard Dickens as the greatest of English authors, remarking that "Gogol resembled him in humor, but had not his broad humane sympathies."* Throughout his life, though he corrected his own works with great care, Tolstoy was almost indifferent to questions of formal style and literary technique.   Of criticism he wrote nothing until after his religious conversion, and then only as a sort of corollary to his religious system.   In his early writings one may find the ideas and the frankness of his idol Rousseau, but very few traces of the literary technique of either Rousseau or Dickens or Sterne.

In a word, Tolstoy, great literary genius though he was, was mercifully free from what we commonly term the literary temperament;   he cared for the substance of life more than he did for its reflection in literature; and in literature he cared for the content more than for the form.   There is no record that he ever read a single poem with pure delight in the melodious sound of the lines.   One of his companions at the university records how he "spoke ironically of verse in general."†   In later years he expressed himself similarly:

In the days of Pushkin and Lérmontov there used to be poetry, but not now.   Verses have gone out of fashion.   And

* Maude: II, 645.   † Biryukóv: I, 126.

what's the good of them? You will agree that prose expresses our thoughts much better—it is easier to read and has more sense in it. Take our conversation, for instance: we say what we want to. But if some one tried to put it into verse, it would come out all upside-down. Wherever a definite, clear expression is wanted, it either spoils the rhythm, or doesn't suit the style: and one has to substitute some other word, often far from the real meaning.—[Quoted by Maude, II, 518; compare p. 347, below.]

The poets, the verse-makers torture their tongues in order to be able to say every possible kind of thought in every possible variety of word and to be able to form from all these words something which resembles a thought. Such exercise can only be indulged in by unserious people. And so it is. —[*Journal*, Feb. 4, 1897; tr. Strunsky, p. 119.]

He himself wrote no verse whatever, if we except some jesting lines on incidents at Sevastopol and similar doggerel composed for the family letter box, an epistle to his friend Fet, and a very few serious lines. He gained a new conception of Pushkin's genius from reading Mérimée's prose version of *The Gypsies*.*

Of painting Tolstoy was fond, but it was not one of his main interests. The art that affected him most strongly was music, to which he was passionately devoted. And of this in his later years he came to have a certain dread, since it aroused his emotional nature without teaching a clear moral lesson.†

Thus one is not surprised to find as a boy Tolstoy made no experiments in literary composition. His

* Biryukóv: I, 246, 299.   † Compare p. 348, below.

art waited until he had experience on which to base his work. His first plans of authorship were formed in 1850, when he thought of writing a story of gypsy life and also an imitation of Sterne's *Sentimental Journey*. Two years later, during his residence in the Caucasus, he set to work in earnest, and at the age of twenty-three he produced a masterpiece in his semi-autobiographical tale, *Childhood*.

CHAPTER II

I N July, 1852, Tolstoy finished his story, *Childhood*, and sent it to the *Contemporary*, then the leading literary journal in Russia, edited by the poet Nekrasov. The work was at once accepted and was printed in the same year, signed only with the initials L. N. Nekrasov himself did not know the real name of the author until he had approved the manuscript. He wrote to Tolstoy, sending him praises but no money, explaining in a second letter that it was not usual to pay writers for their first work, but that in the future he should be glad to receive further contributions from him, and would pay him fifty rubles per printed sheet of sixteen pages, the price received by the best authors. He added that the tale had been well received by the public.

Childhood is an unpretentious narrative of life in a Russian well-to-do family. A growing boy records his impressions of the events and persons around him. In 1853 and 1854 Tolstoy continued the story with *Boyhood*, and in 1856 with *Youth*, after which he abandoned the work, which still remains a torso. The three parts have essentially the same literary qualities and already show the distinguishing marks of Tolstoy's genius. The book is genuinely original, though the form may have been suggested by the *Family Chronicle* of Aksakov. Perhaps *David Copperfield* gave an impulse to the story of child life, and possibly a suggestion for the carousal scene in *Youth*. The author himself acknowledges the strong influence of Sterne and Töpffer (see p. 36), but probably exaggerates its importance.

In this book, as in others that were to follow, Tolstoy paid no heed to plot; the story delights us by the charm of single incidents and scenes. And these incidents, and the characters who take part in them, were with few exceptions drawn from the author's personal experience. No author was more loth to depart from the material of actual life than was Tolstoy, no one was more absolutely a realist in the most literal sense of the term. Thus the kindly German tutor Karl Mauer, the repulsive French tutor St.-Jerome, the French governess Mimi and her daughter, the trusty housekeeper Natalya Sávishna, were all drawn from persons familiar to Tolstoy in his childhood. The narrator, Nikoláy Irtenyev, is naturally, in large measure, a reproduction of the boy Tolstoy; another character, Dmitry Nekhlyudov, also has autobiographic traits. But the book is a spiritual, not a literal autobiography; events are altered and personalities transposed so that the book is not a mere narrative

of happenings in the Tolstoy family. Just as Wordsworth employed in his poetry "a selection of language
really used by men," so Tolstoy built his fiction from a
selection of the experiences of average humanity. And in
Tolstoy as in Wordsworth "the feeling developed gives
importance to the action and situation, and not the action
and situation to the feeling."

In *Childhood, Boyhood, and Youth* one sees already
the two sides of Tolstoy's nature, which run parallel
all through his life, sometimes in sharp conflict with
each other; on the one hand his eager enjoyment of
animal life, his delight in his own physical health and
in the charm of the external world, and on the other
his introspective, brooding temperament, ever seeking
for a moral system by which he may guide his conduct.
The first finds expression in his genius for observation,
in his unique power of selecting just those concrete details that will give the reader the most vivid impression
of the scene described; the second makes itself felt
in his analysis of mental states, his passion for
sincerity, and his ever-present interest in moral
problems.

The descriptions of nature in this early work already
bear witness to that bubbling delight in outdoor life,
to that joy in communion with the life of the universe,
which found its fullest expression in *War and Peace*.
Tolstoy does not see with the eye of a painter; he has
small interest in what is picturesque, or, in a conventional
sense of the word, beautiful. He rather describes the

influence of an outdoor scene on a lad's inarticulate sense
of physical well-being:

Sometimes, rather often in fact, I got up early. (I slept in
the open air on the porch, and the bright, slanting rays of the
morning sun would awaken me.) I dressed quickly, took a
towel under my arm and a volume of a French novel, and went
to bathe in the river in the shade of a birch wood about a half-
mile from the house. There I lay down on the grass in the
shade and read, occasionally tearing away my eyes from
the book to glance at the surface of the river, which showed
purple in the shadow and was beginning to be rippled by the
morning breeze, at the field of yellowing rye on the opposite
bank, at the bright-red morning light of the sun's rays, tingeing
ever lower and lower the white trunks of the birch trees,
which, hiding one behind the other, retreated from me into
the depths of the dense forest; and I enjoyed the consciousness
within myself of just such fresh young strength of life as
breathed everywhere from the nature around me. When in
the sky there were gray morning cloudlets and I was chilled
after my bath, I would often leave the path and set to wander-
ing through the fields and woods, and with a feeling of delight
would wet my feet through my boots in the fresh dew. Meanwhile I dreamed vividly of the heroes of the last novel that I
had read, and imagined myself now a general, now a minister
of state, now a man of extraordinary strength, now a passionate man, and with a sort of trembling I looked ceaselessly
around in the hope of suddenly meeting *her* somewhere in a
glade or behind a tree.—[*Youth*, ch. 32.]

Here, as always, Tolstoy is interested in life itself and
not in the pictures that can be made of it.

But men and women are the usual subjects of Tolstoy's description. By an unerring instinct, in picturing a scene Tolstoy selects its most suggestive features. The traits that appeal to him are apparently obvious, so that the personality of the writer remains unnoticed behind his work. One example of many is the account of how the half-witted religious mendicant Grisha prepares for his night's rest, watched by the boys who have stolen upstairs before him:

After praying and setting his staff in the corner he looked over his bed and began to undress. Ungirding his old black belt, he slowly took off his torn nankeen frock, carefully folded it and hung it on the back of a chair. His face now did not express haste and stupidity, as it usually did; on the contrary, he was calm, reflective, and even majestic. His motions were slow and thoughtful.

When he had stripped himself to his underclothes, he slowly let himself down on the bed, made the sign of the cross over it from all sides, and, evidently with an effort (because he frowned), he adjusted the chains under his shirt. After sitting a short time and carefully looking over his underclothes, which were torn in some places, he rose, raised the candle with a prayer to the level of the shrine, in which there were a few images, crossed himself before them and turned the candle wick down. It sputtered and went out.

Through the windows that faced the forest shone the moon, now almost full. The tall white figure of the mendicant was lit up on one side by its pale, silvery beams; on the other it cast a black shadow, which fell, along with the shadows from the window frames, upon the floor and walls and reached to the ceiling. In the yard the watchman was beating on his brass plate.

Folding his immense arms on his breast, dropping his head, and uttering repeated heavy sighs, Grisha stood silently before the holy images, then with an effort dropped to his knees and began to pray.—[*Childhood*, ch. 12.]

There is here little or no attempt at picturesqueness; the details are such as might impress a lad crouching in the dark. But they are so selected as to give a striking impression of reality. Nor do they cease with this; they make us understand the perfect sincerity and the unaffected piety of the pilgrim. One is not surprised when a moment later Tolstoy exclaims in admiration:

O great Christian Grisha! Thy faith was so strong that thou didst feel the nearness of God; thy love so mighty that the words flowed of themselves from thy lips—thou didst not test them by reason . . . . . And what high praise didst thou offer to His might, when, finding no words, thou didst prostrate thyself on the floor in tears.

At a later period Tolstoy would have been content to let his picture tell its own story, without enforcing its moral, or at all events would have combined his comments with the picture instead of making them a separate passage.

Observation of detail is blended with a boyish shrewdness when little Nikólenka comments on his father's behavior at the funeral of his wife; external acts, quite innocent in themselves, are made to express the vain and shallow character of the man:

His tall figure in a black dress coat, his pale, expressive face, and his movements, graceful and self-confident as ever, when he crossed himself, bowed down and touched the floor with his hand, took a candle from the hands of the priest, or approached the coffin, were extraordinarily effective; but, I do not know why, I disliked in him just that power of seeming so effective at that moment.—[*Childhood*, ch. 27.]

Running parallel with this emphasis on external reality is a constant analysis of the narrator's passing thoughts and feelings. This analysis avoids great emotions, such as love, hatred, and ambition, and lingers over minor sensations, such as crowd upon each of us at every moment of our lives. Hence comes the disconcerting realism of the impression. Tolstoy reveals to each reader the petty thoughts and emotions that he has himself experienced, but which he has thought were his peculiar property, unknown to all outsiders. Nikólenka is standing by his mother's coffin, bowed by the deepest grief of his boy's life. Yet he tells us less of this great sorrow than of the different cross currents of feeling that incessantly crowd upon him:

During the service I wept decently, crossed myself, and bowed down to the floor, but I did not pray with my soul, and I was rather indifferent; I was troubled because the little new dress coat that they had made me wear was very tight under the arms, I was careful not to soil over much the knees of my trousers, and I stealthily made observations on all who were present.—[*Childhood*, ch. 27.]

Here we have that distrust of the grand style in dealing with emotion that will remain with Tolstoy all his life. He could not describe himself as overwhelmed by grief without departing from truth, a truth that every reader will confirm by his own experience. And to desert truth, to be insincere, is contrary to Tolstoy's nature.

Tolstoy, we may remark in passing, may have been affected by a paragraph in his belovèd Rousseau:

Plutarch excels by the very details into which we no longer dare to enter. He has an inimitable, charming art of painting great men in little things; and he is so happy in the choice of his traits that often a word, a smile, a gesture suffices him for the characterization of his hero. With a jesting word Hannibal reassures his frightened army and makes it march laughing to the battle that delivered Italy into his hands. Agesilaus, riding astride a stick, makes me love the conqueror of the great king. Caesar, while passing through a poor village and chatting with his friends, unconsciously reveals the knave who said that he wished to be merely the equal of Pompey. Alexander swallows a medicine without saying a single word; it is the most beautiful moment of his life . . . . . There is the true art of painting. One's physiognomy is not shown in his main features, nor one's character in great actions; one's true nature shows itself in trifles. Public acts are either too common or too affected, and yet it is only on them that our modern dignity permits our authors to linger.—[*Émile*, book IV.]

Sincerity was indeed Tolstoy's idol. A trifling incident in the tale illustrates his worship of it. On grandmother's name-day each of the children is supposed to come to her with his congratulations and some small gift. Nikólenka decides that, like his tutor Karl Mauer, he will write a poem in honor of his grandmother. His doggerel ends with the lines:

> We'll never trouble—do not fear;
> We love you like our mother dear.
>
> [*Childhood*, ch. 16.]

The last verse, despite the fact that it rimed correctly, distressed its small author:

Why did I write, "like our mother dear"? She was not here, and so I ought not even to have mentioned her. To be sure, I love grandmother and respect her, but still she is not the same.—Why did I write that? Why did I lie? To be sure, those are verses, but still I ought not to have done so.

This passage gives a foretaste of the thinker who, as we have seen, later condemned all metrical composition as involving a sacrifice of truth, and who came to reject beauty as an essential element in art.

As the tale advances and Nikólenka becomes a university student, his meditations on life's problems grow more and more important. A chapter on *Dreams* tells of his aspirations for moral purity and perfection:

"Today I shall confess and purify myself of all my sins," I thought, "and I shall no longer—" (Here I called to mind all the sins that most tortured me.) "Every Sunday I shall go to church without fail, and later I shall read the Gospel for a whole hour; then out of the twenty-five ruble note that I shall receive monthly when I enter the university I shall invariably give two and a half (a tithe) to the poor, and in such a way that nobody will know of it—and not to beggars either; I will look up poor people, an orphan or an old woman, of whom no one knows."—[*Youth*, ch. 3.]

These resolves are set down with a full consciousness that they are mawkish and calfish. Crude and immature though they be, they are sincere, not a pose assumed before the world in obedience to others' precepts. Despite continual stumbling and faltering, Tolstoy is striving to follow a moral ideal. With a prophetic voice he adds:

Let no one reproach me with the fact that the dreams of my youth were just as infantile as the dreams of my childhood and boyhood. I am convinced that if I am fated to live to extreme old age, and my tale overtakes my years, as an old man of seventy I shall indulge in the same impossible, childish dreams as now. . . .

Beneficent, consoling voice, which since then so often, in those sad times when my soul silently submitted to the power of life's lies and corruption, hast boldly revolted against all untruth, hast bitterly reproached the past, hast pointed out and forced me to love the bright point of the present, and hast promised good and happiness in the future—beneficent, consoling voice! Wilt thou ever cease to be heard?

These resolves and aspirations are unaffected by any definite religious beliefs. Tolstoy is interested only in

the life here on earth. Though he is not quite an ag-
nostic, he shows in this book no active acceptance even
of so vague a creed as that of his beloved Rousseau, who
prescribed faith in an all-wise and all-beneficent deity
and in a future state of rewards and punishments.
Perhaps for this reason, he emphasizes far less his remorse for the past than his aspirations for the future.
Except in his last years, Tolstoy was not given to brooding over past sins; the Calvinistic atmosphere of *The
Scarlet Letter* is wholly alien to his spirit, as it is to
that of the whole Russian people.* From this calm
indifference to dogma Tolstoy never really departed;
though he ultimately reached a faith in a temporal life
after death he remained indifferent to speculations as
to its nature. Of Natalya Sávishna he here remarks:
"She performed the best and greatest act of this life—
she died without regret and fear."† Though death
never ceased to be a controlling motive in his thought,
Tolstoy at last found other acts better and greater than
"a death without regret and fear."

A somber tone runs through even this youthful work.
The boy narrator sees clearly the frailties of his father
and brother, of his stepmother, of his university comrades, of the high society in Moscow to which he belongs.
To this world one may apply what he wrote at about the
same time in *Sevastopol in May, 1855:*

---

* Stephen Graham, in *The Way of Martha and the Way of Mary*,
pp. 155-160, comments excellently on this national trait.
† *Childhood*, ch. 28.

Vanity, vanity, vanity everywhere, even on the brink of the grave and among men ready to die in behalf of lofty convictions. Vanity! This must be the characteristic trait and peculiar malady of our age. Why among men of former days was there nothing heard of this passion, as of the smallpox or the cholera? Why in our age are there only three sorts of men: some who accept the principle of vanity as a fact inevitably existing and therefore just, and who freely submit to it; others who accept it as an unfortunate but insurmountable condition; and still others who with unconscious servility act under its influence? Why did the Homers and Shakespeares speak of love, glory, and sufferings, while the literature of our time is only an endless tale of Snobs and vanity?—[Ch. 3.]

This emphasis on pretence and conceit, whether conscious or unconscious, at times gives to the book a cynical tone that suggests *Vanity Fair*. But there is a fundamental difference. Thackeray plays the part of a showman, glorifying in the cleverness with which he detects the frailty of the puppets whom he moves across his stage; Tolstoy is a part of the vain world that he is describing, and emphasizes his own vanities quite as much as those of his fellows. His most incisive satire on petty social failings is his account of his own efforts to be in every way *comme il faut*.

Yet vanity is not quite an all-pervading element in Tolstoy's characters. To his mother Nikólenka never attributes it; the little boy's love for her will not allow him to see any defects that she may possess. Nor does vanity affect the humbler people of the story, such as the housekeeper Natalya Sávishna and the half-witted

mendicant Grisha. These persons act from no desire
to be seen of men; Natalya Sávishna husbands the
master's sugar and Grisha, clad in clanking chains, prays
to God, from an inborn moral sense. In a word, the
tone of the book is democratic; the true moral life is
found only among men and women of low estate.

Later in his life Tolstoy condemned this early work as
insincere and affected. His judgment is so remarkable
that it must be quoted entire:

I have re-read them [*Childhood, Boyhood, and Youth*] and
regret that I wrote them; so ill, artificially and insincerely are
they penned. It could not be otherwise: first, because what
I aimed at was not to write my own history but that of the
friends of my youth, and this produced an awkward mixture
of the facts of their and my own childhood; and secondly, because at the time I wrote it I was far from being independent
in my way of expressing myself, being strongly influenced by
two writers: Sterne (his *Sentimental Journey*) and Töpffer
(his *Bibliothèque de Mon Oncle*).

I am now specially dissatisfied with the two last parts,
Boyhood and *Youth*, in which besides an awkward mixture of
truth and invention, there is also insincerity; a desire to put
forward as good and important what I did not then consider
good and important, namely, my democratic tendency.—
[Quoted by Maude: I, 160.]

This harsh verdict is by no means just. An aristocrat
by breeding, Tolstoy always wavered between caste
prejudice and the rejection of it. The democratic sympathies of his early book are like its austere moralizing,

not insincere, but an ideal which the author could not realize in his daily life and to which even his affections could not be constant.

It is noteworthy that in his literary work Tolstoy speaks almost invariably from his best self; not as a prig, but as a man of fervent moral aspirations, for whom conduct is nine tenths of life. Only rarely does he express the unregenerate side of his nature. In *The Two Hussars* (1856) he shows a frank preference for an energetic, vigorous rake over his cool, business-like son; to wrong-doing that springs from animal strength or from easy-going kindliness he is always charitable, while for calculating selfishness he has an unfailing contempt. His scorn of the student carousal in *Youth* is due to the fact that it was undertaken in mere obedience to fashion. Only in two tales, *An Idyl*, and *Tikhon and Malanya*,* which he himself suppressed, but which have appeared in his posthumous works, does he show a cynical point of view. This high seriousness of Tolstoy's artistic work is at the other pole from hypocrisy. Mr. Sellar has admirably stated the true explanation:

Differing infinitely, as they may do, from one another in powers of self-control and obedience to their higher instincts, the greatest poets and artists have one quality in common— absolute sincerity of nature. They give the world of their strongest and best, not because they wish to be thought other than they are, but because it is their strongest and best self which alone deeply interests them and demands expres-

* Neither has been translated into English, so far as the writer is aware,

sion.—[*The Roman Poets of the Augustan Age: Virgil* (Oxford, 1877), p. 94.]

While Tolstoy was serving in the Caucasus important events had been taking place in Europe. In November, 1853, Russia had declared war on Turkey, and the Russians immediately began an invasion of the Danube principalities. Early in the next year Tolstoy received his commission as an officer in the army, went home for a short furlough, and joined the Russian forces in Bucharest in March, 1854. When they were forced to retreat he asked to be sent to the Crimea, where he arrived in November and was assigned to the artillery service. The siege of Sevastopol by the French and English began in October of that year and continued until September, 1855. Tolstoy served throughout the siege in various positions. During April and May, 1855, he was at intervals in charge of the battery on the Fourth Bastion, one of the most dangerous positions in the fortress. From here he was transferred to Belbék, fourteen miles from Sevastopol, in consequence, it is said, of the personal instructions of the Emperor Alexander II, who had been so impressed by the reading of *Sevastopol in December, 1854*, that he gave order to take care of the author and remove him from the place of danger.* His promotion in the service was hindered by some doggerel verses for the composition of which he was partially responsible, and probably also by the

* Biryukóv: I, 259,

displeasure of his superiors at his meticulous honesty in regard to the government money.* At the conclusion of the siege he was sent to St. Petersburg as a courier and never returned to the army, from which he formally retired in November, 1856.

The literary result of Tolstoy's experience of the great siege was three sketches published under the title, *Sevastopol in December, 1854, and in May and August, 1855.* The first of these, composed soon after his arrival in the beleaguered fortress, is marked by a patriotic enthusiasm strongly at variance with his later convictions, but which may be seen to be genuine, not a literary pose, from its agreement with the author's private letters written at this same time. "The spirit of our armies is above all description," he wrote to his brother on December 2, 1854. "In the days of ancient Greece there was never such heroism." Yet even in the first sketch Tolstoy is impressed by the quiet, unassuming courage with which the Russian army endures hardships, not by its aggressive bravery. In the next sketch the atmosphere has changed. Petty vanity Tolstoy now finds to be the master passion of the Russian officers in the field, as of their brothers at home:

Kalugin and the Colonel would have been ready every day to see just such an affair in order each time to receive a gold saber and the rank of major-general, notwithstanding the fact that they were fine fellows. I like to hear people give the

* His attitude is reflected in *Sevastopol in August, 1855*, ch. 18.

name of monster to some conqueror or other, who destroys millions for the sake of his own ambition. But demand a frank confession from Ensign Petrushov, Sub-Lieutenant Antonov and their comrades: every one of us is a little Napoleon, a little monster, and is ready to start a battle at once, to slay a hundred men, merely in order to receive an extra decoration or a third more salary.—[*Sevastopol in May, 1855*, ch. 15.]

In the third sketch the patriotic tone in a measure returns. Speaking generally, one has to exercise some care in the interpretation of these works from this point of view. The censor seriously mangled the second of them, perhaps the others also, before publication; and Tolstoy himself later confessed "that, contending with his desire to tell the truth about things as he saw it, he was at the same time aware of another feeling prompting him to say what was expected of him."*

Though the literary characteristics of *Sevastopol* are, when analyzed, the same as those of *Childhood*, the book made a far stronger impression because of the tremendous appeal of its subject. Tolstoy saw war as suffering and death, unrelieved by any touch of brilliancy or grandeur, and he selected just the right detail to convey his impression:

Now, if your nerves are strong, enter the door at the left; in that room they bandage wounds and perform operations. You will see there doctors with arms covered with blood up to their elbows and with pale, gloomy faces, busy around a

* Maude: I, 134.

bed on which, with eyes open and speaking, as if in delirium, disconnected but often simple and touching words, lies a wounded man under the influence of chloroform. The doctors are occupied with the horrible but beneficent act of amputation. You will see how the sharp, curved knife enters the white, healthy body; you will see how with an awful, piercing cry and with curses the wounded man suddenly comes to his senses; you will see how the surgeon tosses into the corner the severed arm; you will see how on a stretcher in the same room there lies another wounded man, who, gazing at the operation performed on his companion, writhes and groans, not so much from physical pain as from the moral torments of expectation. You will see awful sights that rend your soul; you will see war, not in regular, beautiful, and brilliant ranks, with music and the beating of drums, with waving banners and generals on prancing steeds—you will see war in its true expression, in blood, in sufferings, in death.—[*Sevastopol in December, 1854*, ch. 1.]

Tolstoy agrees with General Sherman that "war is hell." Yet he does not revel in descriptions of carnage and cruelty; his atmosphere is not that of the romantic Sienkiewicz. The force of the book depends on its reserve, on the sense of restraint and self-mastery that makes every word ring true.

In *Sevastopol* the psychological analysis characteristic of Tolstoy's first published work passes to a somewhat broader field. No longer checked by an autobiographic form, Tolstoy tells of the thoughts and feelings of different officers who fight and die for their country. One remarks the same trait as before, the absence of

great, controlling passions, such as patriotic enthusiasm
and self-sacrifice. Ambition there is, but of a petty
sort. Tolstoy does not shrink from portraying the
sensations of an officer during his last moments; the
man is petty even in death:

Praskukhin, closing his eyes tight, heard how the bomb
plumped down on the hard ground somewhere very near him.
A second passed, which seemed an hour—the bomb had not
burst. Praskukhin was afraid lest he might have played the
coward for nothing; perhaps the bomb had fallen far away,
and it only seemed to him that the fuse was hissing just beside him. He opened his eyes and noticed with pleasure that
Mikhaylov was lying motionless on the earth right near his
feet. But here his eyes encountered for a moment the glowing
fuse of the bomb, which was spinning around less than a yard
away from him.

Horror, cold horror, which excluded all other thoughts and
feelings, seized his whole being. He covered his face with his
hands.

A second more passed, a second in which a whole world of
feelings, thoughts, hopes, and memories flashed through his
imagination.

"Whom will it kill, me or Mikhaylov? or both of us together? And if me, then where? If it's in the head, then
I'm done for; but if it's in the leg, then they'll cut it off and
I'll ask 'em to be sure to use chloroform—and I may still sur-
vive. But perhaps it will kill only Mikhaylov—then I will
tell how we were walking together, how he was killed and I was
spattered with his blood. No, it's nearer to me; it will be I."

Then he remembered the twelve rubles that he owed
Mikhaylov, and he remembered still another debt in St.

Petersburg, which he ought to have paid long ago; the gypsy air that he had sung the evening before came into his head. The woman whom he loved appeared before his imagination, wearing a cap with purple ribbons; he remembered a man who had insulted him five years before and whom he had not paid back for the insult, although at the same time, inseparable from this and from thousands of other recollections, the feeling of the present, the expectation of death, did not for a moment abandon him.—[*Sevastopol in May, 1855*, ch. 12.]

Military heroism plays small part in these pages. Officers show their indifference to danger by walking upright along the shallow trenches; but, when they feel themselves free from observation, they are glad to crawl on all fours. Even deeds of valor are performed half unconsciously, by a blind following of the crowd in a night sally.

From the ever-present vanity of the officers the common soldiers are exempt. In war as in peace these men of humbler station do their work willingly and unassumingly. Submitting to destiny, without thought of their personal life, by their very submission they are the only true heroes:

"Really, there seem to be altogether too many men returning," said Galtsin, stopping again the same tall soldier with the two muskets. "What are you coming this way for? Hey, you, halt!"

The soldier halted and took off his hat with his left hand.

"Where are you going and why?" Galtsin shouted at him sternly. "You scoun—"

But meanwhile he had come up close to the soldier and had noticed that no hand could be seen behind his right cuff and that the sleeve was soaked with blood to a point above the elbow.

"Wounded, your honor!"

"How?"

"Here, most likely with a bullet," said the soldier, pointing to his arm. "But I can't tell what struck my head." And, bending forward his head, he showed the hair matted together with blood on the back of his neck.

"And whose is the second gun?"

"A French musket, your honor! I captured it. But I shouldn't have left, if it weren't to help this little fellow; otherwise he'd fall," he added, pointing to a soldier walking a little in front of him, who was leaning on his gun and painfully dragging along his left leg.

Prince Galtsin suddenly felt frightfully ashamed of his unjust suspicions. He felt himself blushing, and, without asking further questions of the wounded or watching them, he walked to the field hospital.—[*Sevastopol in May, 1855*, ch. 7.]

In the third part of his work, *Sevastopol in August, 1855*, however, Tolstoy definitely changes his tone, no longer emphasizing the vanity of the officers, but showing us in the brothers Kozeltsóv two men who are animated by self-sacrificing gallantry and devotion to their country.

In *Sevastopol*, just as in his previous work, *Childhood*, sincerity is the keynote of Tolstoy's writing, and truth is his divinity:

There, this time I have said what I wished to say. But a painful hesitation overcomes me. Perhaps I ought not to have said this; perhaps what I have said is one of those evil truths, which, unconsciously concealed in the soul of each man, ought not to be expressed, in order not to become harmful, like the dregs of wine, which must not be shaken, in order not to spoil it.

Where is the expression of evil, which must be avoided? Where in this tale is the expression of good, which must be imitated? Who is its villain and who its hero? All are good and all are bad.

Neither Kalugin with his brilliant bravery—*bravoure de gentilhomme*—and the vanity that animates his every act, nor Praskukhin, an empty, harmless fellow, though he fell in combat for faith, throne, and fatherland, nor Mikhaylov with his shyness, nor Pest, a child without firm convictions and rules of action, can be either the villain or the hero of the tale.

The hero of my tale, whom I love with all the strength of my soul, whom I have tried to reproduce in all his beauty, and who always has been, is, and will be beautiful—is the truth.— [*Sevastopol in May, 1855*, ch. 16.]

No hatred of French or English is seen in these sketches even among the officers, still less among the private soldiers, who fraternize in the most friendly fashion with their French opponents, whose language they do not understand.

Sevastopol treats of a great war, involving important issues of European politics, and of movements of large armies, involving carefully planned mass action. In all this Tolstoy shows no interest whatever. He is occupied with the individual officer and soldier, with his life as determined by the crushing, revolting circumstances in which he is placed; into the cause of those circumstances he does not inquire. For Tolstoy in a certain sense each man liveth unto himself and dieth unto himself; the private moral life is man's sole concern. He exclaims in sadness:

Yes, on the bastion and in the trench white flags are raised, the flowery valley is filled with dead bodies, the fair sun descends towards the blue sea, and the blue sea, rippling, glitters in the golden beams of the sun. Thousands of men crowd about, gaze, talk, and smile to one another. And will not these men, Christians who profess the one great law of love and self-sacrifice, when they gaze on what they have done, fall suddenly on their knees in repentance before Him who, when He gave them life, implanted in the soul of each man, along with the fear of death, the love for the good and the beautiful; and will they not embrace like brothers? The white flags are lowered, again the engines of death and suffering whistle, again innocent blood is shed and groans and curses are heard.— [*Sevastopol in May, 1855*, ch. 16.]

This passage testifies to the fundamentally religious nature of the gay young officer who was "the soul of his battery,"* and who at times could sink to coarse dissipation. An entry in Tolstoy's diary in March, 1855, speaks even more clearly of his inner life:

A conversation about divinity and faith has led to a great, stupendous thought, to the realization of which I feel myself capable of consecrating my life. This thought is the foundation of a new religion, corresponding to the development of

* Quoted by Biryukóv: I, 256.

humanity, the religion of Christ purified of faith and mystery, a practical religion, not promising future blessedness, but giving blessedness on earth. This thought can be realized, I understand, only by generations consciously working towards that aim. One generation will bequeath this thought to the following, and at some time fanaticism or reason will realize it. To act *consciously* towards the uniting of men by religion, that is the foundation of the thought which, I hope, will draw me on.—[Biryukóv: I, 250.]

No man had previously written of war in such style as Tolstoy. To be sure, Tolstoy himself, with his frequent exaggeration when speaking of his debt to others, has said that he learned from Stendhal's *Chartreuse de Parme* all that he knew of war.* The picture of the perplexed Fabrice, full of Napoleonic enthusiasm, riding over the battlefield of Waterloo and totally failing to understand what is happening all about him, is indeed somewhat in the vein of Tolstoy, but is far more pale and vague. Despite what he may have learned from such a predecessor, Tolstoy is in *Sevastopol* even more independent than in *Childhood*. Other writers, from Homer to Scott, had taken the point of view of the slayer, or perhaps that of the slain man's wife and comrades; Tolstoy dwells on the feelings of the man who is being killed, whether swiftly on the field of battle, or by a lingering death in the hospital, or by still slower tortures in a besieged town, awaiting his turn in the trenches. This book alone would suffice

* Quoted by Biryukóv: I, 270.

to establish its author's fame. Its effect on Russian public opinion has been considerable. War has come to be regarded in Russia, perhaps more than elsewhere, as blood, suffering, and death, rather than as a glorious field of heroic combat. Russians no longer write of war in the tone of their romantic poets, Pushkin and Lérmontov. Men of talent, such as Garshin and Andreyev, have followed in the footsteps of Tolstoy, but without equaling his quiet mastery of reserve force. Andreyev in *The Red Laugh*, though he uses a hundred-fold more lurid tints than Tolstoy, succeeds in making war grotesque rather than terrible.

Nor has Tolstoy's influence been confined to his own country. When we read his book today, fresh from the stories of the European war as related by the newspaper correspondents and the wounded combatants, it seems far less unique than it did at the time of its first appearance. A change has indeed come over the whole style of the descriptions of war, and among those responsible for that change no single man was of more influence than Leo Tolstoy.

Meanwhile Tolstoy's life in the Caucasus had apparently passed without direct reflection in his work, except for some short sketches such as *The Incursion* (1852). In reality he had as early as 1852 begun a story based on his life there,* and in particular on his passing infatuation for a Cossack girl. This he took up

---

* See note by Chertkóv in *The Diaries of Leo Tolstoy: Youth, 1847–52* (New York, 1917), p. 115.

once more in 1860,* and in 1862, in order to satisfy
a gambling debt to the editor Katkóv, he gave him the
book, still unfinished. Owing to the unpleasant memories
connected with the novel, which was published under
the title *The Cossacks*, he never brought it to completion.

The Cossacks is Tolstoy's first attempt at a novel with
a regular plot. Olenin, a young Russian tired of civilized
life in Moscow, enters military service with the troops
stationed on the Caucasus frontier, among the Grebensky
Cossacks. He lodges at the house of an old ensign,
whose daughter Maryana straightway attracts his attention. Introspective and self-conscious, Olenin cannot
flirt and frolic with the peasant girls as does his thought-
less comrade Beletsky. He meditates becoming a
Cossack, marrying Maryana, and abandoning all connection with his old life. Maryana, though attached to
the bold young Cossack Lukashka, seems for a time
to encourage his attentions. Then Lukashka is killed
in a combat with some Circassian raiders. When Olenin
attempts to approach Maryana with words of tenderness,
she drives him from her in a burst of fury and contempt.
Defeated and dejected, Olenin returns home.

No book could be more utterly unheroic and un-
romantic. Yet Tolstoy had been living amid the most
splendid mountain scenery, and amid the same wild,
half-savage life that had inspired Pushkin and Lérmontov to their most typically romantic poems. Push-

* Biryukóv: I, 354.

kin, in fact, had in his *Prisoner of the Caucasus* written a work that is the exact converse of Tolstoy's. A gloomy, disenchanted young Russian officer is captured by the Circassians. A fair Circassian maiden solaces his imprisonment and proffers him her love, but he replies that the springs of tender feeling are quenched within him. Thereupon the maiden brings a file, sets the somber hero free, and, once he is safe across the boundary stream, drowns herself in its depths.

The contrast between these two works is impressive. Pushkin sketches for us two vague, shadowy beings, who owe their existence largely to the poems of Byron; Tolstoy draws a man and woman who are perfectly real and concrete. His Olenin, though no coward, is far from brilliant and dashing; once when he is surprised at nighttime listening by Maryana's window he becomes actually ludicrous: in a word, he is Tolstoy himself, with all his doubts and perplexities, stumblings and failures. Maryana, though chaste and pure, is far from ethereal; she is a good hand at shoveling dung, and is not averse to being kissed by her lover or, on occasion, by others as well. In contrast to Pushkin's eloquent and poetic heroine, she is monosyllabic of speech; when embarrassed, she is given to hiding her face behind her broad sleeve.

In drawing his background, Tolstoy seems absolutely to avoid the descriptions of magnificent landscape in which Pushkin revels, even when they are almost forced upon him by his subject. At the opening of the story, without mentioning a single detail of the mountain scenery, he tells of the overwhelming impression that the first view of it made on the soul of his hero:

It was an absolutely clear morning. Suddenly he saw, about twenty paces from him, as it seemed to him at the first moment, the pure white masses with their delicate contours, and the fantastic, distinct, airy line of their summits and of the distant sky. And when he came to understand the great distance between him and the mountains and the sky, the whole immensity of the mountains; and when he began to feel all the infinity of this beauty, he became alarmed lest it might be a phantom, a dream. He shook himself, in order to wake up. The mountains were still the same.

"What is that? What is it?" he asked of the driver.

"The mountains," the Nogáy answered with indifference....

Owing to the quick movement of the troika along the even road, the mountains seemed to be running along the horizon, their rosy peaks glittering in the rising sun. At first the mountains only surprised Olenin, then they made him joyful; but later, by gazing more and more at this chain of snowy mountains which rose and fled away, not from other, black mountains, but directly from the plain, he gradually began to penetrate into this beauty and to *feel* the mountains. From that moment, all that he saw, all that he thought, all that he felt, assumed for him the novel, sternly majestic character of the mountains.—[Ch. 3.]

But, like other high emotion, the influence of the mountains seems to have been transitory. After this chapter they and their grandeur disappear from view. The Terek is not the fierce, angry stream of Lérmontov's ballad, swollen by the melting snows of spring, but a watercourse dwindling beneath the summer heat, which horsemen can ford. Olenin goes hunting in the woods and is persecuted by the mosquitoes. Life in the Caucasus is like life elsewhere, full of petty discomforts, but made dignified by moral striving. And Olenin amid clouds of mosquitoes becomes absorbed in meditations on moral problems.

The greatest artistic merit in the story is found in the picture of the Cossack community. These men are drunken, deceitful, lustful, cruel, but withal natural, unconscious, self-respecting human animals. Uncle Eroshka is a part of the woods through which he guides Olenin. Lukashka is free as a wolf from thought, and from romantic exaggeration of his own skill, when he shoots the Circassian who is stealthily swimming the stream. With such a community the self-conscious Olenin cannot blend. Tolstoy contrasts him with it so that he seems neither inferior nor superior, but just different. Our sympathies go out both to him and to Maryana.

As for Maryana, she is the first young girl whom Tolstoy introduces into his writings. He wisely does not attempt to analyze her thoughts and feelings, but lets us infer them from her outward life. The following passage shows her at her best; its absolute simplicity and directness place it at the height of Tolstoy's art:

Maryana, after eating her dinner, gave some grass to the bulls, rolled up her half-coat under her head, and lay down beneath the cart on the succulent, crushed grass. She wore only a red silk kerchief on her head, and a faded blue chintz shirt, but she felt unbearably hot. Her face glowed, her legs moved restlessly, her eyes were covered with the moisture of sleep and weariness; her lips opened involuntarily and her breast heaved high and heavily.

The working season had begun two weeks before, and hard, uninterrupted work filled the whole life of the young girl. In the early morning twilight she jumped up, washed her face with cold water, fastened on her kerchief, and ran barefoot to the cattle. She hastily put on her shoes and her half-coat, and, tying some bread in a bundle, harnessed the bulls, and rode off to the vineyards for the whole day. There she rested only for an hour; she cut the grapes and carried the baskets, and in the evening, merry and not tired, leading the bulls by a cord and urging them on with a long switch, she returned to the village. After housing the cattle in the twilight, catching up some sunflower seeds in the wide sleeve of her shirt, she went out to the corner to have a laugh with the girls. But as soon as the light faded she was on her way to the house; and, after eating her supper in the dark shed with her father, mother, and little brother, she went into the house, carefree and healthy, took her seat on the oven, and, half-dozing, listened to the talk of the lodger. As soon as he left, she threw herself on her bed and slept till morning a sound, calm sleep. The next day it was the same.—[Ch. 29.]

CHAPTER III

LIFE AND WORK, 1855–62

THE years immediately following the Crimean war were a time of political discussion in Russia such as had never before been known. The icy oppression of Nicholas I had passed away and new forces were beginning to be felt in the nation. Defeat in war had shown the weakness of the country and the need of internal reforms. The greatest of these reforms was to be the emancipation of the peasantry, the great body of the Russian people, who up to this time had been serfs, the property of the landed nobility, bought and sold like cattle. Once the yoke of serfdom was cast aside, it was felt that Russia would breathe new life. Four schools of political thought had made their appearance, which may fairly be termed political parties, though we must not attach to the term any such definite associations as in England and America.

The first school, the Official Nationalists, were the upholders of the existing order. In their eyes Russia was a peculiar nation: its *autocracy* represented a state order infinitely superior to the constitutional governments of

the west, with their continual parliamentary disputes;
its *orthodoxy*, embodied in the state church, preserved
the true principle of primitive Christian love, in opposition both to the stiff hierarchy of Catholicism, which
erected the church into a rival state, and to the jangling,
rationalistic sects of Protestantism; and its *nationality*,
the simple, patriarchal organization of the people, was
an ideal social order. To the Nationalists were opposed
the second school, the Liberals, whose watchwords were
progress and freedom of thought, and whose ideal
of state organization was contemporary England or the
United States, with their respect for individual liberty
and their guarantees of freedom of speech, of the press,
of conscience. To organized religion they were opposed,
and personally most of them were sceptics and free
thinkers. Their membership was mainly recruited
from the minor nobility of Russia. The third group,
the Socialists, who at this time were still a very small
party, accepted the political program of the Liberals,
but found it inadequate; to political freedom they would
add economic equality. Finally, the fourth school, the
Slavophiles, who were rather a philosophic sect than a
political party, agreed with the Official Nationalists in
regarding the Russians as an elect and a peculiar people,
and accepted the Nationalist trinity of *autocracy*,
orthodoxy, and *nationality*, though their interpretation of
these principles was often radically opposed to that of
the Nationalists; they joined with the Liberals in their
admiration of freedom of thought; they were not neces-

sarily opposed even to the Socialists. Their distinguishing idea was that Russia could progress only by developing its native institutions, not by imitating western Europe. Slavic culture must evolve independently of Germanic or Latin traditions; Russia should take the lead in a new epoch of human history. After 1870 they came to maintain that Russia should place itself at the head of a federation of Slavic nations, of which the capital was to be Constantinople. In opposition to the Liberals, they were animated by religious enthusiasm. Against the Nationalists, the other three parties were united in support of the emancipation movement.

Tolstoy, an individualist to the marrow of his bones, never belonged to any party; but, as time advanced, he developed a stronger dislike for the Liberals, with some of whose leaders he had formerly been temporarily associated, than for any other group. Their emphasis on progress and on public activity proved alien to his spirit. With the Nationalists he was associated by family traditions and by sentimental loyalty to the tsar. Some of his own ideas, as that of the inborn excellence of the Russian common people, coincided with those of the Slavophiles. With the Socialists, who were parvenus and sceptics even more than the Liberals, he had no connections. Yet in his later years, after his religious conversion, he developed points of contact with them at least on the negative side, in his destructive criticism of existing society.

When Tolstoy arrived in St. Petersburg in November, 1855, he naturally became associated with the circle of authors writing for the *Contemporary*, in which his own works had been published. This journal, founded in 1836 by Pushkin, had since 1847 been under the direction of Panayev and the poet Nekrasov, who had made it the chief literary force in Russia, and, above all, the main organ of Russian liberal thought. Among its contributors were Turgenev, Goncharóv, and Grigorovich, the leading novelists of their time, and the dramatist Ostrovsky.

Literature in Russia at this period occupied a far different position from that which it now holds in America or England. It appealed to a very small portion of the nation, for the peasantry was almost entirely illiterate, and the trading classes were impervious to intellectual influences. On the other hand, such a journal as the *Contemporary* had much more powerful influence upon its readers than any one American or English periodical to which it can be compared. Direct discussion of public questions was practically impossible under the rigid censorship of the press that prevailed in Russia. Public opinion was molded by social discussion, and, in an indirect fashion, by the influence of poetry, fiction, and criticism. Even the most arbitrary censor could hardly prohibit an article on *Eugene Onegin* simply because it touched on the social import of the characters drawn by Pushkin. And no writer of stories could describe truthfully any phase of Russian life without at least seeming to pass judgment on it, whether favorable or unfavorable. Once his story was in print it was read hardly less for instruction than for amusement; the "tendencies" of the tale were discussed, and they affected the popular verdict quite as much as did its esthetic merits. Oftentimes tendencies were discovered of which the authors had been profoundly unconscious, or which were even quite contrary to their own fixed opinions. Thus Gogol (1809-52), the great founder of Russian realism, by his satiric portrayal of corrupt Russian officials in *The Inspector-General*, and of stupid landed gentry in *Dead Souls*, had made himself the idol of the Russian Liberals. Later, when Gogol made a direct confession of his faith, he proved to be a defender of the autocracy, the Orthodox Church, and even serfdom itself, which he praised as a divinely ordained institution. His popularity at once vanished. Yet he had not been insincere in his earlier writings; his critics had read into them meanings that the author had never intended.

One may form some conception of the situation if he imagines all free discussion of the problem of capital and labor checked in America, and the public dependent for enlightenment on the works of such novelists as Mr. Herrick and Mr. Churchill, and even ready to interpret Mark Twain and O. Henry from a sociological point of view.

Naturally enough, Russian authors were apt to take themselves very seriously and to pose as teachers of profound truths in politics as well as in personal morals and in art. The *Contemporary* group were united by common liberal principles, though not by a definite political platform; in particular they had an ardent interest in the emancipation movement, in the spread of education in Russia, and in the greater participation of the Russian people in the government of their country. Though they were of various ranks in society, from the wealthy aristocrat Turgenev to the plebeian Chernyshevsky, they were united in opposition to the conservatism of the landed gentry whose prosperity depended on the maintenance of serfdom.

With this group Tolstoy could never be in perfect harmony. He was of higher social station than any of them, and probably looked down upon them as middle-class scribblers. A lady who was intimate with the whole *Contemporary* circle writes of him at this time: "Count Tolstoy was not a timid person, and was aware of the strength of his own talent; and for that reason, as it then seemed to me, he assumed an affectedly free and easy manner."* To say nothing of an inborn spirit of contradiction, which made long cooperation with any body of men difficult for him, Tolstoy, unlike his associates, was little interested in politics. His problems were of the individual life; vague aspirations for the good of humanity, which might accompany a corrupt and dissolute private life, he regarded with contempt. His account of this period of his life in his *Confession* may then be readily understood:

Our mission was to teach men. . . . . I was an artist and a poet [that is, a creative writer], and I wrote and taught, without knowing what I taught.

* Biryukóv: I, 278.

This faith in the significance of poetry and in the development of life was a religion, and I was one of the priests of it. To be a priest of it was very pleasant and profitable. And I lived for rather a long time in this religion, not doubting its truth. But in the second and in particular in the third year of such a life I began to doubt the infallibility of this religion and to inquire into it. My first occasion for doubt was that I began to observe that the priests of this religion were not all in agreement among themselves. Some said, "We are the best and most useful teachers; we teach what is necessary and the others teach incorrectly." But others said, "No, We are the genuine men, and you teach incorrectly." And they disputed, quarreled, wrangled, deceived and cheated one another. Besides this there were many men among us who did not even care who was right and who was wrong, but who simply pursued their own selfish aims with the aid of this activity of ours. All this made me doubt the truth of our religion.

Besides this, when I came to doubt the truth of our writers' religion, I began more attentively to observe the priests of it, and I became convinced that almost all the priests of this faith, the writers, were immoral men, and, for the most part, a poor sort of men, insignificant in character, and much inferior to the men whom I had met in my previous dissipated life, and in my military career, but that they were self-confident and self-satisfied as only men can be who are either absolute saints or who do not know what sanctity is. These men became repugnant to me, and I became repugnant to myself, and I came to understand that this religion was a deception.—[Ch. 2.]

Tolstoy, ever prone to suspect insincerity in others, was unjust to men who united high aspirations with imperfect performance in a way that was really not wholly

unlike his own. But quiet, weak-willed literary men
and professors were never attractive to his passionate
temperament. After 1858 he made no contributions to
the *Contemporary*. His literary work during 1856, when
he was most thoroughly affiliated with this circle, had
been scanty; it consisted only of *Youth, Two Hussars,*
and two short tales, *The Snowstorm* and *A Morning of
a Landed Proprietor*. His growing discontent with
his associates is reflected in an entry in his diary in 1857:
"My stumbling-block is the vanity of liberalism."*
He never again became affiliated with a literary group.

Shortly after his return from Sevastopol occurred
the first serious love affair in Tolstoy's life. As a child
he had had a passion for one Sónichka Kaloshin, which
is presumably reflected in an episode in *Childhood*.
Later came his passing infatuation with a Cossack girl,
to say nothing of boyish dreams of two young women
who scarcely knew of his affection for them.† Now, on
his return from the army, where he had been entirely
deprived of women's society, he looked forward eagerly
to family life, of which he was passionately fond. His
attention was attracted to the pretty daughter of a
neighboring landowner, a girl apparently much younger
than himself, who readily accepted his attentions. Biryukóv, who is the sole source of information as to this
episode, conceals her identity under the initials V. A.
Tolstoy's feeling for her can never have been strong or

* Biryukóv: I, 328.
† Cf. *Diaries: Youth, 1847-52*, pp. 106-11.

unselfish. Soon after the beginning of their acquaintance
V. A. went to Moscow to attend the festivities connected
with the coronation of Alexander II, September 7, 1856.
She frankly enjoyed the gayety and was not displeased
by the admiration of various young men. Tolstoy
thereupon wrote her a series of instructive letters, setting
forth the duties and responsibilities that awaited her as
his wife. Though not even correspondence of this sort
could quench the girl's affection, Tolstoy found that he
was himself growing constantly cooler towards her. In
February, 1857, he left Russia for the west, and from
Paris he sent to his former sweetheart a letter in which
he spoke of their intimacy as a thing of the past. His
conduct towards her had not been above reproach; in
a letter to his aunt he wrote: "As for V., I never loved
her truly, but I let myself be drawn into the wicked
pleasure of inspiring love, which afforded me such joy
as I had never before experienced."* When Tolstoy in
Anna Karenin (part I, ch. 16) wrote of Vronsky's conduct towards Kitty, he was doubtless thinking of his own
youthful experience. Marriage, as we know from one
of his later aphorisms,† he regarded as an engagement
into which a man should not enter lightly, but only
when led to it by an irresistible force.

From this experience Tolstoy drew the suggestion for
his charming story *Family Happiness* (published in
April, 1859), which represents his life with V. A. not as it

* Biryukóv: I, 310.
† *Thoughts on God:* Wiener's translation; XVI, 419.

was but as it might have been. Here for the first time
he gives an analytic treatment of a woman's character.
A girl of seventeen tells of her courtship by a man of
thirty-four and of their marriage; she relates how they
drifted apart owing to her passion for society frivolity
and her husband's absorption in his work and his own
thoughts, and how they later came to understand
each other—and lived happily ever afterwards. The
tale has wonderful freshness and poetic charm. The
portrait of the man is delightful, with his clumsy kindliness, his sincere friendship for the girl whom he has
watched develop from childhood, and his joy when he
perceives that after all she may sometime be able to
love him otherwise than as an affectionate old friend.
The girl, with her genuine sweetness and faithfulness,
combined with an eagerness for admiration that arouses
her husband's jealousy, is even more appealing. This
is a true love story, that of a courtship that does not
cease with marriage.

During this period of his life Tolstoy was restless, not
settling permanently in one place. His first trip abroad
was made apparently partly for mere amusement, partly
as an escape from his unfortunate love affair. He
reached Paris in February, 1857, and spent some time
with Turgenev. On April 6 he made a striking entry
in his diary:

Got up about seven and went to see an execution. The
stout, white, healthy neck and breast; kissed the Gospel and
then—death. What a senseless thing! A strong impression,

which did not pass in vain. I am not a political man. Morals and art I know, love, and can . . . . . The guillotine for a long time would not let me sleep and made me keep looking around me.—[Biryukóv: I, 317.]

Here he vividly characterizes his own talent and gives a hint of his nascent repugnance to acts of violence committed in the name of the state. In his *Confession* he refers to this incident as one of the main causes that made him cease to share the Liberals' worship of progress.

From Paris Tolstoy proceeded to Switzerland, where he met his father's cousin, the Countess Alexandra Tolstoy, maid of honor at the Russian court, and passed the time gaily with her and with congenial Russian associates. With the Countess he formed a friendship which, despite their sharp differences on matters of religion, endured until her death in 1904. Their correspondence is a precious source for the knowledge of Tolstoy's personality. In a short memoir the Countess gives her impressions of the young author after his return from Sevastopol:

He was unaffected, extremely modest, and so full of fun that his presence enlivened everybody. Of himself he spoke very rarely, but he gazed at each new face with marked attention and later he most amusingly told us his impressions, which were nearly always rather extreme. . . . He divined people by his artistic sense, and his estimate often proved amazingly accurate. His homely face, with its kind, clever, expressive eyes, made up by its expression for its lack of elegance; one may say that it was better than beauty.... He was constantly striving to begin his life anew; and, throwing off the past like worn-out clothing, to dress himself in a clean garment.—[*Correspondence with the Countess A. A. Tolstoy*, pp. 3, 4, 6.]

From an artistic point of view this journey is of some importance. Tolstoy was outraged by the indifference of the wealthy guests at the Schweizerhof hotel in Lucerne to a poor musician who had diverted them for a half-hour and then vainly asked pay for his trouble. To shame the crowd, he immediately captured the musician, seated him at table with himself, and ordered champagne. (As Kropotkin intimates,* this stroke caused more pleasure to Tolstoy than to the musician.) This incident he immediately described in his tale *Lucerne*. Kropotkin comments on the honesty with which he depicts the discomfort of the musician in the aristocratic surroundings into which the author has dragged him. The sketch closes with bitter reflections on the way in which external civilization dulls elemental human feeling and fosters hypocrisy.

At about the same time he composed *Albert*, founded on his own attempt, nine years before, in 1848, to befriend a drunken German musician, whom he had taken with him from St. Petersburg to his home at Yásnaya Polyána. But the story is by no means strictly autobiographic, and is more conventional in form than most of his writings.

* *Russian Literature*, pp. 116, 117.

In August, 1857, Tolstoy was back in Russia. The following three years, until July, 1860, he spent mainly on his own estate at Yásnaya Polyána, but with frequent visits to Moscow and elsewhere. In Moscow he was a typical man of society, devoted to gymnastics and distinguished by his dandified clothes. Into dress he could throw himself with the same passion as into other enthusiasms; yet on one occasion (during his second trip abroad) he appeared at an evening reception after a long tramp, without a change of clothes, and with wooden sabots on his feet.

In the beginning of 1858 Tolstoy wrote his notable story *Three Deaths*, in which one may see clear signs of the influence of Turgenev's manner. The three deaths are of a society dame, fretful, peevish, and self-righteous; of a peasant post-driver, calm and resigned; and of a tree, majestically submissive to the laws of nature. Here, even more clearly than in *Childhood* and *Sevastopol*, he makes one's attitude towards death the prime test of character. In a letter to his cousin the Countess Alexandra, Tolstoy, who was little given to criticism of his own works, writes an analysis of this tale that is remarkable in its self-revelation:

You are mistaken in regarding it [*Three Deaths*] from a Christian point of view. My thought was: three beings died; a lady, a peasant, and a tree. The lady is pitiable and horrid, because she has lied all her life and lies in the presence of death. Christianity, as she understands it, does not solve for her the question of life and death. Why should she die, when she wants to live? In the promises of Christianity as to the future she believes with her imagination and her intellect, yet her whole being revolts and she has no other consolation except the pseudo-Christian one—and the place for any other is occupied. She is horrid and pitiable. The peasant dies calmly, for the very reason that he is not a Christian. His religion is different, although in obedience to custom he has performed the Christian ceremonies; his religion is nature, with which he has lived. He himself has felled trees, sown rye and reaped it, killed sheep; and sheep have been born to him and children have been born, and old men have died; and he firmly knows this law, from which he has never turned aside, like the lady, but has looked it straight and frankly in the eyes. "*Une brute,*" you say, but what is there bad about *une brute?* *Une brute* is happiness and beauty, harmony with the whole world, and not such discord as that of the lady. The tree dies calmly, honorably, and beautifully. Beautifully—because it does not lie, does not parade itself, does not fear, does not regret. That is my thought, with which you, of course, do not agree, but which it is impossible to dispute—it exists both in my soul and in yours. That this thought is expressed miserably, I agree with you. Otherwise with your fine feeling you would have understood, and I should not be writing this explanation, which, I fear, will even anger you and make you impatient with me. Do not be impatient, grandmother [Tolstoy's pet name for the Countess]. I possess, and in a high degree, the Christian feeling; but I have this too, and it is very precious to me. This is the feeling of truth and beauty, and that is a personal feeling, of love and calm. How they are united I do not know and I cannot explain; but the cat and the dog sit in the same lumber-room—that is positive.— [*Correspondence with the Countess A. A. Tolstoy*, pp. 101, 102.]

There could not be a clearer statement of the two conflicting sides of Tolstoy's nature. A few months before he had been fascinated by reading at the same time the *Iliad* and the Gospel. He regretted that there was no connection between them. "How could Homer fail to know that God is love?" he wrote in his diary. And he answers his own query: "Revelation—there is no better explanation."*

In February, 1859, Tolstoy was elected a member of the Society of Lovers of Russian Literature, in Moscow, and, according to custom, was required to deliver an initiation speech. In this address he showed his dislike of the Liberal creed by exalting the preeminence in literature of its purely artistic elements over all temporary and accidental tendencies. The president of the society, the noted Slavophile Homyakóv, in a flattering reply, took him gently to task:

A writer, a servant of pure art, sometimes becomes a rebuker of society even without being aware of it, independently of his own will and even against his will. I will venture, count, to take you yourself as an example. You are advancing steadfastly and with no deviation along a definite path of which you are conscious; but are you completely free from that tendency called the literature of rebuke? In the picture of the dying post-driver, for example, who lies dying on the oven amid a crowd of comrades who are apparently indifferent to his sufferings, did you not rebuke a certain social disease, a certain vice? In describing that death did

* Biryukóv: I, 329.

you not suffer from the callous unfeelingness of kind but unawakened human souls? Yes, you have been, and you will involuntarily continue to be a rebuker.—[Biryukóv: I, 351.]

To this convincing argument Tolstoy would have answered, if we may judge by his later reasoning in *War and Peace*, that he had never wished to deny the influence of literature on the moral life of the individual, but that between such influence and any possible effect on the organization of society there is an impassable gulf.

Tolstoy's life on his home estate was wholesome and full of pleasure. With him there lived for some time his sister Marya and a distant relative, his "aunt" Tatyana Ergolsky. Of his companionship with the latter he writes charmingly:

I remember the long autumn and winter evenings, and those evenings have remained for me a marvelous recollection. To those evenings I am obliged for my best thoughts, for the best movements of my soul. You sit in your chair, read, and think, and occasionally you hear her talk with Natalya Petrovna or with the chambermaid Dúnechka, who was always kind and gentle; you exchange a word with her and again you sit and read and think . . . . . The chief charm of this life was in the absence of all material care; in good relations with all; in firm, indubitably good relations with those nearest you, which no one could disturb; and in the absence of haste, the unconsciousness of the passage of time.—[Biryukóv: I, 335.]

Spring had a beneficent effect on Tolstoy as on other authors before him. In April, 1858, he wrote to the Countess Alexandra Tolstoy:

Sometimes you make a mistake and think that a future of happiness awaits not nature alone, but yourself as well; and then you feel splendid. I am now in such a condition, and with the egoism peculiar to me I hasten to write to you of matters interesting only to myself.—I know very well, when I consider the matter sensibly, that I am an old, frozen, rotten potato, boiled and served with sauce, but the spring so acts on me that I sometimes catch myself in a burst of ardent dreams that I am a vegetable which is just about to bud forth along with others, and which will grow simply, calmly, and joyously in God's world.—[*Correspondence with the Countess A. A. Tolstoy*, pp. 98, 99.]

In the next letter this vegetable delight in spring is replaced by a more poetic tone:

At this moment under my very window two nightingales are singing away. I am making experiments on them; and, just imagine, I succeed in attracting them to my window by sixths on the piano. I discovered this accidentally. Some days ago, according to my custom, I was drumming out sonatas by Haydn, in which there are sixths. Suddenly I heard out of doors and in auntie's room (she has a canary) whistling, twittering, and trills to the accompaniment of my sixths. I stopped and they stopped. I began again, and they began (two nightingales and a canary). I passed three hours at this occupation.—[*Ibid.*, pp. 100, 101.]

At this period, in December, 1858, Tolstoy had an adventure which nearly cost him his life, and which he

later narrated, with some changes, in one of his stories
for children. Gromeka, one of his friends, had arranged
a hunt for an enormous she-bear. The gentlemen
hunters were stationed at advantageous points, while
peasant beaters drove on the game towards them.
Tolstoy stood in the deep snow, having neglected to
follow instructions and trample a hard place all about
him. The bear rushed upon him, and was not halted
by a shot which he fired at close range, and which
lodged in its jaw. Knocking Tolstoy down, it tried to
seize his head in its jaws, and tore the flesh above
and below his left eye. Only the timely arrival of a
peasant bear-hunter saved Tolstoy from death.

Two shadows, neither of them very deep, run across
this picture of a decidedly happy life. As a practical
farm manager Tolstoy was far from being an un-
qualified success. In May, 1859, he wrote his cousin
that he was on the point of bankruptcy. But in his
next letter he tells her that she has erred in taking him
too literally: "I cannot become bankrupt, because I
am alone, and I know how (I say it with pride) to earn
my own bread." On the other hand, Tolstoy's literary
work since his return from Sevastopol had been comparatively small in amount, and, great as were its artistic
merits, it had not increased his reputation as a writer.
His one literary friend in the vicinity was the poet
Fet, who owned an estate not far from Yásnaya Polyána,
and with whom he maintained an intimacy that continued interrupted until after his own religious con-

version. To Fet and to Tolstoy, Druzhinin, the critic of the *Contemporary* group, addressed letters in June, 1860, urging them to greater literary activity. Upon Tolstoy he urged his responsibility to the Russian public, which looked to literature for instruction as well as recreation. He reminded him of the serious and high aims of the circle of authors to which they both belonged. Such arguments were not in the least likely to affect Tolstoy.

A main cause of Tolstoy's indifference to his career as a writer of fiction was his revived interest in the problem of popular education. His early experiment of organizing a school for peasant children, in 1849, soon after he left the University of Kazán, in has been already mentioned (p. 11); in 1859, he had renewed his attempt with far more ardor and persistence. He was now eager to study educational conditions in the west in order to prepare himself for his own work. A second motive for a trip abroad was the desire to join his brother Nikoláy, who was suffering from consumption and had been sent to Soden for treatment. He left Russia, accompanied by his sister Marya, in July, 1860.

On this second journey abroad, which lasted until May, 1861, Tolstoy studied works on education and observed diligently the practice of German and French schools. Of his remarks and conclusions something will be said in the following chapter. He visited Berlin, Leipzig, Dresden, Rome, Marseilles, Paris, London, and Brussels, meeting some of the most famous men in

Europe, among them the novelist Auerbach, of whose works he was a devout admirer; the socialist Proudhon, who left on him the impression of a strong man, with the courage of his convictions; and, in London, the Russian exile Herzen. Herzen's daughter has told how, as a little girl, she nestled down in a chair in her father's study, awaiting with trembling heart the arrival of Count Tolstoy, whose works she had read with delight. To her surprise he proved to be a dandified individual, dressed in the latest English style, who talked with her father about cock-fighting and boxing matches.

The health of Nikoláy Tolstoy had not been restored by the visit to Soden. The brothers traveled together from there to Frankfort, and thence to Hyères, on the south coast of France. There Nikoláy Tolstoy died in his brother's arms, on September 20, 1860. "Nothing in my life has ever made such an impression on me," Tolstoy wrote to Fet.* In his *Confession* he couples this event with the sight of the execution in Paris as a chief reason for his loss of faith in the religion of human progress:

Another case in which I was conscious of the insufficiency for life of the superstition of progress was the death of my brother. An intelligent, good, serious man, he fell ill while still young, suffered for more than a year, and died in tortures, not understanding why he had lived and still less understanding why he was dying. No theories could afford any answer to these questions either to me or to him during the time of his slow and painful death.—[Ch. 3.]

* Biryukóv: I, 378.

During his absence from Russia Tolstoy found time
to write *Polikushka*, a powerful story of peasant life on
a gentlewoman's estate. A poor, ignorant manorial
servant, whom his mistress in a futile sort of fashion is
trying to cure of his thieving habits, is sent to fetch
home from town a packet of sixteen hundred rubles. He
loses them on the way and hangs himself from grief and
despair; his distracted wife drowns her baby in the
trough in which she has been washing him. With this
main plot Tolstoy blends a subordinate motif, of the disputes among the peasants as to the selection of recruits
for the army. The usual autobiographic and religious
elements are entirely lacking. Events speak for themselves, and produce an impression of hopeless, deadening
misery. The tale, when it was published in 1863,
aroused the enthusiasm of Turgenev, who wrote to Fet:

> I have read Tolstoy's *Polikushka* and been amazed at the
> strength of that mighty talent. Only he has wasted a terrible
> lot of material and was wrong in drowning the baby son. That
> makes it too terrible. But there are truly marvelous pages!
> It makes the shivers run down my spinal column, which has
> already become thick and coarse. He is a master, a master!

This generous praise by Turgenev, which is only one
of many similar expressions of admiration for Tolstoy's
genius on his part, is the more remarkable because it
followed an acute quarrel between the two great authors.
In the circle of the *Contemporary* Turgenev was beyond
question the man of finest literary talent. Despite the

present tendency to depreciate him in favor of Dostoyevsky, he will probably continue to rank next to Tolstoy among the Russian novelists of the past century. With him Tolstoy had become more intimate than with any other man of the group, despite their fundamental differences of temperament. Turgenev was a kindly man, of delicately artistic nature, but of little force of character, and no moral enthusiasm. In his later life he said that he had come to appreciate landscapes most of all upon the painter's canvas.* The following criticism of *On the Eve*, in a letter to Fet (1860), illustrates Tolstoy's attitude to his friend's work:

I have read *On the Eve*. This is my opinion: generally speaking, to write stories is waste labor, most of all for people who feel sad and who don't really know what they desire from life. However, *On the Eve* is much better than *A Nobleman's Nest*, and it contains splendid negative types: the artist and the father. The others are not only not types, but their very conception, their position is not typical, or they are absolutely insignificant. However, that is Turgenev's perpetual mistake. The girl is wretchedly done: "'Ah, how I love you!' —her eyelashes were long." In general, I am always surprised in Turgenev by his inability, despite his intellect and his poetic sense, to refrain from the commonplace even in his methods. This commonplaceness shows most in his negative methods, which remind one of Gogol. He has no humanity and no sympathy for his characters, and they turn out monsters, whom he rails at and does not pity. This somehow clashes painfully with the tone and flavor of liberalism in everything

* *Correspondence with the Countess A. A. Tolstoy*, p. 17.

else. This was all right . . . in Gogol; and one must add
that if one is not going to pity even his most insignificant
characters one must either curse them so as to make the air
blue, or laugh at them so as to make the reader's sides shake,
not behave as Turgenev does, who suffers from spleen and
dyspepsia. Speaking generally, no one else could now have
written such a story, notwithstanding the fact that it will not
have success.—[Biryukóv: I, pp. 352, 353.]

At another time Tolstoy wrote: "Deuce take him!
I'm sick of loving him!"* Their companionship had
never been harmonious. Tolstoy was irritated by
Turgenev's self-possession and tranquillity, and was
given to teasing him. One of our first glimpses of them
together is in a violent dispute in Nekrasov's apart-
ments. Turgenev is pacing the floor while Tolstoy
lies on a couch in a huff and exclaims: "I won't let
him spite me! He insists on walking up and down
past me and wagging his democratic haunches." †
In 1857, on Tolstoy's first visit to Paris, they are said to
have been on the brink of a duel. Now, in 1861, soon
after Tolstoy's return to Russia, when they were both
visiting Fet, a far more serious conflict occurred between them. Turgenev was telling of the education of
his daughter, and remarked with approval that her
English governess insisted on her mending with her
own hands the clothes of poor people instead of giving
mere money alms. Tolstoy exclaimed that a well-
dressed girl, holding dirty, ill-smelling rags on her

* Biryukóv: I, 340.   † *Ibid.*, p. 273.

knees, was playing an insincere and theatrical part. A sharp quarrel followed, and Turgenev, pale with rage, used the words: "If you talk like that, I'll punch your face." Tolstoy, with his inborn spirit of contradiction, had been irritating, but the blame was on the side of Turgenev. When Tolstoy challenged him to a duel, Turgenev, on reflection, sent a rather stiff apology, with which Tolstoy expressed himself as satisfied. Some months later Tolstoy, in one of his bursts of generous kindliness, wrote to Turgenev expressing his regret for the whole affair. Of the incident he spoke to his cousin: "I may assure you that my part in that stupid episode was not a bad one. I was absolutely in no way to blame, and, notwithstanding my conscious innocence, I wrote to Turgenev the most friendly and conciliatory letter; but he answered it so rudely that I was forced to break off all relations with him."* The broken friendship was restored only many years later, in 1878, after Tolstoy's religious conversion.

Tolstoy's time during the year following his return to Russia was occupied by his peasant schools, by literary work on educational questions, and by his duties as arbiter of the peace between the newly-freed serfs and their former masters. During Tolstoy's absence from Russia, on March 3, 1861, the tsar had issued the great Emancipation Proclamation, which gave freedom to the whole Russian peasantry. In the discussion and agitation that had preceded this greatest reform of

* *Correspondence with the Countess A. A. Tolstoy*, p. 16.

modern Russia Tolstoy had taken no part. Of his attitude towards it he later told Biryukóv:

As for my attitude at that time to the excited condition of all society, I must say (and this is both a good and a bad trait in me, but one that has always been peculiar to me) that I have always been involuntarily opposed to epidemic influences from the outside, and that if I was then excited and joyful, it was with my special, personal, internal interests, which drew me to the school and to communion with the common people. I still recognize in myself the same feeling of resistance to general enthusiasm that existed then, but which showed itself in feeble forms.—[Biryukóv: I, pp. 397, 398.]

His only share in the movement seems to have been signing, in September, 1858, along with 104 other landowners of his province, a resolution favoring the freeing of the peasants and bestowing on them a portion of the land which they tilled, for the loss of which the nobility should be compensated. In 1861 he once remarked to a neighbor at a banquet that the country was really indebted solely to the emperor for the emancipation. Here he showed his usual dislike of the Liberal party, which had taken the leading share in the great reform. Of his own early writings only *A Morning of a Landed Proprietor* and *Polikushka* can be interpreted as implying condemnation of serfdom, and even in them the condemnation is rather of personal stupidity on the part of the serf-owner than of the institution itself.

Towards his own peasants Tolstoy acted fairly, but with no marked generosity. Three or four years before the emancipation he had adopted the liberal plan of placing his serfs on a rent basis, instead of exacting from them the old manorial labor. At the emancipation he gave them no more land than the law required. "The one good thing that I did, or bad thing that I refrained from doing," he wrote to Biryukóv, "was that I did not change the location of my peasants, as I had been advised to do, and that I left the pasture land at their disposal. In general I showed no unselfish feelings in my course of action at that time."*

Tolstoy means by this that he did not act in any such way as the dictates of his later religious views would have led him to do. Among his fellow serf-owners he seems to have been regarded as a dangerous radical. In order to adjust relations between the emancipated peasants and their former lords, the government created officials known as "arbiters of the peace," chosen from among the members of the country gentry who had been in sympathy with the reform. In May, 1861, the governor of the province of Tula appointed Tolstoy as arbiter, despite an energetic protest from the provincial and district marshals of the nobility, who apparently thought him a man not likely in his official duties to serve the interests of his own class. This office as arbiter was the only position under the government that Tolstoy ever held after his retirement from the army. His career in it was, to speak frankly, a failure, owing to his refusal to putter with the petty

* Biryukóv: I, 408.

details of his work. Men and women Tolstoy understood; government documents he despised. One paper
he forwarded to his superiors with the following signature: "To this document, at the request of such-and-
such men, because of their illiteracy, such-and-such a
house servant has set his hand." The obedient servant
had written with Chinese fidelity from the Count's
dictation, without inserting the necessary proper names,
and Tolstoy had sealed and dispatched the document
without even glancing at it.

In his practical work Tolstoy strove for impartiality,
but he leaned always toward the side of the peasants.
His hasty temper made him far from conciliatory to the
proprietors. As early as July, 1861, he wrote in his diary:
"The arbitership . . . has involved me in quarrels
with all the land-owners and has injured my health."*
Thus one Madam Artyukhov made complaint to him
of her former house-serf, Mark Grigoryev, who had
left her, regarding himself as a man "completely free."
Tolstoy wrote in reply:

Mark will immediately, according to my instructions, depart with his wife wherever he pleases, and I beg you most
humbly: (1) to compensate him for the three months and a
half during which he was illegally retained in your service
after the time of the Emancipation Proclamation and (2) for a
beating inflicted on his wife, still more illegally. If you do not
like my decision, you have the right of appeal to the district
sessions and to the provincial board. I shall make no further

* Biryukóv: I, 414.

explanations on this subject. With great respect, I have the honor to be your humble servant, Count L. Tolstoy.—[Biryukóv: I, 410.]

In this case Tolstoy's decision was ultimately confirmed, but in various other cases he was not so fortunate. On May 12, 1862, he passed over his duties to a subordinate, on the ground of ill health, and a few weeks later was formally relieved of his office. In a letter written somewhat later to his cousin the Countess Alexandra Tolstoy, he gives his own view of his conduct as an official:

Outcries against my arbitership have reached even you, but I asked twice for a trial and twice the court announced not only that I was in the right, but that there was no ground for a trial; but not only before their court, but before my own conscience do I know, especially as to the last period of my work, that I softened, softened too much the law in behalf of the nobility.—[*Correspondence with the Countess A. A. Tolstoy*, p. 164.]

Worn out by work and worry over the arbitership and his peasant school, Tolstoy departed for the province of Samara to take the kumys cure. On June 1, while traveling on the steamer, he made the following entry in his diary:

I seem to be born again to life and the knowledge of it. The thought of the folly of progress persecutes me. With the clever and the foolish, with old men and children, I talk of this one subject.—[Biryukóv: I, 457.]

Tolstoy's search for rest and health was interrupted by news from home that aroused him to a burst of fury. His conduct as arbiter, or his work on popular education, in which he was aided by some students who had cherished revolutionary sympathies, had aroused the suspicions of the government authorities, who ordered a search of his premises. His feelings, and the events that occasioned them, can best be understood from his letters to his cousin the Countess Alexandra Tolstoy, who was living in St. Petersburg on intimate terms with the highest officials of the empire; she, he hoped, might aid him to present a complaint to the tsar. The first was written from Moscow, on his way home, early in August:

They write me from Yásnaya: on July 13 there came three troikas of gendarmes, who forbade everybody to leave the house, probably even auntie, and started to search the premises. What they were looking for is still unknown. One of your friends, a dirty colonel, read all my letters and diaries, which I intended to confide only just before my death to the friend who will then be nearest of all to me; he read two sets of letters for the secrecy of which I would have given every thing in the world—and departed, announcing that he had found nothing suspicious. It is my good fortune and your friend's also that I was not there; I should have killed him. Fine! Glorious! That is the way in which the government is making friends for itself. If you remember me on my political side, you know that always, and especially since the time when I fell in love with my school, I have been completely indifferent to the government and still more indifferent to the

Liberals of our time, whom I despise with my whole soul. Now I cannot say that. I feel anger and repugnance, almost hatred, for that dear government, which searches my premises for a lithographic or printing outfit to reproduce proclamations of Herzen which I despise, which I have not the patience to read for very boredom . . . . .

Once I wrote to you that it is impossible to seek a quiet refuge in life, but that one must toil, work, suffer. That is all possible, but only if it were possible to flee somewhere from these robbers whose cheeks and hands are washed with scented soap and who smile courteously. Truly, if my life is spared for long I shall retire into a monastery, not to pray to God—that to my thinking is useless—but in order not to see all the filth of worldly corruption, puffed-up, self-satisfied, and in epaulets and crinolines.—Foh!—How can you, excellent person that you are, live in St. Petersburg! *That* I shall never understand; perhaps you have cataracts on your eyes, so that you see nothing.—[*Correspondence with the Countess A. A. Tolstoy,* pp. 162, 163.]

A second letter, written from Yásnaya Polyána on August 20, is in far greater detail. An extract will give an idea of its tone:

I write this letter after reflection, trying to forget nothing and to add nothing, in order that you may show it to divers robbers, the Potapopovs and the Dolgorukys, who are purposely sowing hatred against the government and lowering the emperor in the eyes of his subjects. I will not and cannot let this matter pass. All my occupation, in which I found happiness and comfort, is ruined. Auntie is so ill that she will not recover. The peasants already regard me not as an honest man, a reputation that I have earned by years, but as a criminal, a man guilty of arson or of counterfeiting, who has escaped punishment only through knavery. "Ah, my friend! You're caught! Quit talking to us of honor and justice; they almost put you in irons." Of the land-owners I need not speak—just a groan of delight. Pray write me quickly . . . how to write and how to forward a letter to the emperor. There is no other way out except to receive a satisfaction as public as the injury done me . . . or to expatriate myself, on which I am firmly decided. I shall not join Herzen; Herzen may take care of himself and I of myself. I shall not dissemble; I shall announce publicly that I am selling my estate in order to leave Russia, where it is impossible to know a moment in advance that I myself, my sister, my wife, and my mother will not be put in irons and flogged—and I shall leave.—[*Ibid.*, pp. 163, 164.]

These letters show Tolstoy's sentimental loyalty to the tsar, which was not mixed with any admiration for government officials; the point of view of the peasant and of the aristocrat of long descent! With it he joined a passionate readiness to revolt when the heel of oppression touched him personally; at the close of the letter he says that he has loaded pistols ready in case of a repetition of the insult. Evidently only his passionate individualism kept him from sympathy with the revolutionary movement. One may add that Tolstoy succeeded in personally delivering a petition for satisfaction to Alexander II during one of his visits to Moscow; "the emperor later, it seems, sent an aide-de-camp to Lev Nikoláyevich with an apology."*

* Biryukóv: I, 462.

Tolstoy had long felt the loneliness of his bachelor existence, but no real love had come into his life. In April, 1858, he had written to his cousin: "When I arrived at my country house it seemed to me that I was a widower, that recently there had been living here my whole family, whom I had lost. And in very truth the family of my imagination did live there. And what a charming family! I regret especially my oldest son! And my wife was splendid, although a strange woman."* Now, almost over night, on his return from the kumys cure, he fell passionately in love with Sofya Behrs, a girl of eighteen, the second daughter of Dr. Behrs, a Russian of German extraction, who had married Miss Islenev, a friend of Tolstoy's childhood. In June, 1856, he had visited this family and noted in his diary: "The children served us. What dear, jolly little girls!" † In the summer of 1862 he went very frequently to their home, and was regarded as a suitor for the oldest daughter, Liza. To Sofya he declared himself in a fashion that he has made famous in *Anna Karenin*. While standing with her by a card table, he wrote on it with chalk the letters: I y f t e a f v o m a y s L y a T s c i. This the girl interpreted correctly as: "In your family there exists a false view of me and your sister Liza; you and Tanya should correct it." He then wrote further: Y y a n o h t v r m o m o a a t i o h, which signified: "Your youth and need of happiness too vividly

* *Correspondence with the Countess A. A. Tolstoy*, p. 99.
† Biryukóv: I, 294.

remind me of my old age and the impossibility of happiness." After this the two fully understood each other.

Meanwhile Tolstoy according to his wont was busily analyzing his own feelings. On September 4 he wrote in his diary: "I fear myself: what if this too is only the desire of love, and not love itself? I try to look only at her weak sides and still I love her."* Finding himself firm in his affection, he made a formal proposal on September 29 and was accepted. He thereupon, with characteristic honesty, which he later reproduced in his hero Levin, handed to his betrothed the diary in which he had recorded all the sins of his youth. The girl, though bitterly undeceived in her fancies as to her future husband, did not waver in her affection for him. They were married almost immediately, on October 5, in the Court Church in the Moscow Kremlin, and after the ceremony they drove to Yásnaya Polyána, where they were welcomed by Tolstoy's brother Sergéy and by his "Aunt Tatyana."

A new period of Tolstoy's life had begun.

* Biryukóv: I, 471.

CHAPTER IV

TOLSTOY AS AN EDUCATOR

EFERENCE has already been made to Tolstoy's experiments in popular education among the peasant children on his estate, and to his study of educational problems during his second trip abroad. One may say without exaggeration that interest in education was Tolstoy's most fervent intellectual enthusiasm up to the time of his marriage, meaning more to him even than his brilliant success as a writer of fiction. Thus on August 19, 1862, he wrote to the Countess Alexandra Tolstoy:

You know what the school has meant to me ever since I opened it. It has been my whole life; it has been my monastery, my church, in which I sought and found salvation from all the anxieties, doubts, and temptations of life. I tore myself away from it for the sake of my sick brother; and, still more weary, and seeking work and love, I returned home.— [*Correspondence with the Countess A. A. Tolstoy*, p. 164.]

Tolstoy's position as arbiter of the peace enabled him to have influence on other schools besides that which he had himself started at Yásnaya Polyána, and he engaged a dozen students to help him in his work. "In 1862, when I was arbiter," he writes, "fourteen schools were opened in a district containing 10,000 people. Besides this there were about ten schools in the same district held at the houses of the church servants and among the servants on various estates."* In this same year, 1862, his enthusiasm led him to establish an educational journal, *Yásnaya Polyána*, in which he printed several articles on educational problems. The periodical had small practical success and cost him much money. After his marriage in October, 1862, Tolstoy became absorbed in new cares and duties, and for some years ceased work in his school; he also soon discontinued his journal, of which but twelve numbers appeared. Yet he had not lost his interest in educational questions; in 1868, before he had quite completed his great novel *War and Peace*, he made a note of a plan for an elementary text-book in reading. This led to the publication in 1872 of a *Primer*, which was divided into four books; this was revised and reissued in 1875 as *A New Primer*, followed by four graded *Readers* in the Russian language and four in the Slavic language (that used in Russia for the church service and for purposes of religious instruction). These little books have had a wider circulation, at least in Russia, than any other of Tolstoy's writings; Biryukóv in 1908 estimated the sale of the *New Primer* at 1,500,000

* *On Popular Education* (1874).

copies.* Meanwhile their author had early in 1872 opened a school for peasants in his own house, and in the fall of that year he was eagerly explaining his methods to teachers whom he had invited to hear him. In 1874 he defended his views at a meeting of the Moscow Committee of Literacy. His theories and those of his opponents were given a practical test, but with no decisive results. In support of them he published an article *On Popular Education* (1874), in which he repeated much the same doctrine as in his periodical of twelve years before. Besides all this, Tolstoy had in 1873 been interested in a project for establishing an advanced school for peasants, "a university in bast shoes," to use his own term, which the pupils should be able to attend without altering their way of life. Setting aside his repugnance for social activity, he sought aid from the provincial council (*zemstvo*), but that body preferred to devote the funds at its disposal to a statue of the Empress Catherine II! Finally, in 1876 and 1877 he had dreams of organizing a teachers' seminary. After his religious conversion in 1878 Tolstoy's views on education naturally assumed an entirely new character, becoming a mere corollary to his religious views.

During the whole period from 1862 to 1874 Tolstoy's writings on education present an essentially consistent body of doctrine, and they may be treated as a whole, without regard to questions of chronology. Aside

---

* Perhaps this figure is too high; in 1901 (in the *Brockhaus-Efron Encyclopedia*) Vengerov estimates the sale as "over 800,000."

from the *Primer* and the *Readers*, and a few minor
pieces that have unfortunately never been reprinted,
they consist of the following articles published in the
journal *Yásnaya Polyána: On Popular Education*
(1862), *On Methods of Teaching Reading*, *A Project
of a General Plan for Organizing Popular Schools* (a
critique of a plan proposed by the government), *Education and Culture, Progress and the Definition of Education,
Who Is to Teach the Art of Writing: We to the Peasant
Children, or the Peasant Children to Us?* and *Yásnaya
Polyána School in November and December [1861]*—and
of the article *On Popular Education* published in 1874.
These articles are Tolstoy's first writings of a distinctly
didactic nature. They make perfectly plain certain
points of view that were implicit in his works of fiction,
and they contain in a rudimentary form many of the
characteristic doctrines that he later developed, giving
to them, however, a different logical basis in his religious system, in his works on ethical, social, and
esthetic questions.

First of all, Tolstoy condemns the whole fabric of
modern education and the principles on which it rests,
and supports his condemnation by remarks on actual
conditions in France and Germany, as he had himself
observed them. The great sin of modern education,
according to Tolstoy, is that it is founded on compulsion, being forced by the government upon an
unwilling people who do not desire it, but who do desire
something quite different.

Popular education has always and everywhere presented, and continues to present, the same phenomenon, which for me is incomprehensible. The common people desire education, and each single individual unconsciously strives for education. The more educated class of men—society, the government—strives to impart its knowledge and to educate the less educated class of the people. It would seem that such a concurrence of needs should satisfy both the educating class and that which is being educated. But the reverse is the case. The people constantly resist the efforts employed for their education by society or by the government, as representatives of the more educated class, and these efforts for the most part are without result. . .

Germany, the founder of the school, has not succeeded by a struggle of almost two hundred years in overcoming the resistance of the people to the school. . .   Notwithstanding the strictness of a law that has existed for two hundred years, notwithstanding the preparation of teachers of the newest fashion in seminaries, notwithstanding all a German's feeling of submission to the law, the compulsion of the school still weighs upon the people with its full force; the German governments do not venture to abolish the law of compulsory education. Germany may pride itself on the education of its people by statistical tables; but the people, as formerly, generally derive from the school only repulsion for the school. . .

Reality has shown me the following: a father sends his daughter or son to school against his own wish, cursing the institution that deprives him of the labor of his son, and counting the days till the time when his son shall become *schulfrei*—the mere word shows how the people regard the schools. The child goes to school with the conviction that the authority of his father, which is the only one he knows,

does not approve the authority of the government, to which
he submits in entering school.—[*On Popular Education* (1862).]

This use of compulsion in education would be justified
if the educated, upper classes who prescribe the school
program really knew what they wished to teach;   that
is, if there were a universally recognized religious sanction for education, such as there was in the middle
ages.

A hundred [mistake for *four hundred?*] years ago, neither in
Europe nor in our own country could the question what to
teach and how to teach have arisen.   Education was insep-
arably connected with religion.   To learn to read meant to
study Holy Scripture.   In Mohammedan countries there survives until today in full force this connection between learning
to read and religion.   To study means to study the Koran and
therefore the Arabic language.   But as soon as religion ceased
to be the criterion of what one must study, and the school
became independent of it, this question was bound to arise.—
[*On Popular Education* (1874).]

Compare the dogmatic school of the middle ages, in which
truths were undoubted, and our school, in which no one knows
what is truth, but to which, nevertheless, the pupil is forcibly
compelled to go, and the parents to send their children. . .
It was easy for the medieval school to know what to teach,
what to teach first and what to teach next, and how to teach,
when there was only one method and when all science was
concentrated in the Bible and the books of Augustine and
Aristotle.—[*On Popular Education* (1862).]

But at the present time, Tolstoy continues, there is no
consensus of opinion as to what should be taught;

"the theological tendency struggles with the scholastic, the scholastic with the classical, the classical with the scientific [real], and at the present time all these tendencies exist, without one's subduing the other, and no one knows what is false and what is true."* "The university does not like the clerical education, and says that there is nothing worse than the seminaries; the clerics do not like the university education and say that there is nothing worse than the universities, that they are only schools of pride and atheism; parents condemn the universities, the universities condemn the military schools, the government condemns the universities, and vice versa." † The most highly educated men justify education as a means of *progress*, by which they mean a change for the better in the condition of humanity as time passes by. But this progress is a pure assumption, incapable of proof:

I, like all men free from the superstition of progress, see only that humanity lives; . . . that the labors of the past often serve as a foundation for new labors of the present, and often serve as a barrier for them; that the well-being of men now increases in one place, in one class, and in one sense, and now diminishes; that, however desirable it might be for me to do so, I cannot find any general law in the life of mankind; and that to subordinate history to the idea of progress is as easy as to subordinate it to any other idea or to any historical dream that you please. I will say more: I see no necessity for searching out general laws in history, to say nothing of the impossibility

* *On Popular Education* (1862).   † *Education and Culture.*

of it. A general eternal law is written in the soul of each man. The law of progress, or perfectibility, is written in the soul of each man and is transferred to history only in consequence of an error. While it remains personal, this law is fruitful and is accessible to each man; transferred to history, it becomes idle, empty chatter, leading to the justification of all sorts of nonsense and fatalism. Progress in general in all humanity has never been proved a fact, and it does not exist for any of the oriental nations; and therefore to say that progress is a law of humanity is just as lacking in foundation as to say that all men are blond with the exception of the brunettes. . . .

We can admit that progress leads to well-being only when the whole people subject to the action of progress shall recognize that action as good and useful, while now in nine tenths of the population, the so-called common, laboring people, we constantly see the opposite; and, in the second place, when it shall be proved that progress leads to the perfecting of all sides of human life, or that all sides of its influence taken together produce more good and useful consequences than bad and injurious ones. The common people, that is the mass of the nation, nine tenths of all men, constantly show a hostile attitude to progress, and constantly not only fail to recognize its benefits, but positively and consciously recognize the harm that it does them.—[*Progress and the Definition of Education.*]

Tolstoy then points out that progress, while aiding some sides of human well-being, such as the improvement of ways of communication and the development of the art of printing, has injured others, such as the primitive wealth of nature, strong physical development, and purity of morals. An unbiased mind, he main-

tains, will see in the celebrated third chapter of Ma-
caulay's *History* evidence of retrogression rather than
of progress. "We personally regard the forward movement of civilization as one of the greatest evils due
to violence to which a certain part of humanity is subject, and we do not regard that movement as inevitable."*

Compulsion in education, Tolstoy proceeds to argue,
can then in no way be justified, since, lacking the universal sanction of religion, teachers do not know what
to teach, and since the ideal of progress for which they
profess to labor is illusory. In practice, the results of
compulsory education are inevitably bad. The experience of France coincides with that of Germany;
the people gain almost nothing from the obligatory
state schools and derive their real education from the
great, free school of life:

A year ago I was in Marseilles and visited all the educational
institutions for workingmen of that city. The proportion of
pupils to the population is so large that, with few exceptions,
all the children go to school for three, four, or six years. The
programs of the schools consist in the committing to memory
of the catechism, sacred and general history, the four rules of
arithmetic, French orthography, and bookkeeping. ... Not
one boy in these schools was able to solve, that is to state, the
most simple problem of addition or subtraction. At the same
time they performed operations with abstract numbers,
multiplying thousands with ease and speed. To questions on
the history of France they replied well by rote, but when I
asked at haphazard I got the answer that Henry IV was killed

* *Progress and the Definition of Education.*

by Julius Cæsar. It was the same in geography and sacred history, the same in orthography and reading. More than half the girls are unable to read anything except the books that they have studied. Six years of school do not give the ability to write a word without a mistake. . . . I became convinced that the educational institutions of the city of Marseilles are extraordinarily bad.

If some one, by some miracle, had seen all these institutions without seeing the people on the streets, in the workshops, in the cafés, in their private life, then what opinion would he have formed of a people so educated? He would surely have concluded that it was an ignorant, coarse, hypocritical people, full of prejudices and almost savage. But one needs only to get on familiar terms with one of the common folk and chat with him to convince himself that, on the contrary, the French people is almost such as it regards itself; clever, intelligent, social, open-minded, and really civilized. Look at a city work-man about thirty years old: he will write a letter with no such mistakes as are made in school, sometimes with none at all; he has some conception of politics, consequently of contempo-rary history and of geography; he knows some history from novels; he has some information as to the natural sciences. He very often knows how to draw and applies mathematical formulas in his trade. Where did he acquire all that?

I involuntarily found an answer to this in Marseilles, when after visiting the schools I started to wander along the streets and to frequent the wine-gardens, *cafés chantants*, museums, workshops, wharves, and bookshops. The same boy who had given me the answer that Henry IV was killed by Julius Cæsar knew very well the history of *The Three Musketeers* and *Monte Cristo*. In Marseilles I found twenty-eight cheap illustrated papers, costing from five to ten centimes. Among 250,000 inhabitants they have a circulation of 30,000, so that if we suppose that ten persons read or listen to one number, they all read them. Besides this there are the museum, the public libraries, the theaters. Next come the cafés, two large *cafés chantants*, which every one has the right to enter so long as he spends fifty centimes in them, and which are daily visited by as many as 25,000 persons, not counting the little cafés, which accommodate as many more—in each of these cafés little comedies and dramatic scenes are produced and verses are declaimed. Thus at the lowest reckoning a fifth part of the population receives oral instruction every day, just as the Greeks and Romans received it in their amphitheaters. Whether that education be good or bad is another thing; but there it is, an unconscious education many times stronger than the compulsory; there it is, an unconscious school that has undermined the compulsory school and made its content almost nil. There remains only the despotic form, almost without content.—[*On Popular Education* (1862).]

Obviously the true course for an educator, Tolstoy concludes, is to reject the element of compulsion in education, and to adopt the methods of the free school of life, giving to the uneducated people the sort of education that they themselves desire. This is even more true in Russia than in western Europe, since in Russia schools have still to be created and no false traditions hamper the educator. "If we become convinced that popular education in Europe is advancing along a false path, then by doing nothing for our own popular education we shall do more than if we suddenly introduce into it by violence all that seems good to each of us."*

For Tolstoy, the two cardinal questions of education are, what to teach, and how to teach it. The sole criterion by which the first can be answered is freedom; the sole method by which the second can be solved is experience.†

Not even reading must be forced on the people if they do not wish to learn it:

If the question be put thus: "Is primary education useful or not for the people?"—then no one can give a negative answer. But if some one asks: "Is it useful to teach the people to read when it does not know how to read and has no books to read?" then I hope that every impartial man will answer: "I do not know, just as I do not know whether it would be useful to teach the whole people to play the fiddle or to make shoes." Looking closer at the results of the ability to read in the form in which it is imparted to the people, I think that the majority will reply unfavorably to reading, taking into consideration the prolonged compulsion, the disproportionate development of memory, the false idea of the completeness of science, the repugnance for further education, the false self-love, and the opportunity for senseless reading that are acquired in these schools. In the school at Yásnaya Polyána all the pupils who enter from the reading schools continually fall behind the pupils who enter from the school of life, and not only fall behind them, but fall behind them the more the longer they have been taught in the reading school.—[*On Methods of Teaching Reading.*]

* *On Popular Education* (1862).   † *On Popular Education* (1874).

But in general, accepting the criterion of freedom, the program of popular schools in Russia is settled, as Tolstoy tells us in his article *On Popular Education* (1874), by the demands of the population; the masses desire to know the Russian and the Slavic languages, and arithmetic, and nothing more. Tolstoy's problem was how to teach these three subjects in the most effective manner. In practice, however, he was far from restricting himself to this program, but introduced any other subjects—such as drawing, natural science, and history—that he found appealed to the children, though presumably not so greatly to their fathers and mothers. There is a wide difference between the rather narrow dictum just quoted from his article written in 1874 and the freer tone of his writings in his own periodical, twelve years earlier. In 1862 he was guided by his own experience in his school, in 1874 by reasonings based on the demands of the adult peasants.

With regard to methods of instruction Tolstoy's experience was similar; he acquired a fervent dislike for western models. The object in the schools he visited was, he concluded, to choose the methods that would make life easiest for the teacher. Great emphasis was laid on external order, which deadens interest and thereby destroys the pupils' ability to learn. Nor did theories of pedagogy seem to Tolstoy of any value. In all pedagogy there is but one principle of real importance, to arouse the interest of the pupil and establish natural, human relations between him and the teacher. This principle he admits is found in the manuals of pedagogy. "The difference between us is only this, that they [the pedagogues] lose this conception that teaching should arouse the interest of the child, in a number of other conceptions about *development*, which contradict it; . . . while I regard the arousing of interest in the child, the greatest possible ease of study, and therefore its naturalness and freedom from compulsion, as the fundamental and the only test of good and bad teaching."*

Tolstoy gives a specific illustration of his point of view in his discussion of methods of teaching reading. The old church method was to make children memorize the Slavic names of the letters, *az, buki*, and so on, and then to spell out words by means of them. Passages of the Psalter, unintelligible to the pupils, had to be committed to memory. The new sound method, imported from Germany, teaches the sound of each letter, not its name, and begins practice in reading with the simplest sentences. The second method cannot be termed an improvement on the first. The energy of the teacher is dissipated in an unsuccessful attempt to make the children pronounce the consonants, such as *b* and *v*, without a following vowel; and the meaningless twaddle that they read arouses the children's contempt. One boy may learn to read from his brother by the old-fashioned method in a few weeks, while his companion may work a year under this improved German method

* *On Popular Education* (1874).

without results. To be sure, Tolstoy himself prefers
still another method, the *be-o, bo* method, to all others,
but he frankly admits that a teacher who had studied
with him made a wretched failure when he tried to apply
it in another school in which conditions were different.
When all is said, the only true method consists of experience and experiment:

The best method for a given teacher is that which is best
known to the teacher. All other methods that the teacher knows
or may invent should aid the teaching begun by one method. . . .
Each separate individual, in order to learn reading in the
shortest fashion, should be taught absolutely separately from
every other, and therefore for each there should be a separate
method. . . . One has a strong memory, and it is easier for him
to memorize syllables than to understand the vowellessness of
a consonant; another takes things in calmly and will understand that most rational sound method; a third has a feeling,
an instinct, and he, while reading whole words, will understand
the law of the composition of words.

The best teacher will be he who has ready at hand an explanation of what has puzzled the pupil. These explanations
give the teacher a knowledge of the greatest number of methods,
the capacity to think up new methods, and, above all, not
the following of one method, but the conviction that all methods
are one-sided, and that the best method would be that which
should answer all possible difficulties encountered by the pupil,
that is, not a method, but an art and a talent.—[*On Methods
of Teaching Reading.*]

In view of his denial of historic progress, Tolstoy's
definition of education is at first sight somewhat sur-

prising. "Education," he tells us, "is an activity of man having as its foundation the need of equality and the unchanging law of the forward movement of education."* With his explanation of this definition, our perplexity vanishes. One man teaches another Latin just as a mother teaches her child to speak, in order to place his pupil on a level with himself, so that they may understand each other. Man feels a need of equality, and the one who knows less strives to approximate his knowledge to that of his more learned companions; hence there is a forward movement in the accumulation of useful knowledge. When equality between teacher and pupil is attained the activity of education ceases. "The school should have but one aim, the transfer of information, of knowledge, not attempting to pass over into the moral field of convictions, belief, and character; it should have but one aim, science, and not the results of its influence on human personality."† In other words, the teacher must not attempt to force upon a child his own corrupt character; that would be an act of violence of the grossest sort. The child has less information than the teacher, but in character he is superior to him:

A healthy child is born into the world, fully satisfying those demands of absolute harmony in regard to truth, beauty, and good that we bear within us; it is near to inanimate beings—to the plant, to the animal, to nature, which constantly represents for us that truth, beauty, and good which we seek and desire.

* *Progress and the Definition of Education.*   † *Education and Culture.*

In all ages and with all men the child has been regarded as a model of innocence, of sinlessness, of goodness, truth, and beauty. "Man is born perfect," is the great word spoken by Rousseau, and this word, like a rock, will remain firm and sure. When born, man represents the prototype of harmony, truth, beauty, and goodness. But every hour in life, each moment of time, increases the extent, the quantity, and the time of those relations, which, at the time of his birth, were in perfect harmony, and each step and each hour threatens the destruction of that harmony, and each following step and each following hour threatens a new destruction, and gives no hope of the restoration of the shattered harmony.—[*Who is to Teach the Art of Writing?*]

To this true aim of education, that of introducing equality among men, Tolstoy adds, there are joined false aims, such as the desire on the part of the powerful to make other people useful to them; thus the government establishes universities in order to train capable public servants. This university education detaches the sons of honest and industrious laborers or farmers from the environment in which they have lived and makes them despise their families and their former associates:

In the university you will rarely see any man with a fresh and healthy face, and you will not see a single man who would look with respect, or even calmly, though with disrespect, at the environment from which he has emerged, and in which he will have to live; he looks at it with contempt, disgust, and supercilious pity. Thus he looks at the men of his own environment, at his kindred, thus he looks even at the activity

which should be his in accordance with his social position.—
[*Education and Culture.*]

This argument is at first sight the same as that used
by some English aristocratic opponents of attempts to
popularize higher education; in reality it is quite
the reverse. The English aristocrat laments any tendency to give to parvenus the education that has been
the privilege of his own class; he will preserve intact
his superior caste. Tolstoy, on the contrary, finds the
university product, whether aristocrats or parvenus,
inferior to the great body of the Russian people. The
university can train only—

. . . either officials, who are convenient only for the government, or professor-officials, or literary-man-officials, who are
convenient for society, or men who are aimlessly torn away
from their former environment, whose youth has been corrupted and who find no place for themselves in life—so-
called men of *university education*, cultivated, that is, irritated,
sickly liberals. The university is our first and foremost educational institution. It is the first to arrogate to itself the right
of education and the first to prove, by the results that it
attains, the illegality and impossibility of education. Only
from the social point of view may the fruits of the university
be justified. The university prepares not such men as are
needed by humanity, but such as are needed by a corrupt
society.—[*Education and Culture.*]

With his contempt for "liberal" innovations and for
all "liberal" thought, with his dislike of government

activity and his desire for natural, human relations in education, it is no wonder that Tolstoy pours forth the vials of his wrath upon the project of a new plan for organizing popular schools brought forward by the government in 1862,* and founded in large measure on the example of the United States. Under the old despotism of Nicholas I the government had itself done next to nothing for popular education, and had prohibited the opening of any private schools whatever. That law was so bad that it was not enforced; it was in fact forgotten, and private persons taught the peasants in whatever way they pleased, or in some cases the peasants themselves opened little schools of their own. The new project attacked a huge problem, which the authorities did not in the least understand, with grossly inadequate means; and, though it legalized the opening of private schools, it laid very considerable restrictions upon them. The defects and inadequacy of the new project Tolstoy shows with convincing clearness. The example of the United States is no just precedent for Russia; to begin with, taxes in one country are voted by the people, in the other they are imposed from above by the government. The danger is that this new law, with its dull, mechanical prescriptions, will not only fail to produce any good, but will be enforced and so will crush independent effort on the part of the population.

* Or perhaps in the year previous; Tolstoy's article was published in *Yásnaya Polyána* for March, 1862.

Tolstoy's own plan, which he set forth a dozen years later in his article *On Popular Education*, (1874), would be to have the district authorities use their money primarily for the encouragement of private effort. They should spend money on the teacher, not on the location; a real school consists of teacher and pupil, not of a stone building with an iron roof. They should not disdain even cheap teachers, who will work for from two to five rubles a month in smoky huts, or in transient lodgings with the peasants. But the authorities should themselves maintain a public school which should serve as an example of right methods, and which would thus raise the standard of private instruction. In other words, Tolstoy would introduce a free organization of educational institutions not entirely different from that which prevails, in differing fashions, in England and America. His recommendations show an intimate knowledge of conditions and much practical common sense. Despite all his utopian idealism and despite his cantankerous refusal to cooperate in the work of other men, Tolstoy had, as he proved at intervals in the management of his own estates, and later by his conduct of famine relief, a considerable share of practical executive ability.

Such are Tolstoy's general principles, which he strove to realize in practice in his own school at Yásnaya Polyána. Of his delight in his own creation he speaks in a letter to his cousin, the Countess Alexandra Tolstoy, written in July, 1861:

I have a poetic, charming occupation, from which I cannot tear myself away, my school. When I break loose from the office and from the peasants, who pursue me from every part of the house, I go to the school, but since it is being repaired, the classes are held nearby in the orchard, under the apple-trees, where you can walk only by bending down, it is so overgrown. And there sits the teacher, with the pupils around him, chewing grass and popping linden and maple leaves. The teacher teaches in the way that I advise him, but nevertheless rather poorly, as even the children feel. They like me better. And we begin a chat which lasts for three or four hours, and nobody is bored. I cannot tell you what sort of children they are; one must see them. Among the children of our own lovely class in society I have seen nothing like them. Just consider the fact that in the course of two years, with a complete absence of discipline, not one boy or girl has been punished. Never any laziness, any rudeness, any stupid jokes or indecent words. The schoolhouse is now almost finished. Three large rooms, one pink, and two blue, are occupied by the school. Besides that, the museum is in the main room. On the shelves and around the walls are arranged stones, butterflies, skeletons, herbs, flowers, physical apparatus and so forth. On Sundays the museum is opened to all, and a German from Jena, who has turned out a splendid young man, performs experiments. Once a week there is a botany class, and we all go to the woods for flowers, herbs, and mushrooms. There are four singing classes a week. Of drawing there are six (the German again) and they go finely. Surveying succeeds so well that the peasants are already asking the boys to help them. There are three teachers in all besides myself. And then the priest comes twice a week. Yet you continue to think that I am an infidel. And then I teach the priest how to teach

them. This is how we teach: on St. Peter's day we tell the
story of Peter and Paul and the whole service. Later on, when
Feofan has died in the village, we explain what extreme unction
is and so on. And thus, without apparent connection, we go
through all the sacraments, the liturgy, and all the holidays of
the New Testament and the Old. The classes are arranged from
eight to twelve and from three to six, but they always continue till two, because it is impossible to drive the children
out of school—they want more. In the evening often more
than half of them stay to spend the night in the orchard, in a
hut. At dinner and supper and after supper we, the teachers,
consult together. On Saturdays we read our notes to one
another and prepare for the coming week.—[*Correspondence
with the Countess A. A. Tolstoy*, pp. 154, 155.]

Of the general organization of his school, and of his
experiments in the teaching of different subjects, Tolstoy
writes at some length in his article on *Yásnaya Polyána
School in November and December* [*1861*]. His aim
was that the children should themselves desire to acquire knowledge, through seeing the value of it, and that
the teacher should merely assist them in their quest.
This concept of freedom is that of the highest university work, which Tolstoy applied to the primary school.
There was no hint of compulsion in any way:

No one brings anything with him, either books or copybooks. No lessons are given to be studied at home. Not
to speak of bringing anything in his hands, the pupil has nothing
to bring even in his head. He is not obliged to remember today
any lesson, anything at all that he did yesterday. He is not

tortured by thoughts of the coming lesson. He brings only himself, his receptive nature, and the confidence that at school today it will be as jolly as it was yesterday. He does not think of class until the class has begun. No one is ever scolded for tardiness and no one is ever tardy—except perhaps the older boys, whose fathers now and then keep them at home for some work. And then that big boy, out of breath, comes running to school. . . .

The teacher comes into the room, and on the floor the screaming children are lying, shouting, "The heap is small!" or, "The boys are squashing me!" or, "Quit, stop pulling my hair!" and so on. "Peter Mikháylovich!" cries a voice from the bottom of the heap to the teacher as he comes in, "tell them to stop it." "Good morning, Peter Mikháylovich!" shout the others, continuing their scuffle. The teacher takes the books and distributes them to those who have gone to the bookcase with him; those who are lying on the top of the heap on the floor also demand books. The heap becomes gradually smaller. As soon as the majority have taken books, all the rest run to the case and shout, "Me too, me too! Give me yesterday's book—and me the *Koltsovish*," and so on. If there still remain two or three excited by the struggle, who continue to tumble about on the floor, then those sitting with books shout to them: "What are you fooling there for? We can't hear anything. Quit!" The excited boys submit and, out of breath, take their books; and only for a short time, while sitting at their books, swing their legs from unallayed excitement. The spirit of war flies away, and the spirit of reading reigns in the room. With the same enthusiasm with which he was pulling Mitka's hair he now reads the *Koltsovish* book (the name by which Koltsóv's works pass in our school), with teeth almost clenched and with glittering

eyes, seeing nothing around him except his book. To tear
him away from reading would be as hard now as it would
have been to stop his fighting a short time before. . . .

According to the program there are four lessons before
dinner, but sometimes there are only three or two, and sometimes on quite different subjects from those set down. The
teacher begins on arithmetic and passes to geometry; he
begins with sacred history and ends with grammar. Sometimes
teacher and pupils grow so enthusiastic that instead of one
hour the class lasts for three. Often the pupils shout of their
own accord, "No, more, more!" and cry out against those
who are bored. "If you're sick of it, go off with the little
kids," they say contemptuously. . . .

The school has evolved freely from principles introduced into
it by the teacher and the pupils. In spite of all the preponder-
ating influence of the teacher, the pupil has always had the
right not to go to school, and even, if he goes to school, not to
listen to the teacher. The teacher has had the right not to
admit a pupil, and has had the possibility of acting with all
the strength of his influence on the majority of the pupils,
on the society that always arises among schoolboys.—[*Yásnaya
Polyána School: General Sketch.*]

Gradually, by the free action of the boys themselves,
this external disorder subsides, and a free order is established far finer than any that could have been devised by the teacher. Despite a somewhat wavering
practice, Tolstoy is convinced that even to stop fighting
among the pupils is a mistake:

How many times have I seen, when children were fighting
and the teacher rushed to separate them, how the parted

enemies would eye each other askance, and, even in the presence of a stern teacher, would not restrain themselves from subsequently kicking each other harder than ever! How many times do I see every day how some Kiryushka, with clenched teeth, flies upon Taraska, pulls his hair, throws him on the ground, and at the risk of his life seems eager to maim his enemy—and before a minute has passed Taraska is already laughing from under Kiryushka, so much easier is it for them to settle scores alone; and before five minutes are over they are becoming friends again and going to take their seats side by side. . . . I am convinced that the school ought not to meddle in that part of education which belongs only to the family, that the school ought not and has no right to reward and punish, that the best police and administration of the school consists in leaving full freedom to the pupils to study and to get along together as they please.

That Tolstoy was the merriest of playmates with the boys in his school and that he was sincerely beloved by them we know from the testimony of Vasily Morozov, one of his pupils. Morozov soon left the village for the city, fell into the depths of poverty, became a tramp, and in his despair determined to drown himself:

And I went to the stream. The day was hot. By the stream there were many people. They were bathing. It was as noisy as in a public bath. I sat down on the bank, took off my boots—and then I suddenly remembered how I and all the pupils of the Yásnaya Polyána school, with Lev Nikoláyevich at our head, used to bathe in the pond and how we would show him our skill; we would jump from the bank one after

another, swim, dive, and chase one another. And Lev Nikoláyevich would lie on the bank with his head propped on his
hand, and would laugh with all his might, especially when some
one wanted to show off and did not succeed.

"Enough, enough, come out!" Lev Nikoláyevich would say
with a laugh. "Dress yourselves. Murzik there is getting
chilled through."

And he would watch us shivering boys, whose arms were
shaking so that we had hard work to get them into the sleeves
of our shirts. Then Lev Nikoláyevich would make us run
races around the pond in couples. More laughter. At last
L. N. would shout: "Boys, let's see who can get to school
first; hurrah!" And he himself would start out at full speed.
We would run after him with shouts and screams, jostling one
another, stumbling and falling. But L. N. was always the
winner. . . .

I was a pupil of the school in Yásnaya Polyána; I loved
the school, and I loved Lev Nikoláyevich also. I remember that
we had the most sincere, childlike attachment for him and
that Lev Nikoláyevich had the most sincere attachment to
us. It was a village commune, but not one depending on
force—rather a commune united by the tie of love. We had
no jealousy of one another in the sense that Lev Nikoláyevich
granted something special to one more than to another. Such
were the feelings that I took away from the school at Yásnaya
Polyána. Like the brand of Jerusalem, it has remained on
my soul and to this day I bear it there.—[In *On Tolstoy* (Moscow, 1909), pp. 128, 129, 132.]

In the teaching of different subjects Tolstoy was not
uniformly successful. Grammar, for example, he could
never make interesting to his pupils, and characteristi-

cally—and with much reason—came to the following conclusion:

> Personally we [I] are not yet able fully to renounce the tradition that grammar, in the sense of the laws of language, is indispensable for the correct exposition of thoughts: it even seems to us that boys studying feel a need of grammar, that in them unconsciously lie the laws of grammar. But we are convinced that the grammar that we know is not at all that needed by the pupils, and that in this custom of teaching grammar there is some great historic misunderstanding.— [*Yásnaya Polyána School: Writing, Grammar and Penmanship.*]

Tolstoy is seen at his best as a teacher of composition, a subject in which even his detractors must admit his competence. He tells touchingly how he suggested the idea of a story, *The Life of a Soldier's Wife*, to two bright boys, about eleven years old, and cooperated with them in the development of it. (Whimsically enough, he reprinted in his complete works his account of how this story was written, and his commentary on it, in his essay, *Who is to Teach the Art of Writing; We to the Peasant Children, or the Peasant Children to Us?*, but did not reprint the story itself, which seems never to have been translated into English.) The tale is a simple one, the life of a little lad who lives with his mother and grandmother while his drunken father is in the army; the boy describes the birth and death of a baby brother and the marriage of an older sister. Finally the father returns, reformed, and "after that we lived well." Tolstoy did no more than keep his pupils' minds

intent on the incidents of the tale; their insight into the
situations proved better than his own. Any attention
to external details, such as handwriting or spelling, was
fatal to interest. The little peasants' work, he claimed,
contained beauties such as could scarcely be found
elsewhere in Russian literature. The story is indeed
excellent of its own sort; perfect handling of detail has
done its work.

One of the two boy artists was Vasily Morozov,
from whose reminiscences of Tolstoy quotations have
already been given. He later became a cabman in
Tula, but occasionally he did bits of writing. A story by
him is printed in *The Messenger of Europe*, one of the
foremost literary magazines of Russia, for September,
1908. Tolstoy's preface to the tale deserves quotation, as an expression of his unvarying literary ideals:

This story was written by my most beloved pupil of my first
school of the year 1862, at that time the dear twelve-year-old
Vaska Morozov, now the honored sixty-year-old Vasily
Stepánovich Morozov.

As then there were especially precious to me in that dear
boy his sensitiveness to all that was good, his affectionateness,
and, above all, his unfailing frankness and truthfulness, so
now I am particularly pleased with the same traits in this
simple story, which is so sharply distinguished by its truthfulness from the majority of literary productions.

You feel that here nothing has been thought up or invented,
but that what is told is just what took place; that a fragment
of life has been seized, and of that peculiarly Russian life with
its sad, gloomy, and precious, spiritual traits.

I think that I have not been bribed by my attachment to the author and that other readers will be as fond of the story as I myself.

In the teaching of literature Tolstoy was similarly an expert, but one of a peculiar sort. His pupils were interested in Afanasyev's folk tales, and in all similar material that had been derived straight from the lips of the Russian common people, and they loved the stories of the Old Testament, but any attempts to guide them up to the reading of Pushkin and Gogol proved futile. Words could not be explained to the children; they must be gradually apprehended by being met again and again. The stuff written by literary men and intended for popular consumption was nearly always a flat failure. Tolstoy felt that a whole course of graded reading was needed for use in the peasant schools, and he set to work to prepare it in his series of *Readers*. On these he labored with far greater ardor than upon *Anna Karenin*. In April, 1872, he wrote to his cousin, the Countess Alexandra Tolstoy:

I am getting on well, except that old age begins to make itself felt; I am often ill and am hastening to work. There is more and more work ahead of me. If they had told me twenty years ago to think up work for twenty-three years, I should have exerted all the strength of my mind and yet should not have thought up enough work for three years. But now if you told me that I should live in ten persons for a hundred years, all of us would not be able to finish all that is *indispensable*. My *Primer* is now being printed at one end, and at the other is still being written and added to. This *Primer* alone could give me work for a hundred years. For it I need a knowledge of Greek, Indian, and Arabic literature; I need all the natural sciences; and the work on the style is terrible. All must be beautiful, short, simple, and above all, clear. Some Frenchman has said: "Clearness is the courtesy of men who wish to teach, when they address the public."—And what is worst of all, people will rail at me for this toil, and you first of all. In your circle you will be sure to find my style *vulgaire*. And I cannot neglect even the opinion of your circle, because I am writing for everybody.—[*Correspondence with the Countess A. A. Tolstoy*, p. 233.]

Tolstoy's labors deserved the immense success that they achieved. His series of five little books contains fables remodeled from Æsop and from Indian sources, stories from the Arabic, bits of natural science, reworkings of Russian ballads, and, most interesting of all for us, original stories for children. From the Bible he gives nothing; he tells us that he found it useless and even injurious to tamper with the language of that book. His own stories are of various sorts; tales drawn from the people themselves such as *God Sees the Truth;* incidents of child life; and bits of his own experience such as his adventure with the bear on the hunt, and stories of the bull-dog Bulka who was his companion in the Caucasus. Unfortunately not all these stories were included in Tolstoy's collected works, and consequently some of the best have never been translated into English. No work by Tolstoy is more perfect, for example, than his story of how little Philip went to school for the first time. In it he has caught the child's point of view and writes without condescension, that most vicious of pedagogical vices; he has the secret of simplicity, even as the man who wrote the story of Joseph and his Brethren. The tale demands quotation:

LITTLE PHILIP (a true story)

Once upon a time there was a boy whose name was Philip. One day all the children were starting off for school. Philip got his hat and wanted to go too. But his mother said to him: "Where are you going, Philip!" "To school." "You're too small; you can't go." And his mother kept him at home. The children went off to school. Early in the morning his father had driven off to the woods; then his mother went away to her daily work. In the hut there were left only Philip and his grandmother, who was lying on the oven. Philip grew lonesome all by himself; his grandmother went to sleep, and he began to look for his hat. He did not find his own; but he took an old one of his father's and started for school.

The school was outside the village near the church. When Philip was walking through his own neighborhood the dogs did not touch him—they knew him. But when he had passed beyond it, Fido jumped out and barked, and after Fido a big dog, Towser. Little Philip began to run, and the dogs ran after him. Philip began to cry, stumbled and fell down. A peasant came out, drove away the dogs, and said: "Where are you running to all alone, you little monkey?" Philip said nothing at all, picked up his skirts and started to run at full speed. He ran to the school. There was nobody on the porch, but in the school he could hear the sound of children's voices. Philip was scared: "What if the teacher drives me off?" And he began to think what he should do. If he went back, the dog would bite him again; if he went into the school, he was afraid of the teacher. A peasant woman came past the school with a pail and said: "They're all studying—what are you standing there for?" So Philip went into the school. In the entry he took off his hat and opened the door. The school was all full of children. Each was shouting his own lesson, and the teacher, with a red necktie on, was walking up and down the center.

"What do you want?" he shouted at little Philip. Philip clutched at his hat and said nothing. "Who are you?" Philip was silent. "Are you dumb?" Philip was so scared that he couldn't speak. "Well, then, go home, if you won't talk." Philip would have been glad to say something, but his throat was dry from terror. He looked at the teacher and began to cry. Then the teacher felt sorry for him. He patted him on the head and asked the children who this boy was.

"That's little Philip, Kostyushka's brother; he's been begging to come to school for a long time, but his mother wouldn't let him, and now he's sneaked off to school."

"Well, sit down on the bench by your brother, and I'll ask your mother to let you come to school."

The teacher began to show Philip the letters, but Philip knew them already and could read a little bit.

"Now then, spell your name."

Little Philip said: "F-i, fi; el-ip, lip."

Everybody laughed.

"Fine boy," said the teacher. "Who taught you to read?"

Philip plucked up his courage and said: "Kostyushka. I'm smart; I understood it all right off. I'm just awful bright!"

The teacher laughed and said: "But do you know your prayers?" Philip said, "Yes, I do," and he began to repeat the prayer to the Virgin, but he said every word wrong. The teacher stopped him and said: "Wait a while before you boast, and just study."

After that Philip began to go to school with the children.— [*A New Primer.*]

Tolstoy's attempts to teach art to his peasant children led him to startling conclusions. He reasoned that the enjoyment of art was a natural human need, to which the children had a perfect right. But he found that neither the children nor their parents could be roused to an appreciation of the Venus of Milo, or of Beethoven, or of Pushkin's lyrics. He came to the characteristically Tolstoyan conclusion that the masses were not below Pushkin and Beethoven, but above them:

I became convinced that a lyric poem, such for example as "I remember the charming moment," that productions of music such as Beethoven's last symphony, are not so unconditionally and universally good as the song of *Vanka the Steward*, and the refrain, *Down Mother Volga;* that Pushkin and Beethoven please us not because there is any absolute beauty in them, but because we are just as corrupted as Pushkin and Beethoven; because Pushkin and Beethoven alike flatter our perverted irritability and our weakness. How commonly do we hear the threadbare paradox, that for the understanding of the beautiful a certain preparation is needed! Who said that, and how is it proved? That is only an evasion, a loop-hole from a hopeless situation into which we have been brought by the falsity of the tendency of our art, by its being the exclusive property of one class. Why are the beauty of the sun, the beauty of the human face, the beauty of the sounds of a folk-song, the beauty of an act of love and self-sacrifice, accessible to all, and why do they require no preparation? . . .

I assume that the need of the enjoyment of art and the service of art lie in each human personality, no matter to what race and environment it may belong, and that this need has its rights and should be satisfied. Accepting this principle as an axiom, I say that if inconveniences and difficulties arise in the enjoyment of art by every one and the production of it for every one, then the cause of these inconveniences lies not in the manner of its transmission, not in the spread of art among many or in its concentration among a few, but in the character and tendency of the art, about which we should have doubts, both in order not to inflict what is false on the young generation, and in order to give the opportunity to this young generation to work out something new both in form and in content.—[*Yásnaya Polyána School: the Arts.*]

True to this conception, Tolstoy concludes his account of Yásnaya Polyána school with the words:

The aim of the teaching of music to the people should consist in imparting to them the knowledge of the general laws of music that we possess, but by no means in the transfer to them of the false taste that is developed in us.—[*Yásnaya Polyána School: Singing.*]

This theory as to the art of our time is essentially the same that Tolstoy expounded twenty-six years later in *What is Art?* (1898), though he there condemns most modern art as *essentially bad*, while here he at first terms it only *less universally good* than popular art, and then insists that its lack of universality comes from its appeal to "our perverted irritability and our weakness." His arguments in his later book are, however, entirely different, being based on his new religious conception of life; they will be considered in due time. One may here emphasize the fact that while his supporting arguments change, his temperamental preference for the popular standard remains the same. This preference is based on the doctrine of Rousseau, that civilization necessarily causes degeneration in the individual man; and it must stand or fall with that doctrine. If we reject Rousseau's teaching in favor of the sounder view that civilization contributes to the growth of certain valuable human capacities, though it may often stunt others, then we have to consider the question whether a given work of art, a lyric by Pushkin or a symphony by Beethoven, appeals to our finer or our baser emotions. The quality of the emotion aroused by a work of art is always a true test of its merit, if the test be applied in a broad and sympathetic manner; the universality of the appeal of a work of art can be used as a test only in connection with other criteria.*

Tolstoy's whole theory of education, no less than his criticism of modern art, is based on a point of view identical with that of Rousseau. His originality con-

* Compare pp. 340-343, below.

sists mainly in applying Rousseau's ideas to Russian conditions; in carrying out in actual experience with a school of peasant children ideas that Rousseau had enunciated with very little regard to working conditions. (The influence of Rousseau on Tolstoy extends even to details; in teaching singing he went so far as to use Rousseau's system of musical notation.) More than this, Tolstoy's ideas are the same as those of a whole series of educational reformers since Rousseau, through Froebel down to Madame Montessori and others. Professor Dewey's *Schools of Tomorrow* is an enthusiastic account of how, under American conditions, different teachers are endeavoring to apply principles that are Rousseau's, and therefore Tolstoy's. The same leaven is working in many different minds.

Tolstoy differs from his fellow reformers only in the unsparing consistency with which he attempts—not always with success—to carry out the principle of individualism in education. His doctrine that the school should convey only information, and not seek to influence individual character, seems to be his own. This principle sprang from the fact that he had not yet worked out a clearly formulated religious and moral philosophy. As he tells us in his *Confession* (chapter 3) he was trying to teach without knowing what to teach. To the doctrine that he professed he could not be true in practice. As we have seen from his own description of his work, his own personality inevitably influenced that of the children with whom he came in contact.

Later, when he had formed for himself a clear moral and religious ideal, Tolstoy straightway demanded that all education should be religious, and laid it down as a principle that the example of a teacher is the most powerful means of education. "I should give two rules for education," he wrote: "not only to live well oneself, but to work over oneself, constantly perfecting oneself, and to conceal nothing about one's own life from one's children."* He had now discovered a religious sanction for education such as existed in the middle ages, a certainty of truth as to ideals of life that justified a man in communicating those ideals to others. But his new religious ideal had as its cardinal principle the doctrine of the non-resistance to evil by violence, that is, an abhorrence of all external compulsion; the communication must come through the infectiousness of true religion embodied in life; force is abhorrent both to religion and to education.

One queries whether Tolstoy was right in his unmeasured repugnance to the use of compulsion in education. The answer is ready at once: if organized society be accepted as right, then compulsion has a place as a last resort in education as in other human relations. The duty of every educator is to let the individuality of his pupils develop with the least possible measure of constraint, yet he must use his best efforts to see that these pupils develop into useful members of society. Merely to acquire a legible handwriting involves the

* *Thoughts on Education and Instruction,* collected by Chertkóv, §2.

subjection of one's personal taste to the convenience of
his fellow men. Force in education, as in government,
is a last resort; voluntary cooperation is the ideal to
be sought. No other follower of Rousseau inveighs
against discipline as does Tolstoy. Rousseau himself
does not reject discipline, but in his theoretic treatise,
Émile, he simply neglects the problem. Tolstoy himself, when he grants the teacher the right not to admit
a pupil, recognizes a sort of negative discipline. Despite
all the beneficent influence on education of Rousseau's
romantic individualism, Rousseau is not the greatest
of educational writers. That place of honor belongs
rather to the moderate and compromising Comenius,
who, starting from a system of Christian anarchy somewhat like that into which Tolstoy developed, emerged
from it into the recognition of broad social service in
the world as it is at present organized.

But can organized society of today itself be justified
as an improvement on a state of barbarism? This
assumption Tolstoy emphatically denies, as we have already seen (pages 93–95), thus showing himself a true disciple of Rousseau. This fundamental quarrel between
Tolstoy and the Liberal worshippers of progress depends on their different standards of value. The Liberals
admire the material advances of humanity and can
point to real achievements. Within historic times the
population of the earth has enormously increased,
waste places have been settled, communication has
become more swift and safe, disease has been checked,

and the average human life has been lengthened. All this can be demonstrated. But there is no proof that the individual man is any happier today than he was two thousand years and more ago, or that his brain capacity has increased. A Hottentot's little girl enjoys her toys as much as a millionaire's daughter; the domestication of the horse probably required as much brain capacity as the invention of the locomotive. An American boy who uses the telephone at five and at fourteen constructs an amateur wireless telegraphic apparatus is not necessarily an inventive genius. Human society is more complicated than it used to be, but there is no proof that the individual man has advanced. Whether we prefer his present state to his former one, whether we accept the commonplaces of the news-papers or the "paradoxes" of Rousseau and Tolstoy depends more on our temperament than on our open-ness to reasoned conviction. Nor can men be blamed for resisting the attempts of a better organized so-ciety to assimilate them; the present struggle against German *Kultur* has in it a certain Tolstoyan element. Individual liberty is valuable in itself, even at the cost of some material welfare.

In revolting from the Liberal faith in western progress and culture, and in recognizing the right of the Russian common folk to educate itself in whatever way it might see fit, independently of western models, Tolstoy ap-proximated to the Slavophiles, with their faith in Rus-sian *nationality* as something distinct and apart from

that of the west. Similarly in his view of the emancipation of the serfs as due to the emperor alone he joined
them in their idea of *autocracy*. He may be said to
have accepted the Slavophile ideal of a free people, taking no part in government, and ruled over by a benevolent
autocrat. At a later time, when he returned to the
bosom of the Russian church, he may be said to have
temporarily accepted their faith in *orthodoxy*. Yet one
would make a great mistake in classing Tolstoy at any
time in his life as a member of the Slavophile party.
He lacked the historic interest that was at the root of
all their teachings. His *autocracy* was the instinctive
loyalty to the tsar of a soldier, an aristocrat, and a
landowner of long descent, joined with a dislike for
Liberal talkers whom he regarded as insincere; his
nationality was a revolt from Liberal theories, joined
with a most genuine affection for the peasants on his
estate; his *orthodoxy* was a conviction of the impotence
of Liberal agnosticism to bring peace to the soul such
as was conferred on his peasant friends by the Orthodox
Church. The Slavophiles, like their Liberal opponents,
reached their mental attitude by a process of abstract
reasoning; Tolstoy was brought to his own opinions
partly by the study of Rousseau, but mainly by his individual personal experience. All three items of the
Slavophile creed he later cast aside with loathing.

To sum up, individualism, expressed in a contempt
for traditional and accepted authority and in an ardent
love of free personal development, is at the basis of all

Tolstoy's educational theories.   The same attitude will later be shown in his critique of the state and of the whole existing social order. His subsequent doctrine of non-resistance to evil by violence, which he made the corner-stone of his ethical system, is not the cause of his anarchistic theories but the prop and support of them. (The parallel to the development of his theory of art is exact and striking.) But his individualism is far removed from the egotistic self-cultivation of a Goethe or the rebellious self-assertion of an Ibsen; it is an individualism of method, not of aim, and is combined with an ideal of service, of self-sacrifice, and of recognition of the claims of other men. Even at this early period, Tolstoy's individuality is most strongly marked in his reluctance to hamper the development of other individualities. And an aversion to the use of force, even for promoting aims the righteousness of which would seem self-evident, is already the mainspring of his instinctive philosophy.

CHAPTER V

O Tolstoy's married life one may apply his own words at the opening of *Anna Karenin:* "All happy families are like one another; each unhappy family is unhappy in its own way." And to this one may add that happy families, like happy nations, have no history. Tolstoy's life in the years following his marriage was prosperous and uneventful; he was absorbed in his wife and children, in literary work, and in the care of his estate.

Tolstoy and his wife were admirably suited to each other, and their devotion, though not their mutual sympathy, remained constant until almost the time of Tolstoy's death. The Countess was an excellent housewife and mother, simple and practical, patient and forbearing, an admirer of her husband's genius and an aid in his literary work. Perhaps Kitty in *Anna Karenin* is her nearest portrait in her husband's writings. To his wife, Tolstoy was absolutely faithful; the loose living of his earlier years he now laid aside forever. The pair had thirteen children, of whom the first was born in July, 1863, and the last in 1888. In the education of the older children Tolstoy himself took a leading part, carrying out so far as he could the principles of Rousseau's *Émile*, and the Countess did her best to act in accord with his views.

In a letter to his cousin the Countess Alexandra Tolstoy, written in the autumn of 1863, Tolstoy describes his joy in his new life, his fresh enthusiasm for literary work, and his consequent loss of interest in the school that had so absorbed him the year before:

You will recognize my handwriting and my signature; but who I am now and what I am you will surely ask yourself. I am a husband and a father, fully content with my situation and so wonted to it that in order to feel my own happiness, I must think of what I should be otherwise. I do not keep pondering over my own situation (*grübeln* has been abandoned) and I only feel my feelings; I do not think about my family relations. This condition gives me an awful lot of mental scope. I have never felt my mental and even all my moral forces so free and so capable of work. And I have work on hand. This work is a novel of the time from 1810 to 1820 [*War and Peace*] which has been completely occupying me since autumn began. Whether it shows weakness of character or strength—I sometimes think both—I must confess that my view of life, of the peasants, and of society is now completely different from what it was the last time that we saw each other. I can be sorry for them, but it is hard for me to understand how I could love them so deeply. However, I am glad that I passed through that school; that latest mistress of mine did much towards forming me. I love children and pedagogy, but it is hard for me to understand myself as I was a year ago. The children come to me in the evenings and bring with them to my mind recollections of the teacher who was in me and who will never return. I am now a writer with all the strength of my soul, and I write and meditate on my work as I never before wrote or meditated. I am a happy and serene husband and father, having no secrets from anybody and no desire except that all should continue as it has hitherto.—[*Correspondence with the Countess A. A. Tolstoy*, pp. 191, 192.]

A letter of January, 1865, tells the same story of complete happiness and contentment at home:

Do you remember, I once wrote you that people were mistaken in expecting any happiness in which there should be neither toil, nor deception, nor grief, but where all should go on evenly and happily? I was mistaken then; there is such happiness and I have been living in it for more than two years, and every year it becomes deeper and more uniform. And the materials of which this happiness is built are the most unbeautiful: children who (excuse me) befoul their clothes and yell; a wife who is suckling one, leading the other about, and at every moment reproaching me for not seeing that they are both on the brink of the grave; and paper and ink, by means of which I am describing events and the feelings of men that never existed.—[*Ibid.*, p. 198.]

The first literary work that Tolstoy undertook after his marriage was *Linen-Measurer* (*Holstomér*), the story of a horse; with this, as he writes in a letter to Fet, he was occupied in the spring of 1863, but for some reason or other the tale was not published until

1888. The story is as thoroughly didactic, though not in so obvious a fashion, as *Black Beauty.* The wholesome, normal, natural life of the horse is contrasted with the dissolute and vain existence of its master and his associates. The concluding pages, which tell of the deaths of the animal and the man, handle in a more drastic fashion the theme that Tolstoy had already treated in *Three Deaths.*

Two comedies that he wrote in this same year, his first experiments in the dramatic form, have unfortunately never been published.

Tolstoy's chief occupation during the early years of his married life was the writing of *War and Peace,* on which, as is plain from the letter quoted above, he began work in the autumn of 1863. He at first projected a novel based on the aristocratic conspiracy of December, 1825, against the Russian government—the conspiracy of the Decembrists, as it is called; then he grew interested in the earlier life of his characters, and composed a huge novel centering on the struggle between Russia and Napoleon. He prepared for it by a study of the archives of his own family and of other historical materials, and during the composition of it he developed the peculiar philosophy of history that he embodied in the book. His habits of work are well described by his wife's brother, Stepán Behrs:

The whole life of Lev Nikoláyevich is industrious in the full sense of the word. . . . He wrote mainly in the winter,

all day long, and sometimes until late at night. . . . Each
morning he sat down at his table and worked. If he did not
write, he prepared himself for writing by the study of sources
and materials. Sometimes before his work and after dinner
he liked to read English novels. Even in summer, when the
children were having a vacation and his wife begged him to
rest and not to work, he did not always yield to her request.
In the most conscientious toiler I have never seen such severity towards idleness as in Lev Nikoláyevich towards himself.—[*Reminiscences*, ch. 3.]

The Countess Tolstoy acted as her husband's secretary in his work; and, according to her brother, she
copied seven times the entire text of *War and Peace*.
This feat seems incredible in connection with her other
work. Of her labors on *Anna Karenin* her son Count
Ilyá Tolstoy gives a description that will presumably
apply equally well to the earlier novel:

My mother's work seemed much harder than my father's,
because we actually saw her at it, and she worked much
longer hours than he did. . . . Leaning over the manuscript and trying to decipher my father's scrawl with her
short-sighted eyes, she used to spend whole evenings at work,
and often sat up late at night after everybody else had gone
to bed. Sometimes, when anything was written quite illeg-
ibly, she would go to my father's study and ask him what it
meant. But this was very rare, because my mother did not
like to disturb him. When it happened, my father would
take the manuscript in his hand, ask with some annoyance:
"What on earth is the difficulty?" and begin to read it out
loud. When he came to the difficult place he would mumble

and hesitate, and sometimes had the greatest difficulty in making out, or rather in guessing, what he had written. He had a very bad handwriting and a terrible habit of inserting whole sentences between the lines, or in the corners of the page, or sometimes right across it. My mother often discovered gross grammatical errors, and pointed them out to my father and corrected them.

When *Anna Karenin* began to come out, . . . long galley-proofs were posted to my father and he looked them through and corrected them. At first, the margins would be marked with the ordinary typographical signs, letters omitted, marks of punctuation, and so on; then individual words would be changed, and then whole sentences; erasures and additions began; till, in the end, the proof-sheet was reduced to a mass of patches, perfectly black in places, and it was quite impossible to send it back as it stood, because no one but my mother could make head or tail of the tangle of conventional signs, transpositions, and erasures.

My mother would sit up all night copying the whole thing out afresh.

In the morning there lay the pages on her table, neatly piled together, covered all over with her fine clear handwriting, and everything was ready so that when Lévochka came down he could send the proof-sheets off by post.

My father would carry them off to his study to have "just one last look," and by the evening it was just as bad again; the whole thing had been rewritten and messed up once more.

"Sonya, my dear, I am very sorry, but I've spoilt all your work again; I promise I won't do it any more," he would say, showing her the passages he had inked over with a guilty air. "We'll send them off tomorrow without fail." But this tomorrow was often put off day by day for weeks or months together.

"There's just one bit I want to look through again," my
father would say, but he would get carried away and rewrite
the whole thing afresh. There were even occasions when,
after posting the proofs, my father remembered some particular words next day and corrected them by telegraph.

Several times, in consequence of these rewritings, the
printing of the novel in the *Russky Vestnik* was interrupted,
and sometimes it did not come out for months together.—
[*Reminiscences of Tolstoy*, pp. 137-139.]

War and Peace is an enormous work, in fifteen parts
and an epilogue. The first two parts, under the title
The Year 1805, were published, like *Family Happiness*,
Polikushka, and *The Cossacks*, in the *Russian Messenger*
(*Russky Vestnik*), edited by Katkóv, who, beginning
life as a moderate Liberal, had become the most prominent Nationalist and reactionary editor in Russia.
To Katkóv's political views Tolstoy, in a letter to his
cousin, expresses the most profound indifference. "He
and I have as much in common," he writes, "as you
and your water-carrier. I do not sympathize with their
prohibiting the Poles to speak Polish, but neither am I
angry at them for it. . . . Butchers kill the cattle
that we eat, but I am not obliged either to take them
to task or to sympathize with them."* This is merely
another instance of his general indifference to political
questions. From Katkóv he received 300 rubles (about
$225) a printed sheet; that is, six times the "best
authors'" price that Nekrasov had promised him for

* *Correspondence with the Countess A. A. Tolstoy*, p. 210.

his early work. His letters to his wife contain references
to rather vigorous haggling over terms. In general,
Tolstoy at this time of his life was eager to make money,
both by his literary work and by the management of
his estate. To quote from Behrs: "The English saying,
'An aristocrat without money is a commoner,' as he
said himself, made him anxious to increase his property
for the sake of his children."* *War and Peace* was not
completed until 1869; the later parts, probably in consequence of some quarrel with Katkóv, were not printed
in the *Russian Messenger*, but were issued as separate
volumes.

"In his farming," to quote once more from Behrs,
"Tolstoy resorted to broad, energetic measures. He
raised fine blooded cattle in great numbers, laid out
apple orchards, planted a large timber patch, and so
on. From intellectual curiosity he was for a time enthusiastic over bee-keeping. He himself managed only
his estate at Yásnaya Polyána; his other properties he
gave over entirely to overseers."† Of his attitude
towards his own farm we can judge sufficiently well from
the portra t of Levin in *Anna Karenin*.

But one incident need be mentioned from these
happy years during which Tolstoy was at work on his
greatest novel. In the summer of 1866 he defended on
a capital charge a private soldier who had insulted and
struck an officer. This was one of the rare occasions on
which he prevailed upon himself to speak in public.

* *Reminiscences*, ch. 4.   † *Ibid.*

His advocacy was unsuccessful and the man was shot.
At a later date Tolstoy bitterly regretted having lowered
himself by taking part in court proceedings. In 1908 he
wrote to Biryukóv:

> This incident had an immense and beneficent influence on
> me. Through this incident I for the first time came to feel:
> first, that every act of violence implies for its performance
> murder or the threat of it, and that therefore every act of
> violence is inevitably connected with murder; second, that
> a state organization that is unthinkable without murders
> is incompatible with Christianity; and third, that what we
> call science is only the same sort of false justification of the
> evil that exists as the church teaching was in former times.
> Now this is clear to me; then it was only a dim consciousness
> of the falsity amid which my life was passing.—[Biryukóv:
> II, 104.]

Of home life in the Tolstoy household Count Ilyá
Tolstoy, the second son, has given vivid pictures in his
Reminiscences. With his boys Tolstoy was a merry play-
mate, amusing them with comic verses, taking them with
him on his favorite sport of shooting woodcock, playing
the bear at a Christmas festival, and inventing for their
benefit an excellent new game of "Numidian Cavalry":

> We would all be sitting . . . . rather flat and quiet
> after the departure of some dull visitors. Up would jump my
> father from his chair, lifting one hand in the air, and run at
> full speed round the table at a hopping gallop. We all flew
> after him, hopping and waving our hands like [*sic*] he did.
> We would run round the room several times and sit down again

panting in our chairs and in quite a different frame of mind, gay and lively. The Numidian Cavalry had an excellent effect many and many a time. After that exercise all sorts of quarrels and wrongs were forgotten, and tears dried with marvelous rapidity.—[*Reminiscences of Tolstoy*, p. 98.]

The children were well brought up in rules of courtesy. "When they needed something of a servant, they were forbidden to give orders. They were obliged to make a request, adding without fail the word *please*. Their parents and the rest of the family set them an example in this."* On the other hand the aristocratic tradition was strong in the home:

We were educated as regular "gentlefolk," proud of our social position and holding aloof from all the outer world. Everything that was not us was below us, and therefore unworthy of imitation. When our neighbor Alexander Nikoláyevich Bíbikov and his son Nikólenka were asked to our Christmas tree, we used to take note of everything that Nikólenka did that wasn't "the thing," and afterwards used "Nikólenka Bíbikov" as a term of abuse among ourselves, considering that there was nobody in the world so stupid and contemptible as he was. And we regarded Nikólenka in this light because we could see that papa regarded his father in the same way.—[Count Ilyá Tolstoy, *Reminiscences of Tolstoy*, p. 308.]

The son speaks with admiration of his father's skill as an educator:

My father hardly ever *made* us do anything; but it always somehow came about that of our own initiative we did exactly

* Behrs, *Reminiscences*, ch. 3.

what he wanted us to. My mother often scolded us and punished us; but when my father wanted to make us do something he merely looked us hard in the eyes, and we understood; his look was far more effective than any command. . . .

My father's great power as an educator lay in this, that it was as impossible to conceal anything from him as from one's own conscience. He knew everything, and to deceive him was just like deceiving oneself; it was nearly impossible and quite useless.—[*Ibid.*, pp. 313, 314.]

Despite his deep feelings, Tolstoy never indulged in outward tenderness towards his children:

There was one distinguishing and at first sight peculiar trait in my father's character—due perhaps to the fact that he grew up without a mother, or perhaps implanted in him by Nature—and that was that all exhibitions of tenderness were entirely foreign to him. I say "tenderness" in contradistinction to "feeling." Feeling he had, and in a very high degree. . . .

During all his lifetime I never received any mark of tenderness from him whatever. He was not fond of kissing children and when he did so in saying good-morning or good-night he did it merely as a duty. It is easy therefore to understand that he did not provoke any display of tenderness towards himself and that nearness and dearness with him was never accompanied by any outward manifestations.—[*Ibid.*, pp. 377, 378.]

Among the inmates of the Tolstoy household was Tolstoy's old "aunt" Tatyana Ergolsky, the best loved of all his elder relatives. It was she who furnished the

model of Sonya in *War and Peace*. She died in 1874. Of
her he wrote:

Auntie Tatyana Alexándrovna had the greatest influence
on my life. She influenced me, in the first place, by teaching
me, while I was still a child, the spiritual delight of love. She
did not teach me this by words, but by her whole being she
infected me with love. I saw and felt how good it was for her
to love, and I came to understand the happiness of love. That
is the first point. The second point is that she taught me the
charm of a leisurely, solitary life.—[Biryukóv: I, 73.]

After the completion of *War and Peace* Tolstoy for some
time undertook no further creative work, but plunged
into a period of reading and study. His first enthusiasm
was Schopenhauer. In September, 1869, he wrote to Fet:

Do you know what this summer has meant for me? An
unceasing enthusiasm for Schopenhauer and a succession of
spiritual delights such as I have never before experienced. I
have procured all his works and have been reading them and
still am doing so—I have also read through Kant. And
surely not a single student in his [university] course ever studied
so much and learned so much as I this summer. I do not
know whether I shall ever change my opinion, but now I
am convinced that Schopenhauer is the greatest genius of
humankind . . . . [His works] are a whole world in an un-
believably clear and beautiful reflection. I have begun to
translate him.—[Biryukóv: II, 78, 79.]

Evidently Tolstoy's pessimistic conception of the outer
world, of which he speaks ten years later in his *Confession*, was already distinctly formed.

In the next year, 1870, prompted by a wish to aid in the education of his eldest son, Tolstoy suddenly took up the study of Greek, into which he threw himself with his usual ardor. Greek appealed to him from the side of his delight in the beauty of the world, and from his passion for clear, concrete expression. His love of Homer has already been noted (p. 68). Now he writes to Fet:

I have read through Xenophon and now am reading him *à livre ouvert*. For Homer I need a lexicon and a little effort. I am impatiently waiting for a chance to show some one this trick. But how happy I am that God has sent this folly upon me. In the first place I am enjoying myself; in the second I am convinced that of all true beauty and simple beauty that has been produced by human speech I have hither-to known nothing, like all men—they know but they under-stand not; in the third place I am sure that I am not writing verbose twaddle and shall never do so any more.—[Biryukóv: II, 170.]

Perhaps the study of Greek was of some influence on Tolstoy's style, leading him more than ever to cultivate simplicity and directness. But on the whole it was important only as furnishing him a tool for his later work on the Gospels. The ascetic, renunciatory side of his nature was already gaining the upper hand, and his native Hellenic joy in life was becoming less important as an influence in his thought.

Owing to excessive study, Tolstoy's health weakened, and in June, 1871, his wife persuaded him to go once more to the province of Samara for a kumys cure. His companion on the trip was her brother, Stepán Behrs, who has given an entertaining account of it in his *Reminiscences*. Like a true aristocrat, Tolstoy never traveled second class; on the steamer to Samara he rode in the third class and he came back in the first:

Lev Nikoláyevich has a remarkable capacity for getting on intimate terms with passengers of all classes. Even when he came across sullen and reserved strangers, he never hesitated to approach them, and, after a few attempts, he successfully engaged them in conversation. His talent as a psychologist and his heart showed him the right methods and he knew how to attract strangers by his sympathy. In the course of two days on the steamer he became acquainted with the whole deck, not excepting even the good-natured sailors, with whom we spent our nights in the bow of the steamer.— [Behrs: *Reminiscences*, ch. 5.]

On the steppes Tolstoy lived for six weeks in a felt tent among the Bashkir nomads, drinking the fermented mare's milk and eating only meat. He had brought his Greek books with him, and he wrote back to Fet: "I am reading Herodotus, who describes in detail and with great fidelity these same galactophagous Scythians among whom I am living."* Ever quick of sympathy, Tolstoy made warm friends even among these semi-savages. Here too he met an Orthodox hermit and a leader of the heretical sect of the Molokane, and listened with attention to their religious discourses. This is the

* Biryukóv: II, 178.

first token of Tolstoy's interest in Russian sectarianism. The Greek lexicon was brought home filled with aromatic steppe flowers.

On this journey Tolstoy bought a large estate in the province of Samara and in the following summers he repeatedly visited it. In 1873 his family accompanied him. At this time the peasants of that region were suffering from a severe famine, the very existence of which had been kept secret from Russian society at large. Prompted by his wife, Tolstoy made a careful personal investigation of conditions and sent to Katkóv's paper, the *Moscow Gazette*, a detailed account of them, with an appeal for aid. He also wrote to the Countess Alexandra Tolstoy in St. Petersburg, begging her to interest in the cause "the strong and the good people of this world, who, fortunately, are one and the same." "Your Magdalens are very pitiable, I know," he tells her; "but pity for them, as for all the sufferings of the soul, is more mental—of the heart if you prefer; but simple, good people, healthy physically and morally, when they suffer from privation, one pities with his whole being—one is ashamed and pained to be a man when he watches their sufferings. So I deliver into your hands this important matter, which is near to my heart."* These appeals were marvelously successful. In the course of 1873 and 1874 contributions to the value of about 2,000,000 rubles were received in aid of the population of the government of Samara;

* *Correspondence with the Countess A. A. Tolstoy, p. 247.*

the empress was one of the first to make a contribution. In 1881, traditions of Tolstoy's personal help were still alive among the peasants of his district; they remembered how he personally visited the most afflicted houses, aiding with grain and with money for the purchase of horses.* This episode in Tolstoy's life is a foretaste of his more famous activity during the famine of 1891–93.

At this period of his life, though his membership in the Orthodox Church was a mere formality, Tolstoy was by no means an opponent of religious ceremonies. In *War and Peace* (part IX, ch. 18) he describes with sympathy the profound impression made on Natasha by the solemn church service. With this one may compare his account of his own feelings given in a letter to Fet written early in 1872:

What do I understand by religious awe? Just this. Recently I visited my brother—and his child had died and was being buried. The priests had come and there was a pink coffin—everything in due form. My brother and I involuntarily expressed to each other a feeling of almost disgust for all this ceremony. But then I thought: What could my brother have done in order to remove finally from the house the decomposing body of the child? How could he finish the matter decently? There was no better way (at least I could think of none) than with a requiem, incense, and so forth. How should one himself grow weak and die? Pray under his breath . . . . and nothing more? That is not

* Biryukóv: II, 188.

right.   One wishes fully to express the significance and the importance, the impressiveness and the religious awfulness of this greatest event in the life of every man.   And I could also think up nothing more decent for all ages, for all stages of development, than the religious setting.   For me at least these Slavic words are redolent of exactly the same metaphysical ecstasy that you experience when you think of nirvana. Religion is marvelous in that for so many ages, to so many millions of men, it has rendered this service, the greatest service that in this matter anything human can render.   With such a problem how can religion be logical?   Yet there is something in it.—[Biryukóv: II, 235.]

In September, 1872, an incident occurred that, like the search of his premises by the police ten years before, proves conclusively that Tolstoy's temperamental dislike for liberalism might have disappeared with advancing experience, had not first his social position and his wealth, and later his literary fame, preserved him from any but the most trifling annoyance by the government authorities.   A letter to the Countess Alexandra Tolstoy tells of both the event and the feelings evoked by it:

Dear Alexandrine: You are one of those people who with their whole being say to their friends: "I will share with thee thy sorrows and thou thy joys with me." * So I, who always tell you of my own happiness, now seek your sympathy in my grief.

Unexpectedly and without warning an event has descended upon me that has changed my whole life.

A young bull at Yásnaya Polyána has killed a herdsman

* The quotation is in English in the original.

and I am held for examination, under arrest—I cannot leave the house (all this by the caprice of a boy called the public prosecutor), and in a few days I must face charges and defend myself in court—before whom? It is terrible to think of, terrible to remember all the abominations that have been inflicted on me, are being inflicted, and will still be inflicted.

With a gray beard, with six children, with the consciousness of a useful and industrious life, with a firm confidence that I cannot be guilty, with a contempt for the new courts that I cannot help having, so far as I have seen them; with the one desire, that I should be left in peace as I leave everybody else in peace, it is unbearable to live in Russia, with the fear that any boy who does not like my face may make me sit on a bench in front of a court, and later in prison—but I will cease showing my anger. You will read all this story in the press. I shall die of anger if I do not vent it; and then let them bring me to trial for the additional offense of telling the truth. I will tell you what I intend to do and what I beg of you.

If I do not die of anger and vexation in the prison where they probably will put me (I am convinced that they hate me), I have decided to move to England forever or until such time as the liberty and dignity of every man shall be made secure in our country. My wife looks forward to this with pleasure (she likes English ways) and it will be a good thing for the children; I shall have sufficient means (I shall get together some 200,000 if I sell out everything). I myself, however much I detest European life, hope that there I shall recover from my anger and shall be able to pass quietly the few years of my life that still remain to me, working at what I still need to write. Our plan is to settle at first near London, and then to select a beautiful and healthful village near the sea, where there are good schools, and to buy a house and land.

For our life in England to be pleasant we need to be acquainted
with good aristocratic families. In this you can aid me and I
beg you to do so. Please do it for me. If you have not such
acquaintances yourself you will surely be able to accomplish
it through your friends. Two or three letters that would
open to us the doors of a good English circle. This is indispensable for the children, who will have to grow up there.
When we leave I cannot yet tell, because they can torture me
here as much as they choose. You simply cannot imagine
my situation. They say that the laws give *sécurité*. In our
country it is quite the contrary. I have arranged my life with
the greatest *sécurité*. I am contented with little, seek nothing,
wish nothing but peace; I am loved and respected by the
peasantry; even robbers let me alone; and I have complete
sécurité, except from the laws. The hardest thing of all for
me is this anger of mine. I so love to love, and now I cannot
help being angry. I repeat Our Father and the Thirty-Seventh
Psalm, and for a moment they calm me, especially Our Father;
but later I boil up again and can do nothing, think of nothing—I
have abandoned work, as being a stupid desire to take vengeance when there is nobody on whom to take vengeance.
Not until now, when I have begun to get ready for my departure and am firmly decided on it, have I become calmer,
and I hope soon again to find myself. Good-bye; I kiss your
hand.—[*Correspondence with the Countess A. A. Tolstoy*,
pp. 235, 236.]

This letter is wonderfully characteristic of Tolstoy's
nature. In it one sees his deep-rooted repugnance to
any constraint visited on him, and in particular to compulsion from the new liberal courts, which, one may
remark, were modeled on French and English institu-

tions. All his life Tolstoy had chafed but little under the
degrading Russian censorship; now he was anxious
to flee to England, where, one may likewise remark,
he might easily have been exposed to similar attacks on
his "liberty." He asserts his individuality, and yet
(as he confesses with shame in a later letter) he has the
covert hope that his kinswoman will spread the news of
the event in her own circle of high government officials.
He runs to religion for help, but finds it no sure resource
against his boiling temper. "In order to accept as a
Christian all that is sent by God," he writes a few days
later, "you must first feel entirely yourself, but while
ants are crawling over you and stinging you it is impossible to think of anything except deliverance. To
accept as a trial sent from on high an itch that is produced in your whole being by insects that swarm over
you is impossible."* The affair ended by the court
authorities confessing that they erred in arresting
Tolstoy, and by their finally admitting that even his
overseer was not criminally liable.

Tolstoy's irritation was increased by his having
undertaken a new piece of literary work, which absorbed all his attention. "And when you are attacked
by that folly, as Pushkin finely called it, you become
peculiarly sensitive to the rudeness of life. Imagine
a man in complete quiet and darkness, who is listening
to a faint rustling and who is scanning faint rays of
light in the gloom, under whose nose they suddenly

* *Correspondence with the Countess A. A. Tolstoy*, pp. 239, 240.

touch off stinking Bengal lights and play a march on trumpets out of tune. It is extremely torturing."[*] On his return from his kumys cure of 1871 he had thrown himself heart and soul into the preparation of his *Primer*, of which an account has already been given, and had finished it. He then suddenly became interested in the study of the epoch of Peter the Great (1682–1725), and particularly of the part played in it by his own ancestors. He buried himself in the study of historical sources, both public and private. In December, 1872, his wife wrote to her brother: "He does not know himself what will come of his work, but it seems to me that he will again write a poem in prose similar to *War and Peace*."[†] After making several attempts at composition, Tolstoy was forced to abandon his project, finding himself unable to re-create in his imagination that distant period, through lack of knowledge of the details of Russian life in the early eighteenth century. He had formed an idea of the personality of Peter in sharp contrast to the prevailing view, and the whole epoch had become unattractive to him. The personality and work of Peter, he maintained, were not only in no way great, but all his qualities were bad. His so-called reforms did not serve the good of the country, but only his personal advantage. In consequence of the ill will that the boyárs (nobles) bore him owing to his innovations, he founded the city of St. Petersburg, in

* *Correspondence with the Countess A. A. Tolstoy*, p. 241.
† Behrs: *Reminiscences*, ch. 4.

order to withdraw from them and to be freer in his
immoral life, among the foreigners and low-born ad-
venturers with whom he surrounded himself. The
class of boyárs was then very influential and was therefore dangerous to him. His innovations and reforms
were taken from Saxony, where the laws were the most
cruel of the time, and corruption of manners the worst,
a fact especially pleasing to Peter. This explains his
friendship for the Elector of Saxony, one of the most
immoral of the crowned heads of the time.* In this
whole conception one may possibly find some influence
of Slavophile thought.

Then, in March, 1873, without conscious preparation,
Tolstoy began the composition of *Anna Karenin*.
Biryukóv's account of the incident demands quotation:

In the year 1873, slowly becoming weaker, the belovèd
aunt of Lev Nikoláyevich, Tatyana Ergolsky, was approaching her end. She was lying in her room on a couch, and the
oldest son of Lev Nikoláyevich, the ten-year-old Sergéy, was
reading to her Pushkin's tales. Sofya Andréyevna was sitting
near by with her work. The old lady dozed off, and the reading
stopped. The volume of Pushkin was lying on the table,
open at the beginning of the story, *A Fragment*. Just then
Lev Nikoláyevich came into the room. Seeing the book, he
took it and read the beginning of *A Fragment*: "Guests had
gathered at a country house."

"That is the right way to begin," said Lev Nikoláyevich.
"Pushkin is our teacher. This at once takes the reader into
the interest of the action itself. Another would have begun to

* Paraphrased from Behrs: *Reminiscences*, ch. 4.

describe the guests and the rooms, but Pushkin gets down to business at once."

Some one of those present jestingly proposed to Lev Nikoláyevich to avail himself of this beginning and to write a novel. Lev Nikoláyevich withdrew to his room and immediately sketched the opening of *Anna Karenin*, which in the first variant began thus: "All was in confusion in the Oblonskys' house."—[I: 204, 205.]

As the kernel of his plot Tolstoy took an incident that had happened in his own vicinity about a year before. A woman named Anna, who had been living with his neighbor Bíbikov, became jealous of the governess in the household, and in despair threw herself beneath the wheels of a railroad train. On this new novel Tolstoy worked fitfully and with small enthusiasm; he was hindered by family griefs, by his labors on educational problems, and probably by his ever-increasing preoccupation with religious questions. In 1875, writing to Fet, he professes complete indifference to the success of his work; in the next year he writes to the same friend: "I am now taking hold of the tiresome and vulgar *Anna Karenin* with but one desire: to get it out of the way and be free for other occupations."* In April, 1876, he wrote to the critic Strakhov of his antipathy for work on the last proof-sheets of the novel: "Everything in them is wretched, and all must be done over, all that is printed; all must be canceled and cast aside; I must swear off and say: 'Excuse me; I won't do so

* *Letters, collected by Sergéyenko* (Moscow, 1910); I, 116.

any more, but will try to write something new which
shall not be so disjointed and helter-skelter!' "*   The
first installments of *Anna Karenin* were published
in Katkóv's *Russian Messenger* in 1875; the last were
not ready until 1877, at a time when all Russia was
seething with patriotic, Slavophile ardor for the war with
Turkey, to secure the liberation of Bulgaria. Katkóv
was a leader in the war party, while Tolstoy, in the concluding chapters of his book, throws cold water on all
military and patriotic enthusiasm. A rupture occurred
between the two men; Katkóv refused to print the last
chapters as they stood, while Tolstoy declined to alter
them. Katkóv was obliged to print a mere statement
as to the conclusion of the novel, while Tolstoy issued
his final chapters as a separate pamphlet.

Before finishing *Anna Karenin* Tolstoy had felt new
interest in *The Decembrists*, his project of years before,
and he now made fresh studies of materials for the
book. But he was unable to obtain permission to use
the government archives that he needed for his work;
and, as he grew more intimately acquainted with the
Decembrist conspiracy, he became convinced that the
source of it was to be found in the influence of the
French Revolution on the Russian aristocracy. A
movement imported into Russia from the west had no
charm for Tolstoy. Besides this, religious doubts and
questionings were now pressing upon him. He definitely laid aside his novel, but in 1884 he contributed

* Biryukóv: II, 213.

to a miscellany a few fragments of it that he had written, partly before *War and Peace* and partly after *Anna Karenin*.

During this period of Tolstoy's life his two most important literary friends were the poet Fet and the critic Strakhov. The former won fame by lyric poems expressing the "esthetic epicureanism that developed on the soil of the sybaritic existence of the Russian landed proprietors."* He later made admirable translations from the Latin poets. Undoubtedly inspired by Tolstoy, he translated Schopenhauer's most important works. Like Tolstoy, he was opposed to the Liberal movement and was politically an indifferent, holding that private citizens should not meddle in government affairs; towards the peasants he is said to have been harsh and oppressive. He must have had attractive personal traits, since Tolstoy's letters to him show intimate affection.

Nikoláy Strakhov, a critic of the Slavophile school, was dear to Tolstoy on both intellectual and personal grounds. With him Tolstoy could discuss religious and philosophical problems, and Strakhov's opinions on his works were almost the only criticism of them that he valued. Strakhov was his intermediary in the printing of his *Primer*. Tolstoy's attachment to Strakhov was apparently never interrupted, while his intimacy with Fet came to an end in his later years, after his religious conversion.

* Skabichevsky: *History of Modern Russian Literature.*

In 1876 Tolstoy became acquainted with the composer Chaykovsky [Tchaykovsky, Tschaikowsky], who
had long been a devoted admirer of his works.   Chaykovsky arranged a musical evening in his honor, inviting Rubinstein to play on the occasion, and was
beyond measure pleased and touched when Tolstoy was
moved to tears by the performance of his music.   But
personally the two men could not become intimate.   Ten
years later Chaykovsky wrote in his diary:

When I became acquainted with Tolstoy I was seized
with fear and a feeling of awkwardness in his presence.   It
seemed to me that this greatest knower of the heart would
penetrate with a single glance into all the little secrets of my
soul.   From him, it seemed to me, it would be impossible to
conceal all the rubbish lying at the bottom of my soul and to
show only the fair side of it.

If he is kind (and such he must be, of course), I thought,
then delicately and tenderly, like a physician who is studying
a wound and who knows all the sore places, he will avoid
touching and irritating them, but thereby he will make me
feel that nothing is hidden from him.   If he is not specially
merciful, he will thrust his finger right into the center of the
pain.   I was terribly afraid of either choice.   But there
was no sign of either.   A profound knower of the heart in his
writings, he proved in his converse with men to be of a simple,
sound, frank nature, showing very little of that universal
knowledge of which I was afraid; he did not avoid touching
sore places, but yet he caused no intentional pain.   It was
evident that he did not at all regard me as a subject for his
observations, but simply wished to chat about music, in which

he was interested at the time. Among other things he liked to run down Beethoven, and openly expressed doubt of his genius. This is a trait not at all characteristic of great men. To bring down to one's own lack of comprehension a genius who is recognized by every one is a peculiarity of men of limited intellect.—[Biryukóv: II, 252, 253.]

This sketch of Tolstoy's life during his greatest creative period may fittingly close with an account of his reconciliation with Turgenev. The two men had ceased their enmity, but had not become friends again; they admired each other at long range. In 1862, immediately after their quarrel, Turgenev had written to Fet: "You may write him or tell him (if you see him) that I (without any phrases or plays on words) *from a distance* like him very much, that I respect him and follow his fate with sympathy, but that near at hand everything takes a different turn."* Turgenev revered Tolstoy's power of picturing external life, but disliked his philosophizing and his incessant brooding over questions of conduct. Of *War and Peace* he wrote in a letter to Polonsky (1868): "Tolstoy's novel is a marvelous thing; but the weakest part of it . . . is the historical side and the psychology. His history is a mere bit of trickery, a flicking of the eyes with fine trifles; his psychology is a capriciously monotonous preoccupation with one and the same feelings. All that has to do with manners, the descriptive and military part, is of the first order, and in it we have no such master as Tolstoy." He made

* Biryukóv: I, 407.

efforts, apparently unsuccessful, to procure the publication of French translations of some of Tolstoy's earlier works. Tolstoy, in his turn, admired Turgenev's limpid, clear style, but despised his lack of moral vigor and moral questioning, the qualities most dear to himself. In 1867 he wrote to Fet a caustic verdict on Turgenev's new novel *Smoke:*

As to *Smoke* I think that the strength of poetry lies in love; the tendency of that strength depends on character. Without strength of love there is no poetry; falsely directed strength, an unpleasant, weak character in a poet is repugnant. In *Smoke* there is scarcely any love of anything and scarcely any poetry. There is love only of light and playful adultery, and therefore the poetry of that story is repugnant. I am afraid even to express this opinion, because I cannot regard soberly the author, whose personality I do not like, but it seems that my impression is common to all. One more man played out. I wish and hope that my turn may never come.—[Biryukóv: II, 77.]

About 1876 he speaks of his former friend with somewhat less lack of sympathy:

I have not been reading Turgenev, but I am sincerely sorry, judging from everything that I have heard, that that spring of pure and limpid water has been fouled with such rubbish. If he would simply recollect in detail one of his own days and describe it, every one would be delighted. However commonplace it may sound, yet in all relations of life, and especially in art, one needs merely a single negative quality, not to lie. In life falsehood is horrid, but it does not destroy life by its horridness; under it the truth of life still remains because somebody always longs for something, is pained or made joyful by something; but in art falsehood destroys the whole connection between phenomena; all scatters like dust.—[*Ibid.*, II, 216.]

In 1878, Tolstoy, whose thoughts were turning more and more on religious questions, and who did not wish to continue to have an enemy, wrote to Turgenev, begging him to forgive him if he had wronged him in any way. Turgenev answered in the same cordial spirit and in the autumn of that year made two visits at Tolstoy's home. The reconciliation was outwardly complete, but no spiritual sympathy between the two men was possible. "He is still the same," Tolstoy wrote to Fet, "and we know the degree of intimacy that is possible between us."* On November 10, in a letter to Strakhov, he referred to Turgenev with whimsical condescension:

Why are you angry with Turgenev? He plays at life and one has to play with him. And his play is innocent and not unpleasant, if taken in small doses. But you too must not be angry with him.—[Letter printed in *The Contemporary World*, July, 1913.]

Soon after this Tolstoy received a letter from Turgenev, who expressed a hope that the "intellectual illness," of which Tolstoy had complained, had now passed away. The tone of the epistle made a disagree-

* Biryukóv: II, 279.

able impression on Tolstoy, who wrote petulantly to Fet:

Yesterday I had a letter from Turgenev. And, do you know, I have decided that it's better to keep away from him and from all chance of trouble. Somehow he stirs me up unpleasantly.—[Biryukóv: II, 279.]

On his side, Turgenev was better pleased with the renewal of friendship. He wrote to Fet:

It made me very happy to meet Tolstoy again and I passed three pleasant days at his house; all his family are very attractive and his wife is charming. He himself has become very gentle and has grown up. His name is beginning to become known in Europe. We Russians have been aware for a long time that he has no rival.—[*Ibid.*, II, 280.]

He himself tried to aid Tolstoy's fame by distributing copies of the French translation of *War and Peace* to such distinguished critics as Taine and About.

All in all, Tolstoy evidently regarded Turgenev as a frivolous babbler, while Turgenev looked on Tolstoy as a wrong-headed prig. Both were mistaken.

CHAPTER VI

"WAR AND PEACE" AND "ANNA KARENIN"

TOLSTOY'S fame as a novelist depends primarily on *War and Peace* and *Anna Karenin*. His earlier works, though they alone would have given him an assured place among the great writers of Russia, may be regarded as in a sense but preliminary studies for these novels. And his religious, ethical, and critical writings, remarkable as they are in themselves, are more widely read owing to the fact that they came from the pen of the author of *War and Peace* and *Anna Karenin*.

War and Peace was the fruit of the happiest and most buoyant period of Tolstoy's life. His activities, hitherto scattered over a variety of aims, were given a definite direction by family ties; conscious of his ripened powers, he applied himself to creative work with all the vigor of his impetuous nature. From a conventional point of view the masterpiece that he produced lacks unity and proportion. A very competent critic has described it as not a novel at all, but rather a vast encyclopedic work like the *Anatomy of Melancholy*, containing material enough for a dozen novels, jumbled together, helter-skelter. Tolstoy himself was fully aware of the nature of his own work. *"War and Peace,"* he told Schuyler, "is not a novel, still less a poem, still less an historical chronicle. It is not presumption on my part if I keep clear of customary forms. The history of Russian literature from Pushkin down presents many similar examples. From the *Dead Souls* of Gogol to the *Dead House** of Dostoyevsky there is not a single artistic prose work of more than average merit which keeps entirely to the usual form of a novel or a poem."†

The book traces the history during the years 1805–12 of five families, all belonging to the higher circles of the Russian aristocracy, and of some minor characters, and it concludes with an epilogue laid in the year 1820. In its two thousand pages we find "God's plenty," and we live with the creations of Tolstoy's art as with the characters of no other novelist; their daily existence has for us the same charm as that of dearly loved friends. In 1871, two years after the completion of his great work, Tolstoy wrote to his wife, mournfully commenting on his own loss of health: "I have no intellectual, and above all no poetic delights. I look upon everything as though I were dead, the very thing for which I have disliked many people. But now I myself see only what exists; I understand, I form ideas, but I do not see through with love as I used to do."‡ That phrase,

---

* *House of the Dead;* compare p. 340.
† Eugene Schuyler, "Count Leo Tolstoy Twenty Years Ago," in *Scribner's Magazine:* V, 548. Tolstoy's generalization is naturally not scientifically accurate. ‡ *Letters to Wife*, p. 82.

"to see through with love," aptly characterizes the unfailing charm of *War and Peace;* the superb excellence of single characters, single incidents, single descriptions makes us impatient of captious comments on the departure of the book from ordinary canons of construction. Formal criticism stands abashed before such a work. One turns with relief to the verdict of Rolland:

In order to be fully sensible of the power of the work, one must take account of its hidden unity. Most French readers, who are a trifle near-sighted, see only its thousands of details, the profusion of which bewilders them and throws them off the track. They are lost in this forest of life. One must rise above it and take in at a glance the free horizon, the circle of the woods and the fields; then one will perceive the Homeric spirit of the work, the calm of eternal laws, the grand rhythm of the breath of destiny, the feeling of the whole with which all the details are united; and, dominating the work, the genius of the artist, like the God of Genesis moving upon the face of the waters.—[*Vie de Tolstoï*, p. 62.]

War and Peace is formed of numerous elements: pictures of Russian home life among the aristocracy, in their St. Petersburg and Moscow mansions and on their country estates, with revels at restaurants and wholesome merrymaking in the family circle and in the fields; and pictures of life in time of war, in the officers' messroom, on the battlefield among the private soldiers, in panic-stricken Moscow, and on the wintry march, among the Russian prisoners carried off by Napoleon on his retreat from Russia. The novel has an historical setting; no small space is given to portraits of Napoleon and of Alexander I, and of the Russian generals, above all to that of the commander-in-chief Kutuzov. Into the work Tolstoy injects whole chapters of historical philosophy, utterly unconnected with the narrative, but justified in his mind as a commentary on the central event upon which the book turns as a pivot, the invasion of Russia by Napoleon. And finally, Tolstoy's ethical point of view, though still unsettled, here becomes more articulate than in his previous works; through the lives of his two chief heroes, Pierre Bezukhov and Andréy Bolkonsky, to each of whom he imparts some share of his own personality, he gives full expression to his maturing philosophy of life.

The first element is the most important. Home life had been Tolstoy's ideal since his boyhood, and now it had been realized. His work is pervaded by his new interests; it is the epic of the family; the family ideal dominates it even more absolutely than it does the work of English Victorian writers of the same period. In portraying family life Tolstoy drew on his own memories and on his family traditions; the two households that occupy the center of the stage in *War and Peace* are modeled on those of his father and mother. The Rostóvs, open-handed, simple-hearted country squires, represent the Tolstoys; Nikoláy Rostóv and his father are portraits of the author's father and grandfather. But Natasha Rostóv was not taken from tradition; in her Tolstoy combined traits of his wife and her sister:

"I took Tanya," he is reported to have said, "pounded her up with Sonya, and Natasha was the result."* The Sonya of the novel was suggested by Tolstoy's beloved "aunt" Tatyana Ergolsky. The Bolkonskys, on the other hand, a reflective, intellectual, independent, forceful family, are modified copies of the Volkonskys, the family of Tolstoy's mother. His mother herself is represented by the pure-hearted but externally unattractive Princess Marya; while his maternal grandfather furnished the model of the eccentric old Prince Bolkonsky. All these identifications, however, must be accepted with a certain reserve. Tolstoy himself, according to his son, disliked questions as to the exact sources of the characters that he created, and "used to say that a writer forms his types from a whole series of people, and they never can or ought to be portraits of particular individuals."†

In his earlier writings Tolstoy had been noticeably chary of feminine portraits. Now he presents a whole gallery of them, drawn and colored with the most exquisite sympathy and skill. One among them stands preeminent.

Wholesomeness and geniality, a hearty delight in mere existence, personal kindliness and freedom from reflection, a whole-souled contentment with the world as it is, and a deep aversion to anxiety and bother over finances, characterize the household of the Rostóvs.

* Biryukóv: II, 32, on the authority of the Countess Tolstoy
† Count Ilyá Tolstoy, *Reminiscences of Tolstoy*, p. 67.

All these qualities, combined with an artistic temperament and a girlish love of the whole world, combine to make Natasha Rostóv Tolstoy's most charming creation, and, one dares to say, the most charming heroine of all prose fiction. The great heroines of poetry and romance, from Helen of Troy to Goethe's Margaret, are all outline sketches, not less true, but less complete and many-sided than this detailed portrait of a real girl and woman, whose life was the reverse of romance, and whose destiny the plainest of humdrum prose. That Tolstoy could infuse pure beauty and poetry into a story such as hers would alone win him a place among the master spirits of literature.

We see Natasha first as a girl of thirteen, scarcely out of the nursery: at a stately family dinner she rises and demands to know what the dessert is to be, and will not be quieted until she is told. Less than a year later she wins the heart of the rough hussar Denisov, her brother's friend, and is childishly grieved that she cannot make him happy, though she has no thought of marrying him:

Natasha ran to her mother in great excitement.
"Mamma, mamma, he's made me!"
"What has he made you?"
"He's made me, made me **a proposal. Mamma, mamma!**"
she cried. The Countess could not believe her ears. Denisov had made a proposal. To whom? To that mite of a girl Natasha, who had only just left off playing with dolls and was still taking lessons.

"Natasha, stop your nonsense!" she said, still hoping that this was a joke.

"Nonsense! I'm talking seriously to you," said Natasha angrily. "I came to ask you what to do, and now you say 'nonsense'!"

The Countess shrugged her shoulders.

"If it's true that Monsieur Denisov has made you a proposal, then tell him that he's a fool; that's all."

"No, he isn't a fool," said Natasha with a grave and injured air.

"Well, then what do you want? You are all in love nowadays. If you're in love with him, then marry him!" said the Countess with an angry laugh. "My blessings on you!"

"No, mamma, I'm not in love with him; most likely I'm not in love with him."

"Well, then tell him so."

"Mamma, are you angry? Don't be angry, darling; how am I to blame?"

"Then what shall we do, my dear? If you wish I'll go tell him," said the Countess with a smile.

"No, I'll do it myself, only you show me how to. Everything is easy for you," she added, answering her smile. "But if you had only seen how he said that to me! I know he didn't mean to say it, but just said it accidentally."

"Well, anyhow you must refuse him."

"No, I mustn't. I'm so sorry for him! He's such a dear."

"Well, then accept his proposal. It's high time you were married," said the mother angrily and mockingly.

"No, mamma, I'm so sorry for him. I don't know how to say it."

"There's no use discussing; I'll tell him myself," said the

Countess, irritated that anybody should have ventured to regard this little Natasha as a grown-up.

"No, no indeed, I'll do it myself, and you just listen at the door." And Natasha ran across the drawing room into the hall, where on the same chair, at the clavicord, his face buried in his hands, Denisov was sitting. He started up at the sound of her light steps.

"Natalie," he said, approaching her with swift steps. "Decide my fate; it is in your hands!"

"Vasily Dmitrich, I'm so sorry for you! No, but you're so splendid . . . but I mustn't . . . this . . . and so I shall always love you."

Denisov bent over her hand, and she heard strange sounds that she could not comprehend. She kissed him on his black, tousled, curly head. At that moment there was heard the hasty rustle of the Countess's gown. She came up to them.

"Vasily Dmitrich, I thank you for the honor," said the Countess in a disturbed voice, but one that seemed severe to Denisov; "but my daughter is so young, and I thought that you, as my son's friend, would apply to me first. In such a case you would have spared me the necessity of a refusal."

"Countess," said Denisov with lowered eyes and a guilty air; he endeavored to continue, and hesitated.

Natasha could not bear to see him in such a pitiable state. She began to sob loudly.

"Countess, I am at fault," Denisov continued with a choking voice, "but be assured that I so worship your daughter and all your family that I would give two lives. . ." He glanced at the Countess and noticed her stern face. "Well, good-bye, Countess," he said, kissing her hand; and, without a glance at Natasha, he left the room with quick, decisive steps.—[Part iv, ch. 16.]

More than three years have passed, and a state ball is given by a St. Petersburg grandee to welcome in the new year, 1810. The Rostóv family prepare anxiously for the great occasion; Tolstoy lingers with delight, in which his readers share, over the scene in the dressing room, which shows us Natasha's eager care that her cousin Sonya and her mother shall look their best. At the ball Prince Andréy Bolkonsky, a young man who has some time before lost his wife, and who has once caught a glimpse of Natasha at the Rostóvs' country estate, now meets her once more:

Prince Andréy, like all men who have grown up in society, liked to meet in society something not marked with the general social stamp. And such was Natasha, with her astonishment, joy, and timidity, and even with her mistakes in French. He behaved and spoke to her with peculiar tenderness and care. Sitting by her and talking with her about the simplest and most insignificant topics, Prince Andréy gazed with delight at the joyous sparkle of her eyes and at her smile, which was caused not by anything that was said but by the happiness that was within her. When Natasha was chosen as a partner and rose with a smile, and danced through the hall, Prince Andréy admired particularly her timid grace. In the middle of the cotillion Natasha, having finished a figure, came back to her place, still panting. A new partner invited her once more. She rose, still out of breath, and evidently thought of declining, but immediately merrily raised her hand once more to the shoulder of her partner and smiled to Prince Andréy.

"I should have been glad to rest and sit a while with you,

for I was tired; but you see they keep inviting me, and I am glad of it, and I am happy, and I love everybody, and you and I understand all that—" this and much more besides was expressed in her smile. When her partner left her, Natasha ran across the hall to select two ladies for the figures.

"If she goes to her cousin first and then to another lady, then she will be my wife," Prince Andréy said to himself absolutely unexpectedly as he watched her. She went to her cousin first.

"What stuff will come into one's head sometimes!" thought Prince Andréy. "But this much is certain, that that girl is so charming, so different from everybody else, that before she has danced here a month she will get married. She is a rarity for this place," he thought, when Natasha, adjusting a rose that had got out of place in her corsage, seated herself beside him.

At the end of the cotillion the old Count in his blue dress coat came up to the dancers. He invited Prince Andréy to call and asked his daughter whether she was having a good time. Natasha did not answer; she only smiled with a smile that said reproachfully: "How can you ask such a question?"

"The best time I ever had in my life!" she said, and Prince Andréy noticed how she quickly started to raise her thin arms to embrace her father and immediately let them fall once more. Natasha was happier than she had ever been before in her life. She was at that highest pinnacle of happiness when a human being becomes perfectly good and kind and does not believe in the possibility of evil, unhappiness, and grief.— [Part VI, ch. 17.]

Prince Andréy makes a proposal for Natasha in due form. She accepts him and falls madly in love with

him, as well she may—for no young man in Russia is
of higher character, of finer talent, or of more brilliant
social position.   Owing to the opposition of Prince
Andréy's father, the marriage must be postponed for a
year, during which time Prince Andréy travels in western
Europe.   Natasha, ill at ease owing to the separation
from him, and treated with rudeness by his family,
meets the rake Anatole Kuragin, who by mere masculine
force of character leads astray the impressionable young
girl and persuades her to elope with him.   Luckily
the shrewd and kindly woman at whose house Natasha
is staying learns of the plot and averts disaster by locking
Natasha securely in her chamber.   Natasha, disgraced,
gradually recovers from her infatuation; the one person
who gives her effective comfort and sympathy is the
slow, fat-witted Pierre Bezukhov, the rich husband of
a bad woman, sister of Anatole Kuragin.   Natasha,
repentant, prepares for communion, and at the solemn
service is bidden to pray for those who hate her.   The
poor child can think of none who do so, since everybody
whom she has known has been fond of her; but, after
reflection, she prays for her father's creditors—who need
her prayers—and for Anatole, who has done her wrong,
though he has not hated her.   The service changes to
prayers for the destruction of the enemies of Russia.
But Natasha "could not pray for the trampling under
foot of her enemies, when a few moments before her
only wish had been to have more of them in order to
pray for them.   Yet she could not doubt the justice of

the prayer repeated by the kneeling throng."* Prince
Andréy, bitter and cynical owing to Natasha's betrayal
of him, is brought wounded from Borodinó into Moscow,
and is carried from the doomed city by the Rostóvs.
Natasha nurses him tenderly until his death and wins
his forgiveness. Later the wife of Pierre dies and Pierre
wins Natasha. The epilogue shows them living happily:

Natasha had married in the early spring of 1813, and by 1820
already had three daughters and one son, whom she had longed
for and whom she was now suckling herself. She had grown
stout and plump, so that it was hard to recognize in this strong
mother the former slender and lively Natasha. Her features
had become defined and had an expression of calm softness and
clearness. In her face there was no longer that ceaselessly
glowing fire of animation that had formed her charm. Now
often only her face and body were visible, and her soul was not
visible at all. There was visible only a strong, handsome, and
fertile female. Very rarely now did the former fire blaze up
within her. That happened only when, as now, her husband
returned from absence, when a child was recovering from an
illness, . . . and very rarely when something accidentally
aroused her to singing, which she had completely abandoned
after her marriage. And in those rare moments when the
former fire blazed up in her mature handsome body she was
still more attractive than before. . . . . .

Natasha did not like general society, but so much the more
did she prize the society of her own kin, of the Countess
Marya, of her brother, her mother, and Sonya. She prized
the society of those people among whom, disheveled and in

*Part IX, ch. 18.

her dressing gown, she could emerge from the nursery with long strides and with a joyous face, and exhibit a diaper with a yellow spot instead of a green one, and hear consoling assurances that the child was now far better.—[*Epilogue:* part I, ch. 10.]

Let us listen to the brilliant Russian critic Merezhkovsky, as he moralizes over this situation, which has disconcerted so many readers:

Natasha has "no words of her own." But, like those statues which, rising aloft in the sky on the very pinnacles of immense complicated buildings, reign over them, complete them and crown them, the picture of Natasha-the-mother, appearing in the epilogue of *War and Peace*, mutely and elementally reigns over the whole boundless epopee, so that the action of a tragedy of universally historic significance—wars, movement of nations, the grandeur and the doom of heroes—seems only the pedestal of this Mother-Female, who, triumphing, exhibits diapers with a yellow spot instead of a green one. Austerlitz, Borodinó, the conflagration of Moscow, Napoleon, Alexander the Blessed may be and may perish—all shall pass away, all shall be forgotten, shall be wiped off the tablets of universal history by a succeeding wave, like letters written on the sands of the shore—but never, in no civilization, after no storms of universally historic significance shall mothers cease to rejoice over a yellow spot on diapers instead of a green one. At the very summit of his production, one of the mightiest edifices ever erected by men, the creator of *War and Peace* unfurls this cynical banner, "diapers with a yellow spot," as the guiding banner of humanity.—[*Tolstoy and Dostoyevsky,* part II, ch. 3.]

Such is our last glimpse of Natasha in *War and Peace*. But, as has been said, Tolstoy had at first planned a novel on the Decembrists, which was to deal with the later life of the same characters that appear in *War and Peace*, and he had written certain fragments of it. In one of these we see Natasha in her old age. Pierre has joined the conspiracy and has been sent to Siberia, whither Natasha has followed him. In 1856 they are allowed to return home—and this is how Tolstoy describes Natasha on her arrival in Moscow:

Natalya Nikoláyevna, after arranging the room, adjusted her collar and cuffs, which were still clean, despite the journey, combed her hair, and sat down by the table. Her fine dark eyes were fixed on some point in the distance; she gazed and rested. She seemed to be resting not merely from the unpacking, not merely from the journey, not merely from her heavy years—she seemed to be resting from her whole life, and the distance into which she gazed and in which there rose before her living, beloved faces, was the rest for which she yearned. Whether it was the supreme act of love that she had performed for her husband, or the love that she had lived through for her children when they were small, whether it was some grievous loss or some peculiarity of her character—no person who glanced at this woman could fail to understand that there was nothing more to be expected of her; that she had long since spent her whole self in life and that nothing remained of her. There remained something fair and sad, worthy of reverence, like memories, like moonlight. It was impossible to imagine her otherwise than surrounded with respect and with all the comforts of life. That she should ever be hungry and eat greedily, that she should wear dirty linen, that she should stumble or forget to blow her nose— nothing of the sort could happen to her. It was physically impossible. Why it was so I know not, but her every motion was majesty, grace, love for all those who had the privilege of seeing her.

> Sie pflegen und weben
> Himmlische Rosen ins irdische Leben.

She knew those verses and loved them, but she was not guided by them. Her whole nature was an expression of this thought, her whole life was but an unconscious plaiting of invisible roses into the life of all men whom she met. She had followed her husband to Siberia simply because she loved him; she did not think of what she could do for him, but involuntarily she did everything. She spread his bed, she packed his things, she prepared his dinner and his tea, and, above all, she was always where he was, and greater happiness no woman could have given to her husband.—[*The Decembrists*, fragment I, ch. 1.]

The same immediate touch with life, the same frank directness, are found in Natasha's prosaic brother Nikoláy, who, devoid of any personal charm, independence of character, or magnetism, develops, after sowing a patch or two of wild oats, into a typical country squire. He is the central figure in Tolstoy's marvelous description of the wolf hunt, the finest picture of out-of-door sport to be found in Russian literature. The feeling in the scene is that of Borrow's Petulengro: "There's the wind on the heath, brother; if I could only feel that, I would gladly live forever." Nikoláy's whole being is absorbed in the tense excitement of the moment:

> Several times he addressed a prayer to God that the wolf might come out towards him; he prayed with that passionate and shamefaced feeling with which men pray in moments of strong agitation that depends on an insignificant cause. "What does it cost Thee," he said to God, "to do this for me! I know that Thou art great, and that it is a sin to ask Thee for this; but for God's sake make the old wolf come out towards me, and make Karáy clutch him with a death grip in the throat."—[Part vii, ch. 5.]

Very different from Natasha and Nikoláy is Sonya, a distant relative and dependent of the Rostóv family. She is good and sweet, but she has no bubbling spring of life within her. Loving Nikoláy with a constant devotion, she wins his heart; then, seeing that he has no ardent affection for her, and that he must make a rich match, she gives him up. Nikoláy retrieves the family fortunes by marrying the wealthy Princess Marya Bolkonsky, sister of Prince Andréy, and Sonya lives on as a dependent in their family. "Sometimes I am awfully sorry for her," Natasha comments. "I used to be awfully anxious that Nikoláy should marry her; but I always seemed to have a premonition that it could never happen. She is a sterile flower; such as grow on strawberry vines, you know. Sometimes I am sorry for her, and sometimes I think that she does not feel it as we should."*

* Epilogue: part i, ch. 8.

Wonderful in another fashion is the account of the home life of old Prince Bolkonsky, formerly a general in the Russian army. A widowed recluse, he passes his time alone on his estate, working at his turning lathe, making mathematical calculations, and giving lessons in geometry to his daughter Marya. The old humorist is a real figure, not a grotesque exaggeration.

The Kuragin family show Tolstoy's skill in still a different sphere. Occupying a high station in court society, they are all corrupt and vicious. The father is a selfish schemer, with no heart whatever, and capable of the dirtiest intrigues. The sons are rakes; the daughter, the statuesque Princess Elena, who married Pierre Bezukhov, is every whit as stupid and as wicked as they, but by her physical beauty and by a certain native tact she holds a secure position as a society queen. As to her Tolstoy preaches no sermons; by hints and suggestions he conveys his loathing for her sensual nature.

In *War and Peace* Tolstoy's methods are the same that have been already analyzed in speaking of *Childhood, Boyhood, and Youth*. But he uses them with a bolder sweep; his tone of cynical probing into motives is replaced by that of joyous, unconscious, benevolent omniscience. He first describes the outward appearance of a man or woman in such a way as to suggest character; then he gradually unfolds that character by acts, great and small, and by detailed analysis of the feelings. Each person grows old before the reader's eyes.

Similarly, Tolstoy's pictures of battles and of war in general show the same peculiarities that we have already remarked in *Sevastopol*. Suffering, not heroism, gives war its individuality. The showy heroism of Prince Andréy at Austerlitz accomplishes nothing; Nikoláy's tales of hussar bravery are mainly folly and pretence. The real actors in battle are the quiet common soldiers, or men like the modest artillery captain Tushin. But now Tolstoy proceeds from mere observation of the details of military life, as masterly as that which he gives of the drawing room and the nursery, to a reasoned commentary on war, of which the finality is not so apparent. Not only valorous officers, he argues, but clever generals are of no account in the progress of a campaign. Napoleon, greatest of military geniuses by common repute, was nothing but a puffed-up nonentity. Circumstances favored him in his early campaigns, and he won them; in his invasion of Russia he showed neither more nor less military talent than before, yet he was miserably defeated, since the trend of events—one may call this fate, though Tolstoy avoids the term—was now against him. Analyzing Napoleon's single acts in the war, Tolstoy shows them to have been foolish and ill-judged. The Russian generals who contrived strategy to meet Napoleon were similarly impotent. Only Kutuzov, fat and sluggish, almost in his dotage, who sleeps through a council of war, is master of the situation by surrendering himself to the spontaneous movement of the Russian people and swimming with the current. Napoleon was defeated by a whole nation of which Kutuzov was the accidental representative.

In all this one sees the individualism and hatred of organization that is a distinguishing trait of Tolstoy's temperament. He can draw the whole man in the case of Nikoláy Rostóv or Pierre Bezukhov or Levin (in *Anna Karenin*); he can show the officer in the mess room or the dreamer in his study, even the capable proprietor superintending laborers on his estate. But more complicated organization, in which one must perforce rise beyond human relations into something like statistical calculations, and in which one deals with ink and paper as well as human beings, or instead of them, is uncongenial to Tolstoy, and he disbelieves in talent so exhibited. Napoleon is futile, but so also is Speransky, the great Liberal minister of Alexander I, whose plan for the transformation of Russia into a constitutional monarchy was thwarted, though Tolstoy does not tell us so, by the treachery of his master. A man's true mission is to shape his own life; when he attempts to guide external events he becomes ineffective.

One is not surprised then, to find *War and Peace* widely different in artistic methods from all historical novels of the school of Sir Walter Scott, Dumas, or Sienkiewicz. *Ivanhoe* and *The Talisman* give pictures of far-off times and countries that add to the narrative a gaudy strangeness; costuming and historic associations lend interest to conventional and vaguely conceived characters; Tolstoy, on the other hand, draws

living men and women whose lives are seen against
the background of a world event which they have no
power to shape or direct. In Scott's stories historical
persons like Richard the Lion-hearted and Saladin
mingle with the creations of the novelist's fancy and
determine their fortunes, or are potently aided by them;
underneath the story lies the tacit assumption that
the individual will is the force determining history.
History becomes a complex of picturesque biographies.
In *War and Peace* Napoleon appears, but as an awkward,
stoutish man, vain and futile, who has no more influence
on history than the meanest soldier in the army that
invades Russia under his nominal leadership.   The
Rostóvs and Bolkonskys are affected not by Napoleon
or Alexander, but by the unseen, mysterious currents of
human destiny.

This conception of history Tolstoy does not leave
to be inferred from his narrative, nor does he convey it
by scattered hints and comments; to it he devotes whole
chapters of abstract reasoning. These are, one must
admit, a blemish in his great work, of which they inter-
rupt the continuity. The theory that they develop is
of no importance except as coming from Tolstoy, as one
stage in the thought of a man of vigorous, though eccentric, intellectual power. In the narrative his skill
as an artist makes us accept for the moment his view
of the impotence of human individuals in the shaping of
history, just as the skill of Homer makes us accept the
contrary assumption of the all-importance of personal

prowess. An artist need see but one side of a question, a philosopher must see all sides; when Tolstoy philosophizes he still sees but one side, and the flaws in his reasoning become apparent. When inspired by moral fervor, as in the religious works of his later life, or when he discusses problems of human life drawn from his own experience, as in his articles on education, Tolstoy is a writer of marvelous power; when, as here, he tries to analyze an abstract problem, he is confused, contradictory, and tiresome.

History, Tolstoy states, has been conceived of as primarily the work of heroes, of representative men, of leaders who have consciously shaped human destiny. To this conception of history, antiquated even in his own time, Tolstoy correctly demurs, but he errs by running to the other extreme, and totally denying the part played by the individual not only in guiding the fate of a nation, but in directing the course of a campaign, or deciding the outcome of a single battle. In a battle, he argues, no general knows what is happening; even subordinate commanders, not to speak of the field marshal, fail to control the men beneath them. A battle depends on a number of factors so infinitely large as to transcend human intellect. Seeing that a general is not omniscient and omnipresent, Tolstoy jumps to the conclusion that he is powerless. He forgets his preparations for the battle, his massing of chosen troops, his wise selection of subordinates, his personal influence on the mind of every private in his ranks. Napoleon, Tolstoy tells us, did not order the invasion of Russia any more than each of his private soldiers did so, for if one corporal had refused to enter the new campaign, and others had followed his example, then the invasion could not have taken place.*

The soldiers of the French army advanced to kill and to be killed at the battle of Borodinó not in consequence of the command of Napoleon, but by their own desire. The whole army, French, Italians, Germans, Poles, hungry, tattered, and worn out by the march, in the sight of an army that barred them from Moscow, felt that *le vin est tiré et qu'il faut le boire*. If Napoleon had now forbidden them to fight with the Russians, they would have killed him and gone on to fight with the Russians, because it was indispensable for them to do so.—[Part x, ch. 28.]

These arguments are hardly worthy of the detailed refutation that General Dragomirov has bestowed on them.† and indeed Tolstoy himself is not always true to them. He tells, for example, how Kutuzov "followed that impalpable force which is called the spirit of an army," and on which victory depends, and how "he guided it so far as that was in his power;"‡ and to guide the spirit of an army is surely much the same thing as to guide the army itself. To say nothing of such minor departures from his own principles, Tolstoy's minimizing of the importance of leaders of men is of

* Part ix, ch. 1.
† *Tolstoy's "War and Peace" from a Military Point of View.* Included in volume of *Sketches:* Kiev, 1898.
‡ Part x, ch. 35.

two sorts, radically inconsistent with each other. On the one hand he makes Napoleon of no more significance than a private soldier in his army; on the other he makes him a blind instrument in the hands of the forces controlling human destiny, thereby recognizing that at least he was a more important instrument than any other man of his time. This fundamental contradiction runs through all his reasoning on the part played by the individual in history.

History, Tolstoy maintains, is the work of all men, and the result of an inscrutable number of minute causes. No man by conscious effort can alter history, which is the result of unconscious human activity. (One queries what Tolstoy would say of the Trans-Siberian Railroad or the Panama Canal.) Its laws are then beyond the reach of human reason; events happened simply because they were bound to do so. In his revolt from hero-worship Tolstoy reaches only blind fatalism, with no glimmer of the modern economic interpretation of history.

In fact the economic interpretation of history contradicts two of Tolstoy's fundamental ideas, those of the *fixity* and the *duality* of human nature. "Life meanwhile," Tolstoy writes after mentioning the events of the years 1808 and 1809, "the genuine life of men with its essential interests of health, disease, work, rest; with its interests of thought, science, poetry, music, love, friendship, hatred, passions, went on as always independently and aloof from political intimacy and enmity with Napoleon Bonaparte, and aloof from all possible transformations."* Here he fails to recognize the fundamental sociological truth, that "personal life is conditioned by certain social forms, which change in consequence of the historical process; and that on these forms, on the whole complexion of social life, depend the fullness, the freedom, and the prosperity of personal existence."† On this transformation of human character by historic conditions rests the whole modern conception of history.

Furthermore Tolstoy makes a strict distinction between the personal and the public life of man:

There are two sides of life in every man: the personal life, which is the more free the more abstract are its interests; and the elemental, swarm life, in which man inevitably fulfils laws prescribed to him.

Man lives consciously for himself, but serves as the unconscious tool for the attainment of the historic aims of all humanity. An act once performed is irrevocable, and its action, coinciding in time with millions of acts of other men, receives historic significance. The higher a man stands on the social ladder, and the more people there are with whom he is connected, the more power does he have over other people and the more evident are the predestined character and the inevitability of his every act.

"The king's heart is in the hand of the Lord." [Proverbs xxi, 1.]

---

* Part vi, ch. 1.
† Kareyev: *The Historical Philosophy of Tolstoy in War and Peace* (St. Petersburg, 1888), p. 8.

The king is the slave of history.

History, that is the unconscious, general, swarm life of humanity, makes use of every moment of the life of kings for itself, as a tool for its own ends.—[Part IX, ch. 1.]

In the personal life Tolstoy *feels* free will, and takes it for granted; in the "swarm life" he denies free will and devotes many pages of ingenious reasoning to the disproof of its existence. His discussion of the problem suffers from a confusion of two distinct questions: the will may be termed bound by the law of causality, no act taking place without adequate cause; or it may be thought of as subject to the operation of certain historic laws, quite external to the individual. The first question is one for metaphysicians to settle, or at least to discuss, and is of small consequence in practical life; but one thing is self-evident, that if the law of causality applies to the "swarm life" of man it applies equally well to the life of the individual soul. And proof that the will is bound in the first sense does not in the least imply that it is bound in the second sense; much less that, if so bound, it could escape bondage by fleeing from the "swarm life" into that of the individual soul. Tolstoy's reasoning is once more an expression of his dislike for public activity, of the same bias that in his articles on education had made him recognize progress in the soul of man and deny it in history. His consciousness, which proclaims freedom as the condition of life, is at war with his intellect, which views every act of man as predetermined; this dualistic view of human nature is his refuge. But this dualism lacks any philosophic justification, and is inconsistent with the economic interpretation of history, which would regard the efforts of certain persons (hermits or monks, for example) to withdraw from the public life of the world, as itself an historic phenomenon of considerable importance.

This brief summary of Tolstoy's views in *War and Peace* shows his total lack of real historic interest. His definition of historic science is a mere negation of the possibility of such a science. Wrapt up in the problems of the individual life, Tolstoy condemns any attempt of the individual to influence history. As a novelist and an historian, he is a realist, drawing individual human life as it is, and striving to represent the historic process in the same fashion. But in the first case he is likewise an idealist, presenting character not only as it is, but in relation to what it should be; his characters are ceaselessly aspiring and ever occupied with moral problems. This strain of idealism pervades all the greatest Russian writers, and distinguishes them from the French Naturalists; it is peculiarly characteristic of Tolstoy. Yet in his reasoning on history, thanks to his fatalistic conception of it, his idealism deserts him; men cannot guide humanity forward by conscious effort. Later, in *What Shall We Do Then?* (1886), Tolstoy will open his eyes and see that any individual, by developing a new life conception, may by infection modify the lives of others, and so be an instrument for bringing in a new social order. Then he will construct his own

theory of historic progress, which will differ from that
of the Liberals not in kind but aim.   And then, in *Why
People Become Intoxicated* (1890), he will condemn discussion on free will and determinism as a futile waste
of time.

Unlike his views on history, Tolstoy's views on personal conduct are expressed not in chapters of abstract
reasoning, but through the figures of Andréy Bolkonsky,
Pierre Bezukhov, and Platón Karatáyev.   To the first
two of these men, the chief heroes of the novel, he
gives what he terms the finest human qualities (those
which are always denied to generals); love, poetry,
tenderness, and searching philosophic doubt.*   The
third, a humble peasant, proves to represent the moral
ideal for which the high-born Pierre has been vainly
seeking.   In each we see Tolstoy's emphasis on moral
personality, as opposed to historic activity.

Prince Andréy Bolkonsky is perhaps the most successfully portrayed "good man" in all fiction.   Most
heroes of poetry and romance that are meant to be
types of strong, efficient character, Achilles, Prince
Hal, Quentin Durward, are mere ardent, vigorous boys,
whose charm is in youthful energy, and who must either
die young or grow into portly and uninteresting middle-
age.   The middle-aged hero is usually a good man with
a weakness or a villain with certain high endowments,
Don Quixote or Colonel Newcome or Macbeth; his
destiny is tragic and he appeals to our compassion quite

* Part ix, ch. 11.

as much as to our admiration. The perfect man, efficient in intellect, virtuous in conduct, and successful
in his career, is generally a prig or a bore: pious Æneas
is the best example for all time, while the mythical
George Washington of the popular imagination may be
a fair second. (Tolstoy's Levin, as we shall see, knocks
for admittance to this mawkish club, but is not quite
permitted to enter.)   Poets and novelists of genius have
understood ardent young men; they have also a sympathy with the human side of usurpers, generals, and
statesmen.   But to expect that they should understand
the technical, special endowments of a statesman or a
general or a captain of industry, of a Speransky or a
Napoleon, is as absurd as to demand that they make
independent contributions to chemistry or botany.
And yet it is just this technical side of a statesman or
a general that counts in his dealings with men, while
the technical endowments of a chemist or a botanist may
never be guessed by men other than chemists or botanists.
Virgil cannot make us see the generalship or the states-
manship of Æneas and he is forced to pour out such
fulsome admiration of the man as defeats its own aim.
Shakespeare or Congreve can make a simple maiden or
a society belle charming by their conversation; they
cannot similarly create a leader of men.   Shakespeare
can write an eloquent speech for Mark Antony, or he
can tell us of the great side of a character like Brutus and
make the man winning by his simple humanity: that
is all.

To return from this long digression, in Prince Andréy Tolstoy has come nearer than any other novelist to solving this impossible problem. To this character he has given his own energy and vigor, along with a conventional society distinction and charm of which he felt the lack in himself. He has made him conscientious, high-spirited, self-sacrificing, with lofty aims. Prince Andréy is an aristocrat by nature as well as by birth; his talents are recognized by all, and the path to distinction in the state service lies open to him. To say all this of a man is easy, but Tolstoy manages to have Andréy's manner and words suggest his distinction. He is efficient, not oratorical; his personal courage is that of a man rather than of a valiant boy such as Nikoláy. By his human failings of pride and uncharity, even snobbery, Tolstoy preserves him from being mawkish. Then comes the characteristically Russian, or shall we say Tolstoyan touch. Prince Andréy suddenly finds meaningless all the public activity that has seemed to him so important; he looks forward to true happiness in life with Natasha. Deserted by her, he is filled with cynicism and despair; then, mortally wounded at Borodinó, he recovers happiness in the hospital, by forgiving Anatole Kuragin, the man who has wronged him, and who now lies on the operating table near by. Tolstoy has created a man fit for action, but has made him see the futility of the active life just as he is winning his first success in it, in order that he may take up the true life of thought and feeling.

Thought and feeling have ever been the portion of Prince Andréy's friend and complement, Count Pierre Bezukhov. He is a stout, short-sighted, ungainly youth, possessed of immense wealth. Incapable of making a good impression in society and not above reproach in his private life, he is valued by Andréy because of his transparent goodness of heart. Tricked into marriage with an evil woman, he finds solace in the mystic mummeries of the Free Masons. For a time these give a moral stimulus to his dreamy nature, but he soon discovers that his belovèd order is becoming a refuge for fashionable hypocrites. His love and pity for Natasha give the girl hope and courage when most she needs them. When Napoleon enters Moscow, Pierre fantastically imagines himself the savior of Russia and sets out to slay the conqueror. He is forthwith arrested by the French, who carry him off on their retreat from the city. On the dreadful march he becomes acquainted with a companion in captivity, Platón Karatayev, whose words and example work a moral transformation within him. When released from duress, he returns to his estate, marries Natasha, and lives in bliss with her, under her welcome yoke; yet his guiding principle in life is always the memory of Karatayev.

And who was Karatayev? An illiterate little peasant, of scanty intelligence, who lived from day to day with no thought of the morrow. He was incarnate simplicity and goodness; unable to reason as to his own conduct, he always instinctively fulfilled the spirit of Christianity:

Karatayev had no attachments, no friendship or love, as Pierre understood them; but he loved all and lived lovingly with all with which life brought him into contact, and in particular with man—not with any special man, but with the men who were before his eyes. He loved his dog, he loved his comrades, loved the French, loved Pierre, who was his neighbor; but Pierre felt that Karatayev, notwithstanding all his caressing tenderness towards him (by which he involuntarily paid what was due to the spiritual life of Pierre), would not for a moment have been grieved by separation from him. And Pierre began to experience the same feeling towards Karatayev.

Platón Karatayev for all the rest of the prisoners was the most ordinary sort of soldier; . . . they bantered him good-humoredly and sent him on errands. But for Pierre, even as he had appeared on that first night, the unattainable, round, and eternal embodiment of the spirit of simplicity and truth, so he remained forever.—[Part xii, ch. 13.]

This simple model is now the culmination of Tolstoy's wisdom: absolute submission to the powers that be, absolute refusal to enforce one's will on a fellow creature, absolute truthfulness, and, above all, universal kindliness and love. In the all-loving self-effacement of Karatayev, and in the maternal love of Natasha, the great epic narrative of Russia, the greatest work of art that has come from the broad plains of eastern Europe, finds its conclusion, so incongruous from the point of view of conventional story-telling, so harmonious with the spirit of Tolstoy, in whose eyes the founding of an empire is of less profit to a man than a single act of personal kindness.

As has already been emphasized, there are two sides to Tolstoy's nature and to his literary genius. He has a marvelous power over concrete detail, the pomp and parade of external circumstance, and he uses it to portray character as no other writer has ever done. On the other hand, he has an overmastering sense of moral responsibility, a compelling interest in the inner moral life. In the works written before his marriage the first element predominates; in *War and Peace* it still holds the first place in the reader's attention, despite the prominence that is given to the moral development of Prince Andréy and Pierre Bezukhov. In *Anna Karenin* the moral point of view has become firmer and more dominating. The grip on externals is the same, but the wealth of them is held in check and directed to a definite end. The book, whether through conscious observation of technical rules of construction, or unconscious following of a moral purpose, has a unity lacking in its predecessor, and, outside of Russia at least, has gained far wider circulation and greater fame. Its Puritan definiteness of moral outlook has probably greatly contributed to its wonderful success in England and America.

In *Anna Karenin* Tolstoy narrows his field, concentrating his attention on two families and on their private life. Like *War and Peace*, this new novel is a hymn in praise of the family. "The idea of *Anna Karenin* is that sexual relations must be guided by pure Christian love and not by the egoistic love of affinity or by the obligatory love of church or society. Hence he takes two pairs of lovers. He endows the first pair, Anna and Vronsky, with more perfections than the second, and shows how permanent thought and fear about personal happiness ruin their lives, and how sacrifice, pardon, and the desire to make happy another (in short Christian love) teach Kitty and Levin to be happy." *

Concentration of purpose then makes *Anna Karenin* the most unified of all Tolstoy's longer works. Furthermore, in the construction of his plot Tolstoy employs a conventional device such as he ordinarily disdains and such as we might anticipate from Sir Walter Scott or from Dickens. At the time when Anna meets Vronsky for the first time, in the railway station, a peasant is killed by a train. Anna, not knowing why, sees in the incident an omen foreboding disaster, and cannot drive it from her mind. Later, during the course of her amour with Vronsky, she dreams of a peasant bending down over a sack, fumbling in it, and uttering incoherent French words: *Il faut le battre le fer, le broyer, le pétrir;* and Vronsky at the same time has a similar dream. And at the catastrophe, when Anna throws herself beneath the train, "a peasant, muttering some-

* From an essay by Mr. F. A. Postnikov.

thing, was working at the iron above her." Thus a sense of impending tragedy pervades the whole work, in contrast to *War and Peace*, in which the reader, like the actors themselves, is quite ignorant what fate may have in store.

The concession to conventional construction, important in the comparison of this novel with other works by Tolstoy, is after all very slight: *Anna Karenin* abounds in episodes and descriptions that have no possible bearing on Anna's story. The contrast of her tragic fate with the commonplace happiness of Levin and Kitty is not worked out with any balancing of detail; the two stories run side by side almost independently: Tolstoy develops one of them to a convenient stopping place and then turns to the other. Often Anna's fortunes seem to be no more than an episode in the novel that bears her name. Her love of Vronsky and its consequences could have been told more neatly, and in a sense more effectively, by a dozen inferior novelists than by Tolstoy, with his apparent prodigality of good material.

One inquires involuntarily whether Tolstoy really fails to understand his own art; whether he actually wastes good material because he does not know how to employ it effectively. A single illustration will show that he is really a master of compressed, vivid suggestion. Anna Karenin is a woman of about thirty, who has been living for eight years with a husband some twenty years older than herself; their life has been, if

not blissful, at least not the reverse. She has respected
and admired her husband and has been faithful to him
from conviction as well as from convention. Then she
leaves him for a few days, in order to visit the family of
her brother in Moscow. There, at a dancing party, she
meets Vronsky, a handsome young officer, and, without
herself being conscious of the fact, she falls in love with
him. He returns to St. Petersburg on the same train
with her, and seizes an opportunity for telling her of
his passion for her. Her mind is filled with her new
interests. At the station in St. Petersburg her husband
meets her:

In St. Petersburg, as soon as the train stopped and she got
out of the railway carriage, the first face that attracted her
attention was the face of her husband. "O heavens, where
did he ever get such ears?" she thought, looking at his cold
and stately figure, and especially at what had so startled her
now, the cartilages of his ears, which supported the sides of his
round hat.—[Part I, ch. 30.]

For eight years she had lived with him and never
noticed his ears, just as no man notices or cares for any
small physical defect or ugliness in those near and
dear to him. Now she sees those ears—and they
continue to stick out during all the rest of the
novel. In a half-dozen lines Tolstoy has shown the profound change that has come over the woman's whole
mind.

Why then is Tolstoy, throughout the book, so lavish

of detail that tells nothing of Anna? Because he is striving to give a picture not of Anna alone, but of a whole world of complicated, conflicting interests. Though he has here chosen a narrower field than in *War and Peace*, he has not essentially changed his ideals and his methods of work. The portrayal of a great company of men and women is his primary interest rather than the telling of an absorbing tale of guilty love. Várenka, Nikoláy Levin, Agafya Mikháylovna, all claim his affection as well as Anna.

Tolstoy's concessions to convention are very slight even in the story of Anna herself. Anna has a premonition that she will die in childbirth. By her bedside her husband and her lover are reconciled: Karenin, a leatherish, documentary person, is touched to the quick so that he shows the inward fineness of his nature and forgives from his whole heart the man who has wronged him; Vronsky has a sudden realization of the sin that he has committed. The scene, as Mr. Howells has said with truth,* rises to heights unmatched in all fiction. By all ordinary rules of literary construction Anna should now die and the two men remain united by a common sorrow. But she recovers. Karenin returns from the heights of emotion to his office routine, and his ears stick out just as they did before. Anna leaves him and lives with her lover. Karenin is minded to give her a divorce, but, falling under the control of some pseudo-religious hypocrites, resists his natural feeling

* In *My Literary Passions.*

of compassion, and refuses to do so. Anna, living with Vronsky, but with no legal claim on him, finds that she is slowly losing her former unbounded power over his affections—and she kills herself in a moment of jealousy and despair.

Indeed this novel, like all Tolstoy's work, impresses the reader as having grown like some living organism, instead of having been put together like a piece of machinery. It is an illustration of a great esthetic truth that has been well expressed by Sellar:

How the great impersonations of poetry and prose fiction, which are more real to our imaginations than the personages of history or those whom we know in life, come into being, is a question which probably their authors themselves could not answer. Though reflection on human nature and deliberate intention to exemplify some law of life may precede the creative act which gives them being, and though continued reflection may be needed to sustain them in a consistent course, yet no mere analytic insight into the springs of action can explain the process by which a great artist works. The beings of his imagination seem to acquire an existence independent of the experience and of the deliberate intentions of their author, and to inform this experience and mold these intentions as much as they are informed and molded by them.—[*The Roman Poets of the Augustan Age: Virgil* (Oxford, 1877), pp. 399, 400.]

Tolstoy himself bears witness to this artistic experience. In a letter to Strakhov he tells how he came to write of Vronsky's attempt at suicide, which immedi-

ately follows the interview with Karenin that has just
been described:

In everything, almost everything that I have written, I
have been guided by a need for the gathering of thoughts,
connected with one another for self-expression; but every
thought, expressed separately in words, loses its sense and
is frightfully degraded when it is taken alone, outside its
connection with others. And the connection itself is formed
not by thought (in my opinion), but by something else,
and to express the basis of this connection immediately
by words is impossible: that can be done only mediately,
by words that describe images, acts, situations. You know
all this better than I do, but I have been interested in the
point recently. One of the most evident proofs of it for me was
the suicide of Vronsky, which you liked. The point was never
so clear to me before. The chapter describing how Vronsky
accepted his part after his interview with the husband had
been long since written. I began to correct it, and quite
unexpectedly for me, but beyond any doubt whatever, Vronsky
started to shoot himself. Now it appears that this was or-
ganically indispensable for what follows.—[Biryukóv: II, 215.]

Anna Karenin is one of the great love stories of the
world. Yet never does one character in the novel pour
out his feelings to another in words of poetic eloquence;
the confessions of love are like those of real life, sometimes through short, earnest speeches, more often by
mere hints and implications: Anna and Vronsky at the
ball learn of their mutual attraction by a subtle mental
telegraphy as they chat on indifferent topics. We fol-

low the course of Anna's passion not by her words, not often even by her conscious thoughts, but by her changed attitude to the world about her, to Dolly's children, to Kitty, to her husband, to St. Petersburg society. We feel her passion rather than learn of it. In the same way, though less subtly, more consciously, we are made to feel Levin's growing happiness. Here, as everywhere, we become acquainted with Tolstoy's men and women as with those of a new city in which we have taken up our home.

Anna Karenin is a novel of the conscience. Scenes of fine, vigorous, physical life abound in it, to be sure, as in the picture of the mowing, where Levin, his moist shirt clinging to his aching back, strains every muscle in order to keep pace with his peasant laborers. With Levin, too, we rejoice in the coming of spring, thawing, gurgling, sprouting, rustling; here we gaze on nature with a farmer's eyes, as in *War and Peace* with a hunter's. Yet the hunter has his share too, even though he be only the unadventurous shooter of woodcock, in a fine chapter describing an evening's sport of Levin and Stepán Arkádyevich. But the spiritual life of the characters furnishes the primary interest of the book. The theories of *War and Peace* have disappeared; Tolstoy is no longer interested in abstract speculation, even of his own nihilistic sort. Plain, ordinary, every-day conduct is his theme; he might be telling the story of the later life of Andréy Bolkonsky and Pierre Bezukhov, after they had recovered from day dreams of public activity.

On one important matter, however, *Anna Karenin* shows us a significant change in Tolstoy's view of the state and of the individual man's attitude towards it. In *Sevastopol* he had described war with a feeling of horror at the sufferings caused by it, but with no attempt to reason upon its existence or to trace its cause. In *War and Peace* it had become the vast, inscrutable product of fate, rebellion at which would be futile. In *Anna Karenin* Levin expresses a more commonplace point of view:

"My theory is this: war, on the one hand, is such an animal, cruel, and terrible thing that no single man, not to speak of a Christian, can take upon himself the responsibility for the beginning of war; of that the government alone is capable, which is summoned to do so and is inevitably brought into war. On the other hand both science and common sense teach us that in state matters, and especially in the matter of war, citizens renounce their personal will."—[Part VIII, ch. 15.]

Tolstoy's conscience rebels at war, but the former artillery officer is still a loyal subject of the tsar, and at the bidding of the state authorities will stifle its demands. Soon conscience will gain the upper hand, and Tolstoy will denounce the very existence of the state as a clog upon it.

Puritan though he be in his point of view, Tolstoy is still broad in his sympathies, showing wonderful charity to sins that come from the animal nature and that have not destroyed goodness of heart. Stepán Arkádyevich Oblonsky, Anna's sybarite, kind-hearted brother, violates nearly every law of the decalogue, and yet he receives from his creator a Fielding-like indulgence. To waste sermons on him would be as foolish as to lecture a kitten for stealing cream; his geniality and freedom from malice preserve him from reprobation. Tolstoy reserves his scorn for creatures like the Princess Betsy, outwardly respectable, but with neither morals nor kindliness to recommend them, who are not only vicious themselves, but the cause of viciousness in others. Yet even for her and for her fellows he shows contempt rather than wrath: such persons are outside the world in which he is interested, though not outside that which he sees. Tolstoy is little attracted even by the most moral men of bookish theories or purely external interests, by the sociologist Koznyshév and the Liberal county politician Sviyazhsky. They debate great questions or adopt public measures without relating them to their personal conduct, which flows on in accustomed, routine channels. Tolstoy reserves his personal attention, so to speak, for Anna and Vronsky, Levin and Kitty, Dolly, the careworn wife of Stepán Arkádyevich, and (to some extent) for Karenin—human beings who have a certain depth of emotion, a " force of life," to use Tolstoy's own term; who both reason about life's problems and feel them, and who strive to shape their lives in accord with this reasoned emotion.

What then is Tolstoy's attitude towards the central figure of his novel, towards the lovely and fascinating Anna, the unfaithful wife and the pitiful victim? Does

he sympathize with her or does he cast a stone? In a
sense he does both. To his book he prefixes the tremendous biblical minatory motto: "Vengeance is mine;
I will repay" (Romans xii, 19). A reader involuntarily
connects this with Anna's fate; vengeance has overtaken
the sinner. But to this simple explanation there are
decided objections. From the point of view of Russian
high society, to which Anna belongs, adultery is a trivial
offence, a mere peccadillo. The Russian critic Skabichevsky compares Tolstoy's treatment of this ordinary
society transgression to the act of a man attacking flies
with an axe. Tolstoy himself sees that from a social
point of view Anna's offence lies not in her unfaithful-
ness, but in her frankness and in her intensity of nature.
Had she been content to live in her husband's house
and keep up the appearance of respectability, according
to his charge, no tragedy need have followed. Princess
Betsy is living in prosperous security at the close of the
novel. Vronsky's mother is gratified when she hears of
her son's connection with Anna, "because nothing, according to her idea, gave the last finish to a brilliant
young man like a liaison in high society, and because
Madam Karenin, who had pleased her so much and who
had talked so much about her own son, had after all
turned out to be just such a person as were all beautiful
and well-bred women, according to the ideas of the
Countess Vronsky";* she is grieved when she learns that

* Part ii, ch. 18. The opinion reflects that of Tolstoy's "Aunt Tatyana": see *Confession*, ch. 2.

this is no mere brilliant and graceful society intrigue, but a deep and lasting passion, which may involve her son in foolish acts and affect his professional career. Later, had Karenin been willing to grant Anna a divorce, so that she and Vronsky might have married and recovered some social position, all might yet have been well, or at least no tragedy need have followed. But he refuses, and Anna lives with Vronsky in defiance not so much of moral standards as of social conventions that are no better than a parody of morality. Anna never in the novel shows any remorse for her desertion of her husband. Her suffering comes first from the snubs that she receives from her former society associates, which force her to concentrate her whole life in her lover; and, second, from her jealous despair when she discovers that her lover is beginning to have a life independent of her own and that she is unable to control his every thought.

In face of this difficulty, one might be tempted to apply the motto to the whole society of which Anna forms a part; to regard the novel as a philippic against modern society like the later *What Shall We Do Then?* or *Resurrection*. But Tolstoy gives no intimation of such an intent in the volume itself; he has not yet become a prophet preaching against the modern Babylon. Or one might interpret the motto in accord with Tolstoy's later cardinal doctrine, that sinful man (in the person of the reader) should not pass judgment on his neighbor's conduct: "'Vengeance is *mine; I* will repay,'

saith the *Lord*." But such an interpretation is impossible, for in the novel Tolstoy constantly forces the moral
issue on the reader's attention, compelling him to judge
between Anna and Levin.

The solution of the enigma may be found in the
peculiar duality of Tolstoy's nature and his art. On
the one side he is a moralist who constantly grows
more strict and ascetic; on the other he is a clear-
sighted painter of life as it actually exists. Breach of
the marriage vows may be a peccadillo for Russian society; for Tolstoy it is a crime of capital moment.
Tolstoy cannot think of adultery as "light and playful";*
he feels that it is serious: his point of view is that of the
Puritan Hawthorne in *The Scarlet Letter*. Levin reflects
his creator's temperament, and in his happy married
life, based as it is on mutual love and self-sacrifices,
realizes his ideal. Anna, led astray by the lust of the
flesh, goes to ruin; Tolstoy is wilfully blind to the
fact that her sin and her fate have no necessary connection. The Princess Betsy and Stepán Arkádyevich
are both outside Tolstoy's moral world; he reasons about
neither, but as a man he despises the one and likes the
other. From his presentation of life, as from life itself,
one may draw various conclusions. Tolstoy's own
spiritual vision is clear and single, but he will not let
it warp his picture of what actually goes on in the
world about him.

To Levin, Tolstoy gives much of his own individuality;

* See page 155.

his own brooding search for spiritual truth, his aversion for government activity, his passion for out-of-door life, his new-found faith in physical labor as a cure for spiritual ills. But he imparts to him none of his own universality of interests, of his high breeding or personal magnetism. Levin attains spiritual salvation in quiet farm work and in his family ties. The church he tolerates, though it means little to him; among the humble peasants he finds the best stimulus to the spiritual life.— As an artistic creation Levin is not a complete success; he resembles too much the pattern good boy of the Sunday-school books. And yet his personality, tiresome at first for readers who are eager to press on with Anna's thrilling story, gains with each fresh perusal of the novel. At last we come closer to Levin and forgive him his virtues. A contrast of the two paragraphs in which Tolstoy says farewell to each of these characters will show us the author's point of view towards them, which is after all our grandmother's point of view, that to which we are all gradually drawing closer as we leave our youth behind us.

This is our last glimpse of Anna in life:

She had intended to fall under the center of the first railway carriage, which had come up opposite to her; but the red bag, which she had begun to take off her arm, checked her, and it was too late: the center had passed by her. She had to wait for the following carriage. A feeling such as she used to experience when bathing, when about to enter the water, seized her, and she crossed herself. The wonted gesture of making the sign of the cross called up in her soul a whole succession of girlish and childish memories, and suddenly the darkness that had concealed everything from her parted, and life rose before her for a moment with all its bright past joys. But she did not lower her eyes from the wheels of the second carriage that was approaching. And just at the moment when the space between the wheels came even with her, she threw aside the red bag, and, drawing her head into her shoulders, fell under the carriage on her hands, and with a light movement, as if preparing to rise again immediately, dropped upon her knees. And at the same instant she was horrified at what she was doing. "Where am I? What am I doing? Why?" She wanted to rise and throw herself back; but something huge and implacable struck her upon the head and tugged at her back. "Lord, forgive me all!" she said, feeling the impossibility of struggle. A peasant, muttering something, was working at the iron above her. And the candle by which she had read the book filled with troubles, deceits, grief, and evil, flashed up with a brighter light than ever, illumined for her all that had before been in darkness, sputtered, began to grow dim, and was extinguished forever.— [Part VII, ch. 31.]

And this is the last thought of Levin, with which the novel closes:

"Just as before, I shall get angry with Iván the coachman, I shall dispute, I shall express my thoughts at the wrong time; there will be the same wall between the holy of holies of my soul and other people, even my wife; just in the same way as before I shall blame her for my own terror and repent doing so; just as before I shall fail to understand with my reason why I pray and yet I shall continue to pray—but my life now, my whole life, independently of anything that can happen to me, every moment of it, is not only not bereft of meaning, as it was before, but has the undoubted meaning of good, which I have power to implant in it!"*

Living on his secluded estate, aloof from the literary circles of Russia, Tolstoy had written the two finest novels of Europe. Now he will turn aside from artistic creation, in order to work out within himself a new religious conception of life. He will attain a place among great religious leaders as well as among great men of letters.

* The writer is indebted here and elsewhere to suggestions from lectures by Mr. Robert Herrick.

CHAPTER VII

THE CRISIS; THE RELIGIOUS SYSTEM

INTO his fiction, as we have seen, Tolstoy has constantly introduced characters who are to a greater or less extent reproductions of his own personality: Nikoláy Irtenyev, Olenin, Prince Andréy Bolkonsky, Pierre Bezukhov, and, above all, Levin. These accounts at second hand, so to speak, of his own spiritual experiences are long and analytical studies that suggest George Eliot. Now, in 1879, he suddenly tells us with startling directness and force the story of his own spiritual life, in his *Confession*. This little book of only eighty pages will ever remain a classic among religious autobiographies. It is so vivid, so compressed, so powerful, that one wishes to cite it entire rather than to give a mere summary of its contents.

Tolstoy tells first of his boyhood, how he was educated in the faith of the Russian Orthodox Church, but very early lost that faith; more accurately, he never had genuine faith, but a mere wavering confidence in what others had taught him. His defection was like that of the immense majority of people of his own class of society, who were forced to remain legally members of the

Orthodox Church, but who were at heart indifferent to it. "Then as now public recognition and profession of orthodoxy was found for the most part among people who were dull and cruel and who regarded themselves as very important. But intellect, honor, uprightness, kindliness, and morality were for the most part found in men who confessed themselves to be unbelievers." As for Tolstoy himself: "I believed in God, or rather I did not deny God—but in what God I should not have been able to say. Neither did I deny Christ and his teaching, but in what his teaching consisted I should also have been unable to say." He tried to lead a moral life, but was ridiculed for his efforts by others. His real faith was in self-perfection, which in practice was merely a struggle to be better than other men according to other men's standards, to be more famous, more important, and more wealthy than others. His life during his young manhood he describes as follows:

I cannot recall these years without horror, disgust, and sickness of heart. I killed men in war, I challenged them to duels in order to kill them; I squandered money at cards, I ate up the toil of peasants; I punished them; I fornicated, I deceived. Lying, theft, lust of all sorts, drunkenness, violence, murder. . . . There was no crime that I might not have committed; and for all that the men of my own age praised me and regarded me, and still regard me, as a comparatively moral man.—[Ch. 2.]

All this means, of course, that Tolstoy's life was that of an average young man of society; one must not take too seriously the words of a convert as to his life before conversion: we have already passed in review the details of his outward existence.*

Winning fame as an author, Tolstoy fancied himself a teacher, though he did not know what he was teaching; he accepted the point of view of his Liberal associates, including their faith in progress. Disenchanted with this, he grew sick, mentally rather than physically, but was saved from despair by his marriage and by the new interests that came with it:

Despite the fact that I regarded authorship as a trifle during these fifteen years [after marriage], I nevertheless continued to write. I had already tasted the seduction of authorship, the seduction of huge financial profit and of the applause given me for my insignificant labor, and I gave myself up to it, as a means of bettering my material position and for stifling in my soul all questions of the sense of my life and of life in general. I wrote, teaching what for me was the sole truth, that one must so live as to gain most prosperity for himself and his family.—[Ch. 3.]

But now questions began to occur to Tolstoy: What is the true aim of life? What permanent meaning can there be to man's existence, and in particular to that of Leo Tolstoy?

In the midst of my thoughts about my farming, which interested me greatly at the time, there suddenly would come into my head the question: "Very well, you will have 16,000

* In particular, compare pp. 9-14, 76, 77, above.

acres in the province of Samara, and three hundred head of
horses—and then?" . . . And I was quite at a loss and did
not know what to think next. . . . Or, thinking of the fame
that my works would gain for me, I said to myself: "Very
well, you will be more famous than Gogol, Pushkin, Shakespeare, and Molière, than all the writers in the world—well,
what of it?" And I could make absolutely no answer. These
questions will not wait; one must answer them at once: if
you do not answer, you cannot live. But there is no answer.

I felt that the foundation on which I had been standing
had broken down, that I had nothing to stand on; that what
I had been living by no longer existed, and that I had nothing
to live by.—[Ch. 3.]

Thus Tolstoy, rich, famous, and prosperous, was
driven to the brink of suicide, and had to hide from
temptations to shoot or to hang himself:

My question, that which at fifty years of age had led me
towards suicide, was the most simple question, one which lies
in the soul of every man, from a silly child to the wisest sage,
the question without which life is impossible, as I had experienced in actual fact. The question is as follows: What
will result from what I am doing now and shall do to-morrow?
What will result from my whole life?

Otherwise expressed, the question will be as follows: Why
should I live, why should I desire anything, why should I do
anything? Or the question may be expressed still otherwise:
Is there in my life a meaning which would not be annihilated
by the inevitable death that awaits me?—[Ch. 5.]

This pondering upon life's ultimate, fundamental
question is the root of Tolstoy's entire religious system,

and, one may add, the root of all religious belief and of all philosophy that is developed independently by a man and not borrowed as a whole from some other person or institution. Such doubts and perplexities come at times into the life of every thinking man. But an Anglo-Saxon is not apt to be driven by them into despair or melancholia; he will reach despair, if at all, through misfortunes of the fleshly, material life, through vice or disappointment. To the brooding, emotional Russian the question is not so much a mental game or business as a vital problem, profoundly affecting conduct. For the proof of this one may turn to the reflection of Russian life in the works of Turgenev and Dostoyevsky as well as in those of Tolstoy himself. Meditation on fundamental problems rather than action on instinctive or half-considered premises, is a characteristic of the Russian temperament.

Having once clearly put the question to himself, Tolstoy set out to solve it. He asked a solution of science, but science could give no answer to his great and fundamental question; it was either vague and equivocal or else contemptuous:

If you turn to the group of sciences that tries to give solutions to the questions of life, to physiology, psychology, biology, sociology, then you encounter a startling poverty of thought, the most extreme obscurity, an utterly unjustified pretense at solving irrelevant questions, and constant contradictions of one thinker with another and even with himself. If you turn to the group of sciences that do not undertake the solution of questions of life, but answer their own special scientific questions, then you are enraptured with the might of the human mind, but you know in advance that there are no answers to questions of life. These sciences frankly ignore the question of life. They say: "To the query what you are and why you live, we have no answers, and that is not our line; but now if you want to know the laws of light, of chemical compounds, the laws of the development of organisms; . . . if you want to know the laws of your own mind, then for all that we have clear, exact, and indubitable answers." —[Ch. 5.]

Tolstoy's question, and his failure to receive a reply, were the same as those of the Persian Omar:

> Myself when young did eagerly frequent
> Doctor and Saint, and heard great argument
>   About it and about: but evermore
> Came out by the same door where in I went.
>
> With them the seed of Wisdom did I sow,
> And with my own hand wrought to make it grow;
>   And this was all the Harvest that I reap'd—
> "I came like Water, and like Wind I go."
>
> Up from Earth's Center through the Seventh Gate
> I rose, and on the Throne of Saturn sate,
>   And many a Knot unravell'd by the Road;
> But not the Master-knot of human Fate.
>
> There was the Door to which I found no Key;
> There was the Veil through which I could not see:

> Some little talk awhile of ME and THEE
> There was—and then no more of—THEE and ME.
>
> Earth could not answer; nor the Seas that mourn
> In flowing Purple, of their Lord forlorn;
>   Nor rolling Heaven, with all his Signs revealed
> And hidden by the sleeve of Night and Morn.

And the plain prose of the modern realist expresses the tragedy of the situation as vividly as the poetry of the Persian sceptic and his translator.

Doubtful of his own powers, Tolstoy wondered whether the wise men of other times and nations had been perplexed by the same problem, and whether they had perchance been able to solve it. And he inquired of Socrates, the wisest man of ancient Greece, of Solomon (or whoever wrote the book of Ecclesiastes),* the representative of ancient Hebrew wisdom, of Buddha, the sage of ancient India, and of Schopenhauer, the greatest philosopher of modern Germany. In each case the reply was the same: life here on earth is evil and futile; death is better than life; the problem of existence is to find an escape from existence. Tolstoy was convinced that his reasoning had been correct; that there was no answer to his query.

But an escape from this reasoning might perhaps be found in the actual experience of the mass of humanity.

---

*Yet, curiously enough, in 1879 Tolstoy wrote to Fet of Ecclesiastes as a new book, which he had just read (Biryukóv : II, 333). In his *Confession* he may have confused dates.

Hence Tolstoy began to trace the paths by which his every-day companions escaped from the dilemma that tortured him:

I found that for men of my circle there are four ways out from the awful position in which we are all placed. The first way out is that of ignorance. It consists in not knowing, not understanding the fact that life is evil and meaningless. People of this class—mostly women or very young or very stupid persons—have not yet understood the question of life that rose before Schopenhauer, Solomon, and Buddha.—[Ch. 7.]

The second way out is through Epicureanism. Seeing that life is evil and meaningless, men say: "Let us eat, drink, and be merry, for tomorrow we die. Let us forget the fundamental misery of life in its fleeting pleasures." Such was the way out chosen by Solomon and by the majority of Tolstoy's associates. And such, we may add, was that of Omar Khayyám:

> Then to the Lip of this poor earthern Urn
> I lean'd, the Secret of my Life to learn:
>   And Lip to Lip it murmur'd—"While you live,
> Drink!—for, once dead, you never shall return."
>
> Ah, make the most of what we yet may spend,
> Before we too into the Dust descend;
>   Dust into Dust, and under Dust, to lie,
> Sans Wine, sans Song, sans Singer, and—sans End!

Tolstoy's comment is decisive, though not perfectly just: "The dulness of the imagination of these people gives them the possibility of forgetting that which gave no peace to Buddha, the inevitability of disease, old age, and death, which today or tomorrow will destroy all these pleasures. . . . These people I could not imitate; not having their dulness of imagination, I could not artificially produce it in myself."

The third class of people are brave and honest: seeing the futility of life, they kill themselves. (It must be remembered that at this time Tolstoy had no faith in a life after death.) "I saw that this was the most worthy way out, and I wished so to act."

The fourth way out is that of weakness. It consists in this, that, understanding the evil and the senselessness of life, men continue to drag it on, knowing in advance that nothing can come of it. . . . This is the way out characteristic of weakness, for if I know something better, and it is in my power, why should I not give myself up to that which is better? . . . I belonged to that class of people.—[Ch. 7.]

Reason had convinced Tolstoy of the necessity and duty of suicide, and yet he was restrained by a dim consciousness of a mistake in his reasoning; by a certain *consciousness of life* working in opposition to his reason. This new force suddenly made him see that his reasoning had been based exclusively on the lives of wealthy, educated men, on Buddha, Schopenhauer, and his own circle, and that he had overlooked the immense majority of mankind, the real working class:

I felt that if I wished to live and to understand the meaning of life, then I must seek this meaning, of course, not among those who had lost the meaning of life and wished to kill themselves, but among those billions of men who had lived and who were still living, who worked and who bore upon their shoulders both their life and our own. And I glanced at the immense masses of simple, unlearned, and poor people who had lived and were still living, and I saw something quite different. I saw that all these billions of people who had lived and were still living, all, with rare exceptions, failed to fit into my classification. I could not admit that they did not understand the question, because they put it themselves and answer it with extraordinary clearness. Neither could I admit that they were Epicureans, because their life is composed rather of privations and sufferings than of enjoyments. Still less could I admit that they irrationally lived to the end of a meaningless life, because they give a clear explanation to every act of their lives and to death itself. And to kill themselves they regard as the greatest of evils. It turned out that all humanity had a sort of knowledge of the meaning of life which I failed to recognize and which I despised. The result was that rational knowledge gave no meaning to life and excluded life; but the meaning given to life by billions of men, by all humanity, rested on a sort of contemptible false knowledge.

Rational knowledge in the person of the learned and the wise denies the meaning of life, but the immense masses of men, all humanity, recognize this meaning in irrational knowledge. And that irrational knowledge is faith, the very faith that I could not help rejecting. That meant God in one and three; it meant the creation in six days, the devils and angels and all that which I could not accept until I should go mad.

My position was frightful. I knew that I should find nothing on the path of rational knowledge except the denial of life,

and in faith nothing but the denial of reason, which is still
more impossible than the denial of life.—[Ch. 8.]

Tolstoy's next step was to see that his original question had been wrongly put, that he had inquired what
was the extra-temporal, extra-spatial, extra-causal meaning of life, and that he had received the answer that life
had no temporal, spatial, or casual meaning.   The
solution to his problem must be given by faith, by a
faith that will connect man's finite life with an infinite
God.   Prepared then to accept any faith which should
not directly contradict reason, Tolstoy now turned to
the study of religion; he studied Buddhism and Moham-
medanism from books, and Christianity both from books
and from the lives of the people around him.   From
cultivated believers he could learn nothing: their faith
was not real faith, but merely one of the Epicurean
solaces of life; it made no practical difference in their conduct.   But the faith of the working classes, though it was
outwardly the same as that of the wealthy, and though
it was blended with much superstition, was intimately
connected with their daily life, was in fact a necessary
condition of it.   It made them, in contrast with the
upper classes, work hard, bear privations patiently,
meet death without terror or despair:

And I came to love these people.   The more I penetrated
into their lives, into the lives of those still living and into
the lives of those who had died, but of whom I had read and
heard, the more I loved them and the easier it became for

me myself to live. I lived thus for some two years, and in me
a transformation came to pass that had long been preparing
within me and the germs of which had always been in me. It
came to pass that the life of our circle, of the rich and the
learned, not only became repugnant to me, but lost all meaning.
All our acts, our reasonings, our sciences and arts—all this rose
before me with a new significance. I came to understand
that all this was mere pampering of the appetites and that it
was impossible to seek meaning in it. But the life of all the
toiling folk, of all humanity which was creating life, rose
before me in its true significance. I came to understand that
this is life itself, and that the meaning given to this life is
truth, and I accepted it.—[Ch. 10.]

Thus Tolstoy returned to faith not through any process of reasoning, but through contact with the masses
of the people and through the infectiousness of their
point of view.

Having rejected reason once, Tolstoy could do so
many times; he had attained the sincerely clerical point
of view:

But with this meaning of the popular faith there is in-
separably connected among our unsectarian folk, in the midst
of whom I lived, much that repelled me and seemed to me inex-
plicable; the sacraments, the church services, the fasts, the
worship of relics and sacred pictures. The people cannot
divide one from the other, and neither could I. However
strange to me was much of what formed part of the popular
faith, I accepted it all; I went to the services, prayed in the
morning and in the evening, fasted, prepared for communion—
and at first my reason did not oppose any of this. The very

thing that before had seemed to me impossible now aroused in me no opposition.—[Ch. 13.]

This point of view is that adopted by Levin in the last chapter of *Anna Karenin,* when he reflects: "I am willy-nilly united with other men into one company of believers, which is called a church."

But there was a point beyond which Tolstoy could not strain his reason; the reception of the communion was a hard task:

I shall never forget the feeling of torture that I experienced on the day when I took the communion for the first time after many years. . . . The communion itself I explained as an act performed in memory of Christ and signifying purification from sin and full acceptance of the teaching of Christ. Even if this explanation was artificial, I did not notice its artificiality. It was so joyous for me, humiliating and abasing myself before the confessor, a simple, timid priest, to turn out all the filth of my soul, repenting of my vices; it was so joyous to merge in thought with the humility of the fathers, who wrote the prayers of the rules; so joyous was the union with all who have believed and do believe, that I did not feel the artificiality of my explanation. But when I came up to the royal doors, and the priest made me repeat what I believed, that what I was going to swallow was the true body and blood, then I was cut to the heart: this was more than a false note; this was the cruel demand of some one who evidently had never even known what faith is. . . . Knowing in advance what awaited me I could not go there a second time. —[Ch. 14.]

Yet Tolstoy was finally turned away from the church not by rational objections to its doctrines but by moral objections to its practices. He was shocked by its exclusiveness, by its denunciation of Catholics, Protestants, and Russian sectarians and dissenters as people living in spiritual darkness. This was indeed opposed to the Christian precept of brotherly love. On the pretence of preserving in all its purity the Greco-Russian Orthodox faith, the church was merely seeking the best means of performing in the sight of men certain human obligations [the sacraments]. Worse than this was the church's attitude towards war, and in particular towards the war between Russia and Turkey of 1877-78; and towards capital punishment, and in particular towards the execution of certain revolutionary agitators in the times immediately following this war:

At that time war occurred in Russia. And the Russians began in the name of Christian love to kill their brothers. Not to think of this was impossible. Not to see that murder is an evil opposed to the very first foundations of every religion was impossible. And at the same time in the churches they prayed for the success of our arms, and the teachers of religion recognized this murder as an act resulting from religion. And not only these murders in war—but during the disorders that followed the war I saw officials of the church, its teachers, monks and ascetics, who approved the murder of erring and helpless young men. And I turned my attention to all that is done by men who profess Christianity, and I was horrified.—[Ch. 15.]

Thus Tolstoy became convinced that in the faith which he had accepted false elements were mingled with truth. In 1878, after three years of faithful adherence to the church, he abandoned it forever, and set himself to the task of separating the central elements of truth in the Christian teaching from the dirt and filth with which it was defiled in the church's presentation of it. This he sought to do first negatively, by the examination and criticism of a manual of theology recommended by the church, and second positively, by a similar study of the Gospels, which he felt must contain the essential teaching of Christ.

Before proceeding to an examination of Tolstoy's religious and ethical system as he developed it in the works that sprang immediately from his conversion, we may pause a moment to consider the causes of that conversion.

Nothing is more obvious than the intimate connection of the conversion with the concrete facts of Tolstoy's life. His whole doctrine he derived primarily from his own experience, and only secondarily from the study of other thinkers. His conversion, as he himself expounds it, sprang from his own dichotomy of the world into two classes, the idle and sceptical rich and the industrious and believing poor. These two classes he represents as almost mutually exclusive. But such a dichotomy has no basis in reality, not even in Russian reality, not even in Russian reality as portrayed by Tolstoy in his works of art. Idle men may be found among the poor, and industrious men among the rich, even in Russia. Tolstoy is blinded to this fact by his refusal to regard intellectual work as anything but Epicurean relaxation, or at best as a pretence at real work, a mere self-delusion. Karenin in Tolstoy's novel is probably busy with his tasks, if we average all the days of the year, more hours than even an exceptionally industrious peasant. That some of the documents that he writes lead to no result should not be laid up against him; even so some of the peasant's fields may be trampled by horses or ruined by droughts: Karenin and the peasant have each done their best. Kitty understands the meaning of life for which Levin searches in vain,* yet by Tolstoy's later theory she belongs in the first or ignorant class rather than in the fifth, of the true believers. Nor even at this period can Tolstoy in his more discreet moments have believed in the universal power of faith among the peasantry; types of character such as he pictured later in *The Power of Darkness* cannot have escaped his attention. Tolstoy has seen peasants such as Karatayev and rich men such as Anatole Kuragin or (not to be unfair) such as Vronsky, and from them makes a viciously simple generalization. Only a year or two later he has shifted his point of view, and proclaims that, far from the church's being a moral inspiration to all its humble followers, any peasant, when once the moral sentiment is awakened within him, turns from it to one of the dissenting bodies.† To establish a

* *Anna Karenin:* part v, ch. 19.
† *Critique of Dogmatic Theology* (Conclusion): see p. 226.

dichotomy like Tolstoy's as a basis for religious life in America would be yet more futile.

Tolstoy is not disturbed by his own scepticism with regard to God, but by his own conviction of the meaninglessness of life. The existence of God, Kant has satisfied him, cannot be proved by the argument from cause; hence the pessimistic outcome of all reasoning as to the causal, temporal, spatial universe. He becomes satisfied of the existence of God through his awakened moral sense. One may suspect that he was influenced here— though in his *Confession* (ch. 12) he seems to imply the contrary—by Kant's doctrine of the immanent, underived moral sense, and the proof of God from it. His divining of God's existence through human need of it is valid if this part of Kant's doctrine is valid; it falls to the ground with it. For Kant's reasoning again rests on a dichotomy between feeling and intellect that cannot be accepted; the moral sense is no more independent of time, space, and causality than is the intellect. Once having become convinced of God's existence, Tolstoy does not reason upon it, for reasoning, he feels, simply removes him from God. Laying aside any attempt at theology, and paying small attention to metaphysics, he devotes his energy to constructing a system of practical ethics, and to applying that system to the solution of social questions. On pragmatic grounds he may be justified in his rejection of a strictly logical foundation for his system. Tolstoy's system can be justified, if at all, only by the contention that it works

well in actual practice: it is not a strictly logical system
of philosophy, nor a system of social ethics, developed
by observation of the world about him, but a religious
system of personal morality, founded on man's instinctive moral sense and having as its aim the guidance
of his practical life.

On the development of this religious system Tolstoy
labored with whole-souled devotion. Beginning work
towards the close of 1879, by the end of 1881 he had produced his *Critique of Dogmatic Theology* and his *Harmony
and Translation of the Four Gospels*. In his preface to
the *Harmony* he speaks of the "concentrated, continually
ecstatic spiritual tension that I experienced in the course
of all this long work." A tutor in his household, Vasily
Ivánovich Alekseyev, a former revolutionist, made an
abridgment of the *Harmony*, which, with some revision
by Tolstoy himself, was published under the title, *A Short
Exposition of the Gospel*. In 1883 Tolstoy composed a
summary of his creed, in half-autobiographical form,
to which he gave the name *My Religion*. The doctrine
contained in these books forms a single system, that
by which most readers the world over have judged
Tolstoy's thought. They too often forget that this
system is not consistent either with Tolstoy's view of
life in his earlier period, when he wrote his great novels,
nor with some of his teachings in his latest years, after
the composition of *My Religion*. During the years of
storm and stress which we have just reviewed, in the

course of which he threw off his former caste prejudices
and became a lover of all humanity, Tolstoy developed a
system of thought that seemed to him consistent as well
as convincing. But in truth it still contained elements
of compromise. As he grew older Tolstoy became more
rigidly consistent in his point of view and rejected positions that he had previously maintained with stirring
eloquence.

The *Critique of Dogmatic Theology* is the least interesting of all Tolstoy's writings. Tolstoy takes a manual
of dogmatic theology by Makary, Metropolitan of Moscow, and proceeds to analyze its doctrines, following its
arrangement from chapter to chapter. He is thus busy
with theology, in which he has small interest, instead of
with ethics, on which he writes with understanding and
fervor, and he is engaged in mere destruction instead of
in building up a system of his own. The theology of the
Russian Orthodox Church differs only in details from
that of the Roman Catholics or from that of evangelical
Protestants: there are the same teachings of the Trinity,
the miraculous birth of Christ, his taking upon himself
the sins of the world, his redemption of mankind and
resurrection, and of salvation by faith in him. Against
all this Tolstoy tilts with a crusader's fury. He will make
an impression upon but few readers. To some he will
seem to be attacking doctrines that have utterly lost
their hold on thinking men, and which should be passed
over with silent contempt or studied as relics of a bygone
stage of thought, like the Homeric theology; to others

he will seem a blasphemous foe of a great church, which preserves intact a body of doctrine that needs only spiritual interpretation in order to guide men today as it has done for nearly two thousand years. In the ardor of his invective one misses the concrete illustrations, the shrewd humor, the direct connection with actual life that make Tolstoy's other didactic writings so powerful. But in his Conclusion Tolstoy rises to sudden eloquence:

I remember when I did not yet doubt the teaching of the church and was reading the Gospel, the words: "Blasphemy against the Son of Man shall be forgiven you, but blasphemy against the Holy Ghost shall not be forgiven, neither in this world, neither in the world to come"*—I could in no way understand those words.

Now they, those words, are too terribly clear to me. Here it is, that blasphemy against the Holy Ghost, which shall not be forgiven, neither in this world, neither in the world to come.

That blasphemy is the horrible teaching of the church, the foundation of which is the teaching about the church.

The Orthodox Church?

I can now connect with this word no other concept than that of several unshorn men, very self-confident, deluded, and ill-educated, in silk and velvet, with diamond panagias, called bishops and metropolitans, and thousands of other unshorn men, who are in the most crude, slavish servility to these dozens of men, and who are occupied, under the pretext of performing certain sacraments, in cheating and fleecing the people. How can I believe in this church, and believe in it

* Loosely quoted from Matthew xii, 31, 32.

when to the deepest questions of man about his soul it replies with pitiable deceptions and stupidities, and moreover maintains that no one must dare reply otherwise to those questions, that in all that forms the most precious part of my life I must not dare be guided by anything else than by what it points out? The color of my trousers I may choose, my wife I may choose according to my taste, but as to the rest, the very thing in which I feel myself a man, as to all that I must take counsel of them, of those idle, deceiving and ignorant men. In my life, in the sanctuary of my soul, my guide is a pastor, my parish priest, a befooled, illiterate lad discharged from the seminary, or a drunken old man whose only care is to gather in as many eggs and kopeks as he can. They bid that in prayer the deacon should half the time shout "many years" for the orthodox, pious harlot Catherine II, or for the most pious Peter, the robber and murderer, who mocked at the Gospel, and I must pray thus. They bid me curse and burn and hang my brothers, and I must follow their example in shouting anathema. These people bid me regard my brothers as accursed, and I must shout anathema. They bid me come drink wine from a spoon and swear that it is not wine but the body and the blood, and I must do so.

But this is horrible!

It would be horrible if it were possible. But in fact it does not occur, but not because they have weakened in their demands: they still yell anathema at whom they are bidden to, and "many years" at whom they are likewise bidden to—but in fact for a long, long time nobody has been heeding them.

We, experienced and educated people (I remember my thirty years outside the faith), do not even despise them; we simply pay no attention to them, do not even have the curiosity to know what they are doing and writing and saying. A priest has come—give him half a ruble. A church has been built for vanity's sake—consecrate it, call in a long-maned arch-priest, and give him a hundred. The common people pay still less attention to them. In the week before Lent we must eat pancakes, and in Passion Week prepare for Communion; but if a question of the soul arises for us we resort to wise and learned thinkers, to their books, or to the lives of the saints, but not to the priests; and the men of the people, as soon as religious feeling is awakened within them, join the dissenters, the Stundists, or the Molokane. So that the priests have long since been performing the service for themselves, and for feeble-minded folk, rascals, and women. Evidently they will soon be instructing in life only one another.

One can understand that the Russian Church, once Tolstoy's teaching had become famous, could hardly do otherwise than publicly proclaim him no longer a member of its flock. It is a wonder that it took that action only in 1901.

This book was the last which the Countess Tolstoy copied for her husband.* Her influence was always exerted towards modifying his more drastic expressions, and in the first edition of the *Critique* the final paragraphs quoted above do not appear; they are printed in the edition published by Chertkóv in England in 1903. Beginning with the *Confession*, nearly all of Tolstoy's religious and moral writings were prohibited in Russia by the censorship, and were issued in Switzerland, England, and Germany.

* Ksyunin, *The Departure of Tolstoy* (St. Petersburg, 1911), p. 38.

From the *Critique* one turns with a certain relief to the *Harmony and Translation of the Four Gospels.* Now that he has refuted the false doctrines of the church, Tolstoy seeks to learn in what the true teaching of Jesus consists. He studies the Greek text of the Gospels in the spirit of a Protestant theologian, making a revised translation, seeking to explain inconsistencies, and casting aside as interpolations passages that contradict the spirit of Christ. The Greek text, the Russian accepted version, and Tolstoy's own rendering are printed in parallel columns, after which follows Tolstoy's commentary, with frequent quotations from other interpreters and refutation of them.

Tolstoy's attitude towards the Gospels is logically indefensible. His doctrine of the deity is so vague that he cannot be regarded as believing in a personal God. Later, in his *Journal* for July, 1896, he wrote directly: "I even know as a matter of fact that He is not personal, because the personal is finite and God is infinite." * Towards Christ he takes a position like that of Unitarians or agnostics: Christ was for him a man like other men, a great teacher of religion. He never says directly that Jesus was inspired or infallible, and yet he assumes for his teaching an infallibility that he does not assert. When he has once determined to his own satisfaction the original teaching of Jesus, he accepts it with reverent faith. Taking as his foundation the simplest and most

* *The Journal of Leo Tolstoy, 1895–1899,* translated by Strunsky (New York, 1917): p. 67.

intelligible portions of the text, he interprets the rest
in accord with them. Passages that seem to him false
or hopelessly obscure he either rejects as interpolations
or boldly alters, sometimes, though not always, fortify-
ing himself by the comparison of manuscripts or by
the use of the lexicon. All the miracles, including the
crowning miracle of the resurrection, he casts aside as
useless and injurious to the correct understanding of the
teaching. The falsity of the story of the resurrection,
he tells us, is shown by the fact that the narrators could
not make Christ say anything worth while after he rose
from the dead. The truth of the narrative of his life
is attested by the words of his message.* This is the
Protestant attitude run mad, individual liberty of interpretation carried to its farthest extreme, while still
the dogma of infallibility lurks in the background. A
scientific critic will seek to determine the real teaching
of the Gospels, feeling at liberty to reject it when he
has found it. In contrast to this, Tolstoy's method results in the development of his own thought rather
than in the discovery of the true teaching of Jesus.

The origin of Tolstoy's attitude is obvious. Certain
parts of the Gospels have appealed to him from his
childhood, as utterances of the deepest truth, corresponding to his own heartfelt demands. Confronted by
the soul problem before him, he feels that thorough study
of the book containing these utterances will yield him
fuller comprehension of them. But he fails to see that

* *Harmony*, ch. 12.

his study is really throwing light on his own system, and only secondarily on that of the Gospels. From one point of view his book is the product of misdirected energy; from another it is a monument of keen intellectual labor, in which we see the processes that led to the building of a great religious classic in *My Religion*.

Two examples of Tolstoy's methods of interpretation must suffice. Tolstoy's fundamental problem, as stated in his *Confession*, has been to find an explanation of the riddle of life; some faith that will give a meaning to his futile existence. The author of the Fourth Gospel has understood his difficulty. For the opening words of that Gospel: "In the beginning was the Word, and the Word was with God, and the Word was God. The same was in the beginning with God"—become in Tolstoy's version: "The understanding of life became the beginning [or, first principle] of all. And the understanding of life took the place of God. And this understanding of life became God. It became the beginning of all in place of God." God is a concept infinitely above man's comprehension, and is replaced for him by a true knowledge of life. Surely the unhistorical and personal interpretation of scripture can go no farther than this! Biblical scholars may have a right to scornful laughter. And yet there is something winning and pathetic, even inspiring, in Tolstoy's struggles with a mystic text which he forces to correspond with his own spiritual history.

Jesus said to men, "Love your enemies," 'Aγαπᾶτε τοὺς

ἐχθροὺς ὑμῶν. In Greek there are two words for enemy, one meaning a public foe and the other a personal enemy; the latter is used in this case. The saying has been generally interpreted as a command to have no hostile feelings, to love men who do evil to us. But the literal-minded Tolstoy exclaims (in *My Religion*, ch. 6): "To love one's enemies? This was something impossible. This was one of those fine sayings which cannot be regarded otherwise than as an indication of an unattainable moral ideal. This was either too much or nothing at all. It is possible not to injure one's enemy, but to love him is impossible." Christ could not have prescribed the impossible. The escape is obvious; the enemy meant in the text is a public enemy, a man of another race. One should love all men alike, making no difference between Russians and French, English, or Germans. To such an ideal Tolstoy felt that he might attain; hence he made no comment on the philological objections to his interpretation. Characteristically enough, Tolstoy abandoned this position with advancing years. In March, 1891, he wrote in a private letter (to Rakhmanov): "Do not think that I defend my former point of view, expressed in *My Religion*. I not only do not defend it, but I rejoice that we have outlived it."* He now tells us that one element of perfection is to have no enemies—the conventional interpretation of the passage—and doing good to one's enemies is one stage of progress towards it.

Letters collected by Sergéyenko (Moscow, 1910) : vol. I, p. 200.

Similarly Tolstoy came to see that the truth of his own doctrine was in no way dependent on the historical existence of Jesus. As early as 1882 he wrote: "It now seems to me that if Christ and his teaching had never existed, I should myself have discovered this truth, so clear and simple does it now appear to me."* He wrote to Biryukóv, in 1899, that the supposition that Christ never existed was "like the destruction of the last outskirts opposed to the enemies' attack, in order that the fortress (the moral teaching of goodness, which flows, not from any one source in time or space, but from the whole spiritual life of humanity in its entirety) may remain impregnable."† In 1909 he speaks with assurance:

The teaching of Jesus is for me only one of the beautiful religious teachings that we have received from Egyptian, Jewish, Hindu, Chinese, and Greek antiquity. The two great principles of Jesus: the love of God, that is to say of absolute perfection; and the love of one's neighbor, that is to say of all men without any distinction whatever, have been preached by all the sages of the world: Krishna, Buddha, Lao-tsze, Confucius, Socrates, Plato, Epictetus, Marcus Aurelius, and, among the moderns, Rousseau, Pascal, Kant, Emerson, Channing, and many others. Religious and moral truth is always and everywhere the same. . . . I have no predilection for Christianity. If I have been particularly interested by the teachings of Jesus, it is because, first, I was born and

---

* *Letter to N. N.: On Non-Resistance to Evil by Evil.*
† Maude: *Tolstoy and His Problems,* p. 209; cf. *Journal,* tr. Strunsky, p. 381.

have lived among Christians; and, second, I have found
great spiritual joy in separating the pure teaching from the
surprising falsifications made by the churches.*

In *My Religion* Tolstoy gives the results of his study
of the Gospels in short, pithy form, with personal illustrations that show the novelist's power. The system
that he develops is simple on the side of theology, and
almost equally so on that of ethics.

Tolstoy's theology may be dismissed briefly. God
Tolstoy never seeks to define; God exists, but is un-
knowable except as the source of faith. More positive is
Tolstoy's attitude on the second great dogma of Christianity, one held so universally that it is felt by many
to be synonymous with faith of any sort, the belief in
immortality. This Tolstoy directly and emphatically
repudiates:

The idea of a future personal life came to us not from the
Hebrew teaching and not from the teaching of Christ. It entered into the church teaching from absolutely different
sources. However strange it may appear, it is impossible not
to say that the belief in a future life is a very low and crude
conception, founded on a confusion of sleep with death,
and peculiar to all savage peoples, and that the Hebrew
teaching, not to speak of the Christian, stood immeasurably
above it. We are so convinced that this superstition is something very elevated, that with great seriousness we try to prove
the superiority of our teaching over others by the very fact

*Quoted by Rolland (ch. 10) from a letter to the painter Jan
Styka, printed in *Le Théosophe*, Jan. 16, 1911.

that we hold this superstition, while others, like the Chinese and the Indians, do not hold it.—[*My Religion*, ch. 8.]

The true eternal life is that which each man receives through the understanding of life which is the beginning of all. "Christ contrasts with the personal life not the life beyond the grave, but the general life, connected with the present, past, and future life of all humanity— the life of the Son of Man."* "All the teaching of Jesus consists in this, that his disciples, understanding the phantasmal quality of the personal life, should renounce it and transfer it into the life of all humanity, into the life of the Son of Man. But the teaching of the immortality of the personal soul not only does not summon one to renounce his personal life, but forever confirms this personality."* " To all men is given the possibility of true life. He who wishes takes it; he who does not wish does not take it. He who receives true life has it; and it is not exactly the same for all, but to it there cannot be applied our concepts greater and smaller, earlier and later. It is outside the categories of space, time, and causality, they would say in philosophic language." † "The Kingdom of Heaven is outside time and space; it is within you, in your present life."‡ For this life death has no meaning; it cannot be destroyed by carnal death. "For God there is no time; and therefore, uniting with God, man escapes from time, consequently from death."‡

My Religion, ch. 8.   † *Harmony*, ch. 8.   ‡ *Ibid.*, ch. 9.

One may surmise that Tolstoy, unable to accept the popular doctrine of the future life, which he cannot justify by reason, builds up his own view on the basis of Kant's conception that the moral principle is independent of space and time. This view he later elaborated in his most important metaphysical book, *On Life* (1887), in which he strives to show the extra-spatial and extra-temporal nature of the regenerate life. His reasoning is not such as would be accepted by a Kantian; into it he blends elements that he probably derived from Plato.* His leading thought is of the dual nature of human life, which is divided into animal, carnal, personal life on the one hand, and the life of reason on the other. The carnal, personal existence is not real life (*On Life*, ch. 8). "True life man knows within himself as a striving for the good, attainable by the subjection of his animal personality to the law of reason" (ch. 14). "Reason itself cannot be defined, and we have no need to define it, because we not only know it, but know nothing but reason" (ch. 10); that is, the foundation of the moral life is immediate, inborn knowledge. This rational life "is manifested in time and space, but is defined not by temporal and spatial conditions, but only by the degree of subjection of the animal personality to reason. To define life by temporal and spatial conditions is like defining the height of an object by its

---

*The problem of Tolstoy's indebtedness to formal philosophy is important, and has not, so far as the writer knows, been discussed with any thoroughness. This book can do no more than indicate its existence.

length and breadth" (ch. 14). "The renunciation of the good of personality is . . . the indispensable condition of the life of man" (ch. 15). Yet personality itself for a rational man is the indispensable condition of life. "One should not renounce personality, but renounce the good of personality and cease to recognize personality as life" (ch. 21). No man's life vanishes through his corporeal death; it lives on in the memory of him, in his influence on other men. "My special relation to the world was established not in this life and began not with my body and not with a series of stages of consciousness in time" (ch. 28). "Christ died very long ago, and his carnal existence was short, and we have no clear idea of his carnal personality, but the force of his rationally-loving life, his relation to the world—no one else's—acts till this very time on millions of men who receive into themselves this relation of his to the world and live by it" (ch. 31).

This true meaning of life Tolstoy defends against the Pharisees and the Scribes, that is, against churchmen and materialistic scientists. The former

profess in words the teachings of those enlighteners of humanity, in whose traditions they were educated; but, not understanding their rational sense, they turn these teachings into supernatural revelations of the past and future life of men and require only the performance of ceremonies. This is the teaching of the Pharisees in the broadest sense of the term, that is, of men who teach that a life in itself irrational may be set right by faith in another life, acquired by performance of external ceremonies.

Others, not recognizing the possibility of any other life than the visible life, deny all marvels and all that is supernatural and boldly maintain that the life of man is naught else than his bodily existence from birth to death. This is the teaching of the Scribes, of men who teach that in the life of man as an animal there is nothing irrational.—[*On Life*, ch. 2.]

Tolstoy's rejection of personal immortality was a passing phase of his thought, though a very important one. Before his religious conversion he had at least a flickering belief in it. In 1859 he had written to his cousin that during his life in the Caucasus (1851–53) he had "found out that immortality exists, that love exists, and that one must live for others in order to be eternally happy."* In 1865 he had again written to her: "I now know that I have a soul that is immortal (at least I often think that I know it), and I know that God exists."† And in his latest years he seems to have come to a firm faith in it. Passages in his *Journal*, from November, 1897, to February, 1898, show, to be sure, that he had not yet attained such a faith.‡ But in May, 1898, he wrote to his wife:

I rode home through Turgenev's wood. . . . And I thought, as I think continually, of death. And it became so clear to me that it will be just as good, though in a different way,

* *Correspondence with the Countess A. A. Tolstoy*, p. 131; compare p. 16, above.
† *Ibid.*, p. 210.
‡ *The Journal of Leo Tolstoy, 1895–1899*, translated by Strunsky (New York, 1917): pp. 168, 189, 205.

on the other side of death, and I could understand why the Jews represented paradise as a garden. The purest joy is the joy of nature. It was clear to me that there it will be just as good—no, better. I tried to call forth in myself doubt of the other life, such as I used to have, and I could not as I could before, but I could call forth confidence within me.— [*Letters to Wife*, p. 545.]

And in his *Course of Reading*, which he compiled in the last years of his life, he writes boldly: "Only he can disbelieve in immortality who has never seriously thought of death."*

The vital part of Tolstoy's teaching is, however, not his theology or his metaphysics, but his ethics. Reading the Gospels, he discovered that the central doctrine of Christ was contained in the precept: "I say unto you, That ye resist not evil" (Matthew v, 39). When he read the Sermon on the Mount with a Jewish rabbi, the rabbi could cite for all sayings of Jesus parallels in the Old Testament or in the Talmud. "But when we came to the verse about non-resistance to evil, he did not say, 'This is also in the Talmud,' but only asked me with a sneer: 'And do the Christians observe this? Do they turn the other cheek?' I had nothing to reply, the more so since I knew that at this very time the Christians were not only not turning the cheek, but beating the Jews on the cheek turned towards them."†

This rejected teaching Tolstoy made the corner-stone

* *Course of Reading* (Moscow, 1910): I, 117.   † *My Religion*, ch. 2.

of his edifice. Starting from it, he reduced the Sermon on the Mount to five commandments:

1. Be not angry. Live in peace with all men; never regard your anger at men as just.

2. Do not make for yourself a sport of the lust of sex relations: let every man have a wife, and the wife a husband; and let the husband have one wife, and the wife one husband. And under no pretext must they violate the carnal union with each other.

3. Swear not at all. Never take oath to any man in any matter. Every oath is required from men for evil.

4. Resist not evil by force. Do not reply to violence by violence: if they strike you, endure it; if they force you to work, work; if they wish to take from you what we regard as our own, give it up.

5. Love all men alike, making no distinction of races and peoples; recognize neither kings nor kingdoms.

Of these commandments the first pertains to man alone with himself in his heart; the second to his relations with woman, to the family; the third to man in his private worldly relations with other men; the fourth to the relations of man to his own state and its laws; the fifth to his relations with all humanity, to men of other nations.*

In these rules there is not at first sight anything startling; they are much like what each of us has learned at his mother's knee. The trouble comes in Tolstoy's drastic application of these principles, which he clearly

* *My Religion*, ch. 6; *Harmony*, ch. 4.

sees will destroy all human society as at present organized. A man who will take no oaths, that is, who will not submit his will to that of another, who will not resist evil by force, and who loves all nations equally, can obviously take no part in war, whether as officer or private. Just as obviously, he can take no part in the state administration, as judge or member of a jury. Furthermore, he can hold no property, since force is required to defend this from others:

This faith has changed my estimate of what is good and what is bad and low. All that formerly seemed to me good and high—riches, property of every sort, honor, the consciousness of one's own dignity and rights—all this now has become bad and low; and all that seemed to me bad and low— work for others, poverty, humiliation, renunciation of all property and all rights—has become good and high in my eyes. If now in a moment of forgetfulness I may be so far carried away as to use violence for the defense of myself or others or of my own property or that of others, I can no longer calmly and consciously serve that temptation, which destroys myself and other men. I cannot acquire property; I cannot use violence of any sort against any manner of man, with the exception of a child, and then only to save him from some evil that hangs over him; I cannot take part in any activity of the authorities having as its aim the defense of men and their property by violence; I can be neither a judge nor one sharing in court duties; I cannot be an executive or one sharing in an executive position; I cannot contribute to having others take part in courts and executive positions.—[*My Religion*, ch. 12.]

Under Tolstoy's system a faithful Christian must become a beggar, a pious mendicant. Tolstoy sees this consequence with perfect clearness, stating in his *Harmony* (ch. 4) that "only the beggar and the wanderer can enter into the Kingdom of God." This conclusion was in accord with the whole tendency of his religious thought. We have already noted in his first work, *Childhood*, his admiration for the half-witted pilgrim Grisha.* In a letter to Strakhov of 1877 he writes: "If I were alone, I should not be a monk, I should be a pious mendicant; that is, I should prize nothing in life and should do no one harm."† In his posthumous drama, *The Light Shineth in Darkness*, written in 1900–02, he makes his double Saryntsov exclaim, near the close of the play: "Humility, pious mendicancy. Yes, if I could only rise to it!" And his final flight from home, at the age of eighty-two, was beyond doubt an attempt to realize this ideal.

In *My Religion* Tolstoy makes prominent this ideal of pious mendicancy, the same that inspired the friars of medieval times. But here, since he is no longer laying down abstract principles, as in the *Harmony*, but a practical guide for daily life, he involuntarily introduces elements of compromise, pronouncing "work, physical work that gives appetite and sound, refreshing sleep," and the family, to be "undoubted conditions" of human happiness.‡ The same point of view, as we shall see later, will be emphasized in *What Shall We Do Then?*

* Page 29, above. † Biryukóv: II, 304. ‡ *My Religion*, ch. 10.

(1886). Now work is not the most prominent characteristic of pious mendicants, and family life is inconsistent with their aims. The family ideal, one may say,
represents a survival, a dearly loved survival, of Tolstoy's worldly period, which at last he will be obliged
to cast aside as inconsistent with his ascetic system.

Thus the wealthy aristocrat Tolstoy has developed
on the basis of the Gospels a system of ethics that is
thoroughly anarchistic, destructive of all organized
society. Regarding Christianity as fundamentally a
simple code of moral rules, he pours out his scorn upon
St. Paul, the first corrupter of Christianity, "who did
not know the ethical teaching expressed in the Gospel
of Matthew, and who preached a metaphysico-cabalistic
theory foreign to Christ." The process of degeneration
was completed in the time of Constantine, "when it
was found possible to dress the whole heathen mode of
life, without change, in Christian garments, and thereby
recognize it as Christian."* So Tolstoy joins the group
of fervent spirits who through the ages have denounced
the donation of Constantine.

Such is Tolstoy's religious and moral system. One
is at once led to inquire how far his writings are of
value as an exposition of the real teaching of Jesus, as
embodied in the Gospels. However unscientific his
method of study, his insight may of course have led him
to correct results. In theology, the two great doctrines
of the Gospels are that of the personal fatherhood of

* *My Religion*, ch. 11.

God, and that of personal immortality. The second of these Tolstoy rejects, exercising his utmost ingenuity in reading it out of the text; the first he accepts in a nerveless, attenuated form, as the result of the moral teaching of Jesus rather than the source of it.

But with Tolstoy's ethical system the case is different. Though he felt himself to be the discoverer and restorer of the true teaching of Jesus, Tolstoy was here treading on ground often trodden by other reformers. His teachings are similar in their essentials to those of the Bohemian Brethren in the fifteenth century, and of the English Quakers in the seventeenth, and, most important, to those of the Dukhobors and other Russian peasant sects in the eighteenth and nineteenth centuries. We may even say that the wide acceptance of the doctrine of non-resistance in Russia during the present crisis is probably due less to the influence of Tolstoy than to that of less famous teachers. To such ideas the Russian common folk lend a willing ear; and the Russian common folk, one cannot too often repeat, were a primary source of inspiration for Tolstoy. Furthermore, all of the sects that have been mentioned, including the Russian, were inspired directly by the Gospels, the precepts of which their members endeavored to carry out in their daily lives. And the interpretation was in each case just.

Whether the teaching of Jesus was itself a sound and final system of ethics is a different question. Let us listen to a modern biblical scholar, whose estimate of the nature of Jesus' teaching, if not of its universal validity, is the same as Tolstoy's:

Broadly speaking, it may be said that there are two aspects of ethical teaching. The first is that with which in modern times we are so familiar, the teaching which says that the first thing a man has to do is to be a good citizen. This is the world-affirming ethic which says that this world as we have it is God's world. That is a perfectly true statement: We are put here to work, and if we scorn society, and do not do our fair share, we are shirking the responsibility which has been put upon our shoulders. Therefore it is our duty to take part in all such things as social, political, and national duties (which may not appeal to us very much in themselves), because they are the things which we are put here to do.

But there is also another kind of ethical teaching—the teaching which denies the world; which says that these social and national claims are doubtless valid, but there is something beyond them all, and a man is more than a good citizen. There are times when he has the right and the duty not to be hurrying about, and busily doing something, but rather to go aside and think about the meaning of life. There come times when he will not even be able to do his work in the world properly, if he do not throw aside the world altogether for a moment, and stand apart from the hurry and toil of life as it is now, to ask himself what he will do in the end thereof. This is the world-renouncing ethic which says that, although many possessions and wide interests enable a man not only to enjoy life, but also to do much good to other people, if he be not able at times to throw off all their claims he becomes the slave of his own surroundings.

Stated in terms of modern life, it reminds us that although

it be true that society, so far as we can see, is permanent, and that the world is not speedily coming to an end by means of some dramatic cataclysm, it is nevertheless true that we personally are coming to an end, so far as the world or society is concerned, within a period which, after all, cannot be so very long. And, stated in the terms of ancient Jewish life, it is this ethic which is presented most vividly and most strongly in just those parts of the New Testament which represent the teaching of Jesus when he and his hearers were looking at life under the influence of the eschatological expectation.

The effect of that expectation was to hide almost entirely the more obvious duties of a "world-affirming ethic" in daily life, but in the darkness thus induced some of the eternal lights shone out, as the stars during an eclipse.—[Kirsopp Lake, *The Stewardship of Faith* (New York: Putnam, 1915) pp. 37–40.]

Jesus, like other Jews of his time, thought that the present state of the world was transitory, soon to pass away and to give place to the Kingdom of Heaven. Hence his teaching gave no place to state duties and taught primarily preparation for a better world to come; it was emphatically world-renouncing. This ethic, untenable as an all-including system, nevertheless puts in clearer light certain spiritual values that are apt to be smothered by our own complacent world-affirming ethic. Herein lies the great value of Tolstoy as a moral and social teacher, that he interprets the world-renouncing ethic of Jesus in terms of modern life. His peculiarity is that he upholds so powerfully this ethic while denying or neglecting the theological beliefs that lay back of it. With him a pessimistic emphasis on the ills of the present social world takes the place of confidence in a world to come; yet his emphasis on inward spiritual blessedness is the same as that of Jesus.

That the Gospels were a source of Tolstoy's ethical system we may admit, and that his use of them was sound and logical. But whether they were the only source of his system, or even the real starting point of it, may be doubted. Tolstoy's developed system is in thorough accord with the temperamental tendencies that he had shown all through his life. Its roots may be defined as individualism, a dislike of civilization and a Rousseau-like passion for a return to nature, pessimism, asceticism, and—love.

The intense individualism of Tolstoy's temperament, as shown both in his life and in his works of fiction, has already been amply emphasized. Tolstoy disliked public activity, resisted mass movements, instinctively swam against the stream. His philosophy of history in *War and Peace* has for its foundation the futility of outward effort, while he regards the perfecting of one's inward character as the true aim of man. So in his ethical system individual perfection, in whatever that may consist, is at first all with which he is concerned. Man must shape his conduct by the inward light that is given him and let the results take care of themselves. Church and state, Tolstoy sees, will be destroyed by the adoption of his teaching, but in church and state he is not interested. It is only later that, in *What Shall We Do Then?*, he formulates the new order of society to which his system will lead.

Formerly Tolstoy had preferred barbarism to civilization (as in *The Cossacks*), or had glorified the life of toiling field laborers in opposition to that of luxurious aristocrats (as in *Anna Karenin*), because civilized luxury enfeebles man and makes difficult his struggle with nature.* His position was that of Rousseau: it is too late to destroy civilization; we must try to mitigate its ills while preserving its finer sides. Rousseau, and Tolstoy following him, had weighed the bad sides of modern culture against its benefits, and had deplored its rise. Rousseau had seen the inconsistency between patriotism and the Christianity of the Gospels: one cannot be a good Christian and a good soldier. But so convinced was he of the necessity for state organization that he banished Christianity from his ideal community and replaced it by a sort of official deism, with reverence for the laws as a cardinal doctrine. With this state religion individual Christianity must make its peace as best it may. Now, after his religious conversion, Tolstoy sees the same dilemma, and forthwith sacrifices the state, since it is necessarily inconsistent with Christianity; patriotism, which leads to violence and war, becomes a cardinal sin. Now he sees the chief evil of civilization in the fact that it forces a man to exploit the labor

* Behrs: *Reminiscences,* ch. 6.

of his fellow men, since without such exploitation riches and idle ease are impossible.

Of his own despair and pessimism Tolstoy tells us eloquently in his *Confession;* we may judge of it indirectly by his long devotion to Schopenhauer. Yet Tolstoy's pessimism was after all superficial; it was a deepening of Rousseau's dislike for modern society, combined with personal discouragement at his own failure to solve the riddle of existence. But in his view of human nature Tolstoy was never a thorough pessimist; he never lost faith in the optimism of his earlier master Rousseau. Pessimism is a belief that the non-existence of the universe would be preferable to its existence. Such a belief steals into our minds as we read the novels of Hardy or the tales of Guy de Maupassant. The offence lies not in the portrayal of sin and shame, but in the denial of any possibility of improvement or in the negation of all standards of right and wrong. Tolstoy's joy in the beauty of the world, his delight in physical strength and vigor, and his confidence in the possibility of moral progress, exclude any such tone from his novels previous to his religious conversion. *War and Peace* and *Anna Karenin* are books wherein "all noble lords and ladies" "shall find many joyous and pleasant histories and noble and renowned acts of humanity, gentleness, and chivalry. For herein may be seen noble chivalry, courtesy, humanity, friendliness, hardiness, love, friendship, cowardice, murder, hate, virtue, sin. Do after the good, and leave the evil, and it shall bring you to good fame and renommee."* And, unlike Malory, Tolstoy is so convincing in his picture of this checkerboard world that "all noble lords and ladies" find themselves constrained "to give faith and belief that all is true that is contained herein." The vital force that saved Tolstoy from suicide kept his picture of the world from becoming black and despairing.

In the artistic work that followed Tolstoy's religious conversion there is, as we shall see, a decided change of tone. The author's altered point of view shows in his darker picture of the world as at present organized, which indeed would better perish and pass away. When pessimism has lost its hold on his philosophy it becomes more prominent in his fiction. From *The Death of Ivan Ilyich*, *The Power of Darkness*, *The Kreutzer Sonata*, and *Resurrection* the former instinctive joy of life has vanished, while the new gospel of love and hope is expressed only in a pale, ineffectual fashion. The artist and the preacher in Tolstoy never worked in perfect harmony.

The ascetic element in Tolstoy's thought may be detected even in his earliest novels. Though Tolstoy instinctively admires beauty and strength, when he begins to reason on conduct he preaches self-sacrifice, self-abnegation, self-limitation; each of his heroes, Olenin, Pierre Bezukhov, Levin, struggles upward by a process that contains distinct ascetic elements, though it may also contain elements of a quite different sort. Now, in his *Harmony of the Gospels*, when he proclaims

* Caxton's preface to Malory's *Morte Darthur*.

that all property is a hindrance to the moral life, and bids men be beggars and vagrants, he expresses the ascetic ideal with perfect distinctness:

Jesus Christ nowhere bids us give to the poor in order that the poor may be well fed and content; he says that one should give all to the poor in order that he himself may be happy. . . . He bids us give up property only in order that it may not be an obstacle to life; and afterwards, when a man gives up his property, he teaches that a man's happiness consists in pitying and loving men.—[*Harmony,* ch. 6.]

Denial of the personal life, of the animal life of the body, is at the foundation of Tolstoy's religious system. The distinction that he makes between the monk and the pious mendicant is only one of external form; the monk and the mendicant follow the same aim, the salvation of their own souls, and by essentially the same means.   In a letter to his wife (1898) he quotes with enthusiasm the following passage from a book that he has been reading: "Luxury and effeminacy hinder the soul from understanding itself.   In the same way asceticism, the torturing of one's body, also hinders.   In both cases man thinks of the body. But one must forget it."*   Yet it is so obvious that sincere forgetfulness of the body is itself a form of asceticism.

Tolstoy himself always stoutly denied that his teaching

* *Letters to Wife,* p. 559.

was ascetic. The following passage, written in 1882, is characteristic:

Some men, seeing in the teaching of Christ a teaching about the salvation of the soul for the sake of a crudely conceived eternal life, have withdrawn from the world, taking pains only about what they should do for themselves, how they should perfect themselves in solitude—which would be ridiculous were it not pitiable. And terrible efforts have been wasted by these men—and there have been many of them—on what is impossible and stupid, on doing good for oneself in solitude, away from men. . . . I love these people, but with all the strength of my soul I hate their teaching. . . . Truth is only in that teaching which points out an activity, a life, which satisfies the needs of the soul, and which is at the same time a constant activity for the good of others.—[*Letter to N. N.: On Non-Resistance to Evil by Evil.*]

All this means that the ascetic element in his teaching, which in time will become more prominent, is as yet overshadowed by his ideal of service, of universal love.

If asceticism be related to the reflective, intellectual side of Tolstoy, his ideal of love springs from the warm, emotional element in his personality. From his childhood Tolstoy was a man of passionate nature, constant in his affection for his brothers and kinsfolk, and later on he was equally constant in his devotion to his wife and children. He was a steadfast friend to a few chosen persons both in his own circle and among the common people, though his decided opinions, and his pugnacious, uncompromising support of them, prevented him from

having many intellectual intimates.   His aristocratic
prejudices also hindered him from extending his personal
ties.   Now, under the influence of the Gospels, his whole
nature softened, and from being a haughty noble he
became an open-hearted lover of all humanity, ready
to receive each and every visitor and converse with him
on questions of the soul.   His kind heart led him to assist
any peasant in misery, whether by personal toil or by
gifts of the money that he despised.   Logic would have
made him see that if property, and money in particular,
is a sin, then to force goods on others leads them into
sin; his emotions restrained him from that logical consequence.   His family affection made him erect the same
ideal for other men;   later his asceticism will force him
to tear down his own edifice.

In *My Religion* (1884) Tolstoy makes most prominent
the negative side of his teaching, the five prohibitions.
But in his *Preface to Bóndarev's Work*, "*On Labor for
One's Daily Bread*," written in the same year, he points
out that "all Christ's positive teaching of truth is expressed in one phrase, 'Love God and thy neighbor as
thyself!'"   The five prohibitions are merely sign-
posts erected to show man where he is likely to stray
from the true path.   And in his work *On Life* (1887) he
lays all emphasis on *love*, which springs from the renunciation of the animal personality:

Not in consequence of love for father, for son, for wife,
for friends, for good and dear people, as is ordinarily thought,

do men renounce their personality, but only in consequence of a consciousness of the vanity of the existence of the personality, of a consciousness of the impossibility of its good; and therefore in consequence of renunciation of the life of personality man recognizes true love and can truly love father, son, wife, children, and friends.

Love is the preference of other creatures to himself—to his animal personality. . . .

This condition is a condition of good will towards all men, which is present in children, but which in a grown man arises only on the renunciation of the good of personality and increases only in proportion to that renunciation.—[*On Life*, ch. 24.]

True love is life itself.—[Ch. 25.]

They say: "Disease, old age, senility, a decline into childishness are an annihilation of the consciousness and life of man." For what manner of man? I imagine to myself, according to the tradition, John the Evangelist, who declined from old age into childishness. He, according to the tradition, said only: "Brothers, love one another!" The hundred-year-old man, barely able to move, with watering eyes, mumbles only these same monotonous three words, "Love one another!" In such a man the animal existence barely glimmers—it has been all consumed by a new relation to the world, by a new living creature, which no longer finds a place in the existence of the carnal man.—[Ch. 30.]

In conclusion, it may be worth while to indicate very briefly the formal characteristics of Tolstoy's ethical system. Ethical theories may be divided into two types, jural and teleological: theories of the first sort regard conduct as obedience to a set of rules laid down by some authority; those of the second sort regard conduct as directed to a certain end, and inquire what end is the most appropriate. The hedonists find that this end is pleasure, whether of the individual or of humanity as a whole, while the eudæmonists find it in the complete, harmonious development of all human powers and capacities. Such development may produce pleasure, but pleasure is not the aim of the development. On the other hand, some at least of the hedonists would maintain that pleasure demands as its tool (though not as an end in itself) the harmonious development that the eudæmonists regard as an end in itself. Thus the two types of teleological theory in their best forms meet on a common ground.

Tolstoy's ethics are of the jural type. Like Kant, he regards conduct as obedience to an ideal of duty, an inborn moral sense, a categorical imperative imprinted on the soul of each individual man. This is the characteristic Puritan point of view, though the Puritan may regard conduct as laid down by an external deity rather than by man's inborn moral sense. Tolstoy gives the name *reason* to the source of moral conduct, and he may rightly be regarded, like Kant, as a rationalist.

Every jural system of ethics may, however, be regarded from a teleological side. The Jews presumably had a distinct idea of the purposes of the Lord in ordaining the decalogue. Here Tolstoy must be regarded, ridiculous as the term seems at first sight, as a hedonist; he has absolutely no points of contact with the characteristic Greek eudæmonism of Plato and Aristotle, with its ideal of the harmonious development of the human faculties. For asceticism is after all only a distorted and perverted type of hedonism, its aim being to gain pleasure in the next life, as with monks, or to ward off misery in this life, as with Schopenhauer and Tolstoy. And Tolstoy's theory of universal love and self-sacrificing service has as its aim the greater happiness of the mass of humanity; that is, it is a utilitarian hedonism. Each of these doctrines neglects the harmonious development of personality that was the aim of Greek eudæmonism and the method of the best Greek hedonism. As an ethical thinker no man was ever more un-Greek than Tolstoy.

Tolstoy has a further point of contact with Kant in his insistence on the universality of any principle of human conduct. He will have no division of humanity into monks and laymen such as came to pass both in Christianity and Buddhism, where an ideal system of conduct was admitted to be beyond the reach of the mass of humanity. His ideal, he insists, may be attained by every man.

But this formal classification of Tolstoy's system does it no justice. Tolstoy is primarily a preacher, a religious leader, not a philosopher. His great service, one should repeat again and again, is not the formulation of any consistent and valid system of ethics, but the powerful application to modern conditions of the world-renouncing ethics of Jesus.

CHAPTER VIII

OR five years (1878–83) Tolstoy was wholly absorbed in meditation and writing on religious topics. He seemed to have abandoned forever his work as a novelist. Earnest and sincere, he felt the incongruity of his own life with the ideas and the ideals which he had formed and which he was now working out into a system. The new faith did not bring with it an entire change in his life, for the habits of fifty years were not to be laid aside suddenly like a garment. Its first effect was to bring on fits of depression and irritability. His son Ilyá tells of the altered atmosphere in the family:

As a boy of twelve [1878], I felt that my father was getting more and more estranged from us, and that our interests were not merely indifferent to him, but actually alien and repulsive. He got gloomy and irritable, often quarreled with my mother about trifles, and from our former jovial and high-spirited ringleader and companion was transformed before our eyes into a stern and censorious propagandist. His harsh denunciations of the aimless life of gentlefolk, of their gluttony, their indolence, and spoliation of the industrious working-classes, grew more and more frequent. . . .

When I recall this period, I am filled with horror at the thought of what he must have been suffering mentally. When he utterly repudiated everything he had delighted in before, repudiated that patriarchal order of country-house life which he had lately described in his novels with such affection and which he had built up for himself, repudiated all his former interests, from war down to literary fame, family life and religion—how terribly his solitude must have weighed upon him! All the more terribly because it was the solitude of a man in the midst of a crowd of people with whom he had nothing in common.—[*Reminiscences*, pp. 261, 266.]

His cousin the Countess Alexandra Tolstoy tells how he poured forth upon her, when she met him in Moscow in 1882, his derisive mockery of the church beliefs to which she was devoted:

"I have no reply to make to you," I answered, "and will say only that, while you were speaking, I saw you contending with someone who is now standing behind your chair."

He turned about quickly. "Who is that?" he almost shouted.

"Lucifer in person, the incarnation of pride," I answered.

He jumped from his seat, overwhelmed by this phrase; then he tried to calm himself and immediately added:

"Certainly I am proud to have been the first who has at last laid his hand upon the truth." . . .

In the evening I went to call on them and found the so recently infuriated Leo a meek lamb. Beside the numerous family, outsiders were present, and the conversation was general; but Leo guided it with evident care that nothing unpleasant should touch me; he gazed at me with gentle eyes, as if asking forgiveness, and the whole evening paid attention to me with that enchanting kindness which is a distinctive trait of his beautiful nature.—[*Reminiscences,* in *Correspondence with the Countess A. A. Tolstoy,* pp. 29, 30.]

An early result of Tolstoy's new faith was a letter to the young tsar Alexander III, begging him to give the world an example of Christian forgiveness by pardoning the assassins of his father. On March 13, 1881, Alexander II had been murdered on the streets of St. Petersburg by a group of revolutionists who desired the transformation of Russia into a democratic state, organized on socialistic principles. Tolstoy's letter, full of eloquence, animated at once by a scorn of revolutionary violence and by the loyalty to the tsar that ran in Tolstoy's blood, reminds the new ruler that both severe repression and liberal concessions have failed to restore peace to Russia, and urges him now to adopt the one true path, that shown on men by Christ himself. The letter reached the tsar, but failed of its purpose.

On October 10, 1883, Tolstoy made one modest step towards the realization of his teaching by refusing, on the ground of religious convictions, to serve on a jury, and paying the fine imposed on him.

Property was the great stumbling-block when Tolstoy tried to apply his convictions to life. The recognition of private property as a sin and form of violence is fundamental in his religious system; it had probably been maturing in his mind long before his conversion. In 1861, as has been said, Tolstoy had met Proudhon in Brussels, and had presumably been impressed by his maxim: "La propriété—c'est le vol." In 1865 he made in his diary the following startling entry, which might have been written by one of the Russian Social Revolutionists:

The problem of Russia in universal history consists in bringing into the world the idea of the communal organization of land property.

"La propriété—c'est le vol" [property is theft] will remain truer than the truth of the English constitution so long as the human race shall exist. This is an absolute truth, but there are also relative truths flowing from it—applications. The first of these relative truths is the Russian people's view of property. The Russian people denies property of the most stable sort, that which is the most independent of toil, the property which more than any other cramps the right of other people to acquire property—namely, property in land. This is not a dream; it is a fact, expressed in the communes of the peasants and the communes of the Cossacks. This truth is understood alike by the learned Russian and by the peasant, who says: "Let them enroll us as Cossacks and the land will be free." This idea has a future. The Russian revolution can be founded only on this. The revolution will not be against the tsar and the despotism, but against land property. It will say: "Take from me, take and strip from man all that you wish, but leave us the land in its entirety." The autocracy does not hinder but aids that order of things.

All this I saw in a dream on August 25. [Biryukóv: **II, 69**.]

This passage is another illustration of the fact that Tolstoy's new faith merely gave new emphasis and a new logical foundation to ideas that were already latent in his mind. It is of interest in connection with the present revolution in Russia, which is striving to deal with the question of property in land.

After his conversion Tolstoy was confronted with a dilemma. He could not live in luxury and be true to his principles; neither could he force his wife and children to abandon their accustomed way of life. The consistent solution would have been to abandon wife and children and go forth from home as a religious beggar, like so many thousands before him. For this choice Tolstoy frankly admitted that he had not the courage. Family life had saved him from dissoluteness and had long kept him from despair. His love of it, almost worship of it, persisted long after the formation of a religious ideal which, as he himself finally perceived, was fundamentally inconsistent with it. In May, 1881, he noted in his diary:

The family is flesh. To abandon one's family is the second temptation—to kill oneself. The family is one body. But do not yield to the third temptation: serve not the family, but God alone. This is an indication of the place on the economic ladder that man should occupy. It is flesh; as for a weak stomach light food is necessary, so for a pampered family more is needed than for one wonted to privations.—[Biryukóv: II, 381.]

The change was gradual. In 1881 a letter to his wife shows him much interested in an edition of his

works and very much alive to financial considerations.*
In the next year a letter from the province of Samara
shows him occupied with the practical success of his
estate there.† Later on he simply neglected his property, trying to treat it as if it did not exist. A letter to
his wife on November 5, 1884, shows him thoroughly
dissatisfied with this course and resolved on a compromise:

I have been thinking much and well about the fact that
while we live and as we live I must conduct the estate myself.
Begin at Yásnaya. I have a plan how to conduct it in accord with my convictions. Perhaps this is hard, but I must
do it. My general reasoning is as follows: to say nothing of
the fact that if we take advantage of the conduct of business
on principles (false) of private property, then we must, nevertheless, conduct it in the best fashion in the sense of justice,
harmlessness, and, if possible, of kindness. To say nothing
of this, it has become clear to me, that if what I regard as
truth and the law of men is really to become that law in life,
then this will occur only if we, rich oppressors, shall voluntarily renounce riches and oppression; and this will occur not
suddenly, but by a slow process, which will lead to it. This
process can occur only when we ourselves shall direct our
own affairs, and, above all, enter into relations with the
common people who work for us. I wish to try to do so. I
wish to try with complete freedom, without violence, and in
accordance with goodness, to conduct this business at Yásnaya
myself. I think that there will be no great mistake or loss,
perhaps none at all. And maybe it will be a good deed. I

* *Letters to Wife*, p. 127.   † *Ibid.*, p. 136.

should like at a favorable moment, when you are listening, to tell you about it, but to describe it is hard.   I think of beginning right off.   To take over the whole thing from Mitrofán and arrange it, and during the winter to make occasional trips, and beginning with spring to occupy myself with it constantly. Perhaps here, unconsciously, I am bribed by a desire to be more frequently in the country, but I feel that my life has been ill ordered by this turning aside, this ignoring of work which was being done, and done for me, and which was absolutely contrary to my convictions.   In this ignoring there was also the element that I, denying property on principle, in the sight of men, from *fausse honte* did not wish to occupy myself with property, in order that I might not be reproached with inconsistency.   Now it seems to me that I have outgrown this. I know by my conscience just how consistent I am.   But, my darling, please bear in mind that this matter is one that touches me very nearly, and do not oppose me heedlessly and hastily and do not disturb my frame of mind.   I am sure that no harm will come of this and perhaps something good and important will result.—[*Letters to Wife*, pp. 223, 224.]

And in this same letter Tolstoy asks his wife to advertise the sale of some horses.

Apparently nothing came of this plan for Christian farming, and Tolstoy lapsed into his previous indifference.   His wife was at one time ready to appeal to the authorities to have his property put under guardianship, in order to preserve it for the children, when he wished to distribute it to outsiders.*   In 1891 the vexed question was settled by Tolstoy's dividing his estates

* Behrs: *Reminiscences*, ch. 6.

among his wife and his children, his wife retaining the copyright in his earlier works. The works written after *Anna Karenin* became the property of every man. This was against the protest of the Countess Tolstoy, who had a real grievance in the case of *The Death of Iván Ilyich*, which her husband had given her as a name-day present, to be included in a new edition of his works.* After 1891 Tolstoy lived as a guest in houses belonging to others.†

Tolstoy burned with eagerness to communicate to his wife something of his own new faith. In May, 1892, he wrote to his disciple Feinermann:

I am terribly eager to give her at least a part of the religious consciousness that I possess (though feebly, still to a degree that gives me the possibility of sometimes rising above the griefs of life), because I know that only this, this consciousness of God and of one's own sonship to him, gives life; and I hope that it will be imparted to her—of course, not from me, but from God. Although this consciousness is imparted to women with great difficulty.—[*Letters, collected by Sergéyenko* (Moscow, 1910): I, 214, 215.]

His wife looked up to him with all her old devotion, and regarded him as a man in advance of his age. Yet devotion to her children kept her at her post. She told her brother with tears in her eyes:

It is hard for me now; I have to do everything alone, while formerly I was only a helper. The property and the education

* *Letters to Wife*, pp. 354–57.   † Maude: II, 426, 427, 513.

of the children are entirely in my hands. They blame me because I do this and do not go begging alms! Would I not go forth with him if I did not have little children! But he has forgotten all for his teaching!*

This difference in ideals made constant friction and discord between the Count and the Countess, which alternated with bursts of passionate affection. Tolstoy, feeling that his new teaching had brought strife into his life rather than peace, pathetically told Feinermann that love of those distant from us is a sin that hampers our love of those near at hand.† Yet at the bottom of his heart his love of his wife survived with all its youthful fervor. In May, 1897, he wrote to her in Moscow, whither she had returned after a two days' visit to Yásnaya Polyána:

What sort of a trip did you have, and how are you now, my dear? By your coming you left such a strong, cheerful, good impression, even too good a one for me, because I feel the lack of you the more strongly. My awakening and your appearance [in the early morning of a marvelous May day] is one of the strongest joyful impressions that I have ever experienced, and that at the age of sixty-nine, from a woman of fifty-three.—[*Letters to Wife*, p. 523.]

Once at least before his last journey Tolstoy resolved to make the supreme renunciation and to go forth into the world alone. Less than two months after the out-

* Behrs: *Reminiscences*, ch. 6.
† Teneromo: *Living Words of L. N. Tolstoy*, pp. 1, 2.

burst of affection that has just been quoted he wrote to his wife the following letter:

DEAR SONYA, I have long been tortured by the inconsistency of my life with my beliefs. To force you to change your life, your habits, to which I myself have trained you, I have been unable; to leave you I have hitherto also been unable, thinking that I should deprive the children, while they were still small, of even that little influence which I might have on them, and that I should grieve you; but to continue to live as I have lived for these sixteen years, now quarreling with you and irritating you, now myself submitting to the temptations to which I am accustomed and by which I am surrounded, I am also no longer able, and I have decided to do now what I wished to do long ago, to leave: in the first place, with my continually advancing years, this life becomes harder and harder for me, and I more and more long for solitude—and in the second place, because the children have grown up, my influence is no longer needed in the house, and you all have more living interests, which will make my absence little noticed by you.

The principal thing is that as the Hindus at the age of sixty retreat into the forest, as every old, religious man wishes to consecrate the last years of his life to God, and not to jokes, puns, gossip, and tennis, so I, entering on my seventieth year, with all the strength of my soul long for that calm and solitude, and if not perfect agreement, at least not clamorous disagreement between my life and my beliefs, my conscience.

If I should do this openly, there would be requests, reprovals, quarrels, complaints, and I should remain, perhaps, and should not carry out my decision—and it should be carried out. And therefore please pardon me if my act pains you, and in your soul, above all, Sonya, let me go with good will and do not seek me, and do not complain of me, do not condemn me.

That I have left you does not prove that I have been discontented with you. I know that you *could not*, literally could not and cannot see and feel as I do, and therefore could not and cannot change your life and make sacrifices for the sake of a truth that you do not recognize. And therefore I do not condemn you; but, on the contrary, I remember with love and gratitude the long thirty-five years of our life, especially the first half of that time, when you, with the motherly self-sacrifice natural to your character, so energetically and firmly bore that to which you regarded yourself as called. You gave to me and to the world what you could give, and gave much motherly love and self-sacrifice, and it is impossible not to value you for it. But in the last period of our life, for the last fifteen years, we have become separated. I cannot think that I am to blame, because I know that I have changed not for my own sake nor for that of men, and because I could not act otherwise.

I cannot blame you for not following me, but I thank you, and with love I remember and shall remember you for what you have given me. Farewell, dear Sonya.

Your loving,
LEO TOLSTOY.

[*Letters to Wife*, pp. 524–26.]

But Tolstoy's strength was still insufficient, and he remained at home in the old compromising circumstances.

He gave the letter to a friend, charging him to deliver it to his wife after his death. Consciousness of his weakness never left him. In 1882 he had written in his tract *On Non-Resistance to Evil by Evil* (*Letter to N. N.*): "If I know the road home and walk along it drunken, tottering from side to side, does that prove that the path along which I am walking is not the true one?" And in February, 1884, he wrote to his wife: "I read Montaigne, go snowshoeing to no purpose, but get very tired, make shoes and think, and try to injure no one. I do not even try to do anything useful for others, it is so impossibly difficult."* At last, in his eighty-third year, he summoned up his resolution to take the great step, and he left home on the journey that closed with his death.

All this history Tolstoy strove to clothe in artistic form in the drama *And the Light Shineth in Darkness*, on which he worked in 1900 and 1902. This work he never completed, but it was published in fragmentary form after his death. Here he depicts the struggles of an elderly landed proprietor, whose aspirations are the same as his own, with the apathy and passive resistance of his family. The piece is perhaps the only failure among all Tolstoy's works of art inspired by the life about him; he could not or would not make his double a hero, and he fails to make him even a pathetic figure.

Tolstoy's aversion to the life of the wealthy, and to money and property in general, was strengthened by his life in Moscow. In 1881 his eldest son, Sergéy, was ready to enter the university; and the Countess

* *Letters to Wife*, pp. 216, 217.

desired better educational advantages for the other children as well. In September of that year the family moved to Moscow and settled in a rented house; in the next year they bought a permanent residence there. Life in the city brought Tolstoy face to face with the problem of poverty in a totally different form from that which he had known in the country. Hitherto he had felt merely that his own life lacked meaning; now his eyes were opened to the ills of society, and he met men who sympathized with his own point of view. On October 17, 1881, he noted in his diary:

A month has passed. The most torturing in my life. The move to Moscow. All are settling themselves, but when will they begin to live? All is done not in order to live, but in order to act like other people. And there is no life.

Stink, stones, luxury, beggarhood, vice. Villains have gathered together, who have plundered the people; they have gathered soldiers and judges in order to protect their orgies, and—they feast. The common people have nothing further to do than, taking advantage of the passions of these men, to coax back from them what has been plundered from themselves. The peasant men are the more clever at this. The women stay at home; the men rub floors and bodies in bath houses and serve as coachmen.—[Biryukóv: II, 401.]

These scattered phrases contain the essential idea of *What Shall We Do Then?*

Tolstoy spent his time partly in literary work; then he would relieve his feelings by walking outside Moscow and sawing and splitting wood with peasants. He found true joy in his acquaintance with the peasant sectarian Syutayev. This man had abandoned his trade as a stone-cutter in St. Petersburg, and had moved to the village, where he had taken the humble post of herdsman, wishing to do good even to animals. He and his family rejected the church, disapproved of military service, shared their goods in common, and endeavored to guide their lives by the precepts of the New Testament, by non-resistance and by love. The living sincerity of Syutayev was an inspiration to Tolstoy; here was a man who had really altered his life from religious conviction.

It was at this time that Tolstoy took up the study of the Hebrew language. With the aid of a Jewish friend, Rabbi Minor (compare p. 237), he made rapid progress in it. Reading only the portions that interested him, he went through the Old Testament as far as Isaiah.

Of his life in Moscow, and the conclusions to which it led him, Tolstoy gives an account in *What Shall We Do Then?*, written in 1886, four years after the events that it records. In this powerful book, part autobiography and part sociological speculation, he naturally shows the same point of view as in *My Religion* (1884). Yet the book makes a far different appeal. Tolstoy's argument is of a sort more cogent with men of this generation: he is not citing Gospel texts, to which he attaches a mandatory power, or appealing to the abstract moral sense of man; he is picturing actual social conditions and demanding that they be changed. Only the title is biblical; it is taken from Luke iii, 10, the question that the people asked of John the Baptist, when he bade them prepare the way of the Lord.

On the negative side *What Shall We Do Then?* is a social tract of marvelous power. Tolstoy, like Jacob Riis, in *How the Other Half Lives,* or like hundreds of lesser writers in American ten-cent magazines and sociological reports, simply tells of conditions as he has seen them. But Tolstoy is a writer of genius and in his picture of slum conditions he shows the same mastery as in his drawing of the ball-room or the hospital. And moral fervor gives to his denunciation of the pagan world of modern society an eloquence like that of St. Paul.

Stirred by the suffering that he beheld, Tolstoy tried to start a sort of informal charitable organization, and in January, 1882, issued a public appeal to society, *On the Census in Moscow.* The coming census offered an opportunity for the census-takers to become acquainted with city conditions and to help the poor. They could wisely distribute alms that would be contributed by the kind-hearted rich. After the census they would remain in touch with the poor and aid them by work rather than by money; they would become brothers to the poor. Through the united efforts of society poverty would be abolished.

But the scheme failed. The rich were apathetic. Tolstoy himself was a poor worker. "On the first day appointed the student census-takers started at dawn, but

I, the benefactor, joined them about noon. I could not come earlier, because I got up at ten, then drank my coffee and smoked, waiting for digestion to take place."*

Furthermore, the distribution of charitable funds proved to be useless without an alteration in the life-conception of the people who were to receive them. And this life-conception, on examination, was found to be exactly the same as that of the rich who gave the funds. Tolstoy was horrified when he found a prostitute bent on bringing up her daughter to her own trade. Reflection convinced him, however, that the prostitute was acting in precisely the same fashion as the ladies of his own acquaintance:

This daughter may be taken by force from the mother, but the mother cannot be convinced that she is doing evil by selling her daughter. If there was any one to save, it was this woman, the mother; above all she must be saved from that view of life, approved by every one, according to which a woman may live without marriage, that is without the bearing of children and without work, serving only the gratification of sensuality. If I had thought about this, then I should have understood that the majority of those ladies whom I wished to send here for the saving of that girl, not only themselves live without the bearing of children and without work, serving only the gratification of sensuality, but even consciously educate their little girls for this very life: one mother takes her daughter to the tavern, another to the court or to balls. But both mothers have one and the same life-conception, namely, that woman should gratify the lust

* *What Shall We Do Then?*, ch. 5.

of man and that for this she should be fed, clothed, and pitied. So how shall our ladies correct this woman and her daughter?—[*What Shall We Do Then?*, ch. 8.]

Tolstoy himself took a boy from the slums into his own kitchen, but the lad ungratefully ran away and joined a circus. The boy had discovered the possibility of a merry life without work; he would neither stay with Tolstoy nor work with Syutayev, the peasant, who offered him a place in his own family:

I might have understood how silly it was for me, who was educating my own children in the most complete idleness and luxury, to be correcting other people and their children, who were perishing from idleness in the Rzhanov house, which I called a den, but in which nevertheless three quarters of the inmates worked for themselves and for others. But I understood nothing of this.—[Ch. 9.]

Syutayev opened Tolstoy's eyes to his error. Tolstoy must first reform himself before he tried to correct others; he must become a laborer, a brother to his fellow men, and so infect them with his own view of life. This is Syutayev's solution of the problem:

"Let us divide them [the idle folk of the slums] up between us. I am not rich, but I will at once take two. You took a lad into your kitchen; I invited him to join me, but he did not come. Let there be ten times as many; we will divide them all up. You will take some, and I will take some. We will go and work together; he will see how I work, will learn how to live, and we will sit down to the bowl together at one table, and he will hear a word from me and from you. That is charity, but that society of yours is mere folly."— [Ch. 14.]

The idle rich, supported by the labor of the poor and setting them the example of a useless and dissolute life, are the cause of the continued existence of poverty. Tolstoy is one of this class, and is personally responsible for the misery of the Moscow slums. The clean, educated, luxurious rich can never help the poor.

Tolstoy now proceeds to examine the nature of money itself, the symbol of wealth. Money, he finds, is only incidentally a medium of exchange; it is primarily an instrument of oppression, by means of which a small number of men make slaves of all the rest. In early times conquerors made slaves of men subjugated in battle; later feudal lords made slaves of men by seizing their lands; now the government, by the collection of taxes, forces men into a third, financial slavery. For in order to raise money to pay taxes Russian peasants are obliged to leave their own lands and work on those of the neighboring proprietors, or, worse yet, to go to the city and work in factories:

So evident is this, that if the government would only make the experiment for a year of not collecting direct, indirect, and land taxes, all the work on other men's fields and in the factories would cease. Nine-tenths of the Russian people hire themselves out during the time of the collection of taxes and to raise money for taxes.—[Ch. 20.]

The use of money to alleviate poverty only increases the evil. What then can be the real cure? It is that indicated by Syutayev, and has two stages. A man must first be honest with himself and recognize that he is supported in idleness by the labor of others; that men and women are toiling at injurious trades in order to maintain him in luxury. Conscious of his guilt, he will seek to escape from it, not by distributing a portion of his ill-gotten gains, but by ceasing to depend upon others. He will support himself, will engage in manual labor, will live a simple life in the country instead of a luxurious life in the city. Others, imitating him, will likewise take up a simple life, tilling the soil. Some men, with a talent for metal work or for teaching, will make plowshares or teach the children of the community instead of plowing and reaping. But their activity will be recognized as necessary by the whole community, nor will it lead to any distinctions of property. Gradually the whole world will adopt this mode of life, luxury and government will disappear, and men and women will be once more free and equal.

To this book Tolstoy appends eloquent pages inculcating on women the duty of childbearing, as on men that of labor. The logical connection is not obvious, except that in each case he preaches a revolt against the luxurious, self-indulgent habits of modern society.

Thus in *What Shall We Do Then?* Tolstoy temporarily lays aside his ideal of pious mendicancy and inculcates useful work for society; he is guided not by the ascetic impulse, but by love. His ethic is to a certain extent world-affirming instead of world-renouncing. Through fixing his attention on social conditions instead of on personal conduct he is unconsciously driven into a compromise position, one that we may define as Christian anarchy.

Tolstoy's diagnosis of the causes of modern conditions and his proposed remedy for them are as inadequate as his presentation of the ills of modern society was masterly. Even in Russia taxation has been but a minor factor in determining the rise of modern industrialism and city life; in other countries the part played by taxation has been of still less account. Money has made possible modern conditions, but it was devised centuries before they arose; to say that money is primarily a means of oppression is as absurd as to say the same thing of steam or electricity. Neither money nor steel knives are bad in themselves, though they may be put to evil uses.

It is a striking fact that in this work Tolstoy pays little attention to the industrial conditions that are shaping modern society, and yet shows clearly the influence of modern socialistic thought, with which he may have become acquainted through his friend the ex-revolutionist Alekseyev. His three stages of slavery, personal slavery, land slavery, and taxation slavery, suggest those of Karl Marx. But for the wage slavery of Marx, of which he has small personal knowledge, he substitutes taxation slavery, of which he has watched the dire effects on his peasant neighbors. And, while the Socialists concentrate their attention on problems of the production of wealth, Tolstoy considers rather the problem of consumption. By limiting his consumption, by simplifying his life, a man will benefit society more efficiently than by increasing his production through the use of machines.

If Tolstoy had never formally abjured his doctrine of the impotence of the individual man to influence historic events, he had ceased to emphasize it, had indeed forgotten it. This is strikingly seen in the remedy here proposed for existing ills, in which we reach the ultimate limit of Tolstoy's individualism. Once he had denied the possibility of progress in history, but had admitted it for the individual man. Now, opening his eyes, he sees that the perfected human character may become an object of imitation by others, and that thereby the structure of society may be modified, may become Christian instead of pagan, altruistic instead of predatory. What the man of action like Napoleon could not accomplish the humble peasant sectarian may perform. This is a buoyant individualism like that of Emerson. "Gods are we, bards, saints, heroes, if we will!"

In this remedy for modern ills may be seen not only Tolstoy's uncompromising individualism, but also his aversion to artificial civilization, his passion for the return to nature, for life next the soil and in the free air. A temperamental instinct has now become a religious duty.

The weakness of Tolstoy's remedy is seen in its essentially reactionary character, and in its exclusive insistence on the moral life, to the neglect of other sides of human existence; or, to put the same thing more exactly, in its insistence on a narrow and unsound ethical ideal.

Tolstoy had constantly denied the value of material progress and had hated external civilization, so that he contemplated with equanimity the sloughing off of such institutions as railroads and printing-presses. He was a kindred spirit to his English contemporary Ruskin. Ruskin had found modern machine-made goods unlovely, and so had been brought to a study of their production and to a yearning for the revival of simpler industrial conditions that did not crush the worker. Tolstoy had found city conditions morally vicious and so had longed for their abolition through the growth of a new social consciousness. Each man preached a gospel of simplification. Each thereby placed himself in opposition to the current of modern history, which tends to more diversified wants, to cooperation in industry, to specialization. Tolstoy was the more extreme. He lacked the saving common sense of his master Rousseau, who, despairing of a return of mankind to a happy barbarism, wished to organize civilization on the basis of justice—to see that the new conditions should not hamper the development of the individual. The aim of all constructive reformers, of whatever type, notably of the Socialists, has been to introduce justice, equality of opportunity, into the social order. Tolstoy, a voice crying in the wilderness, is almost alone among great men of our time in his wish to destroy the material advances that mankind has made.

To this pitch of enthusiasm—let us frankly term it absurdity—Tolstoy was brought by his concentration on the moral life of the individual man. He views men as wholes; a man who does not lead a moral, that is, a self-sacrificing life, can accomplish no good in the world. Thus he ridiculed the Russian political exiles because their lives were often selfish and licentious, and he mocked at his literary associates for the same reason. But men of common sense do not judge a ballot-reform law by the private life of its framer, or condemn one of Poe's poems because of its author's moral weakness. Life is not all morality, or at least not all self-abnegation. If dry and sanitary houses, pure water, clean streets, knowledge of what is taking place in the world about us, are not worthy objects of ambition, then Tolstoy may be right in his insistence on his peculiar type of ascetic, altruistic morality. But common sense will suspect that an ethical doctrine that leads to contempt for such things is fallacious, and common sense will be confirmed by ethical theory. Tolstoy's ethical and social writings are eloquent and stirring, but they are based on premises that we must admit are unsound.

Naturally Tolstoy tried to carry out in his own life the ideal of self-sacrificing physical labor that he had formed. He toiled in the fields with his peasants: Repin's picture of the stalwart old man trudging behind the plow has become familiar to us. He learned the cobbler's trade, but so poorly that the boots he made "couldn't be worse."* He built a stove for a peasant, with similar ill success.† But as his years advanced, and his physical strength declined, he gradually ceased from labors in the fields.

In this behavior men are accustomed to see something of the mountebank, and perhaps the reproach is to some small degree just. Possibly there was in it just a suspicion of that yearning for admiration which Tolstoy confesses was one of his distinguishing traits. But it is better to regard it as the pathetic effort of a great man to realize his own ideal in actual life, however imperfectly and poorly he might do so. The work was good for him, even if it did not benefit the recipients. It was valuable for the spirit of brotherly love behind it, which was real and sincere. Similarly Tolstoy, who disapproved of money alms in principle, continued to give them, in order to cultivate better feelings in himself, and because his family still enjoyed the use of his property.

Of course this queer exterior, these external traits, were easily imitated by the disciples, many of them mere soft-headed cranks, who now began to flock to Yásnaya Polyána. Had Tolstoy desired to found a religious sect, there might easily have grown up a Tolstoyan

* Maude: II, 347.   † Ibid., II, 227.

ritual of plowing and boot-making. But he had no such desire. "My father had good reason for saying," his son writes in his *Reminiscences* (p. 302), "that the 'Tolstoyites' were to him the most incomprehensible sect and the furthest removed from his way of thinking that he had ever come across. 'I shall soon be dead,' he sadly predicted, 'and people will say that Tolstoy taught men to plow and reap and make boots; while the chief thing that I have been trying so hard to say all my life, the thing I believe in, the most important of all, they will forget.'"

Beyond certain limits Tolstoy never carried the application of his teaching. He claimed the right, for example, to have a quiet room in which to do his writing,* though he must have seen that even this modest luxury was inconsistent with his scheme of life. He never even tried to learn how to prepare his own food. His wife cared for him most tenderly, adapting the kitchen to his wants when in 1885 he became a vegetarian. Separation from such care was not good for him. His son Ilyá, who was strongly affected by his father's teaching and was trying to live the simple life with his wife, tells amusingly of a visit from his father:

My father helped us as well as he could, but I must confess, I came to the conclusion that he was extremely little fitted for the Robinson Crusoe life. It is true that he was not at all exacting, and always vowed that everything was first rate. But habit told—he had been accustomed for so many years

* Maude: II, 528.

to a particular order of life, a particular diet, that every departure from that order, even when he was only s`*ty, had a disastrous effect on his health. It happened again and again that when he had gone away quite healthy from home and found himself in new conditions, he came back ill; even when he had been staying with people who knew all his habits and looked after him like a little child.—[*Reminiscences of Tolstoy*, pp. 331, 332.]

Tolstoy was now a changed man; his aristocratic aloofness had vanished and he became accessible to all visitors, ready to give counsel when asked, yet never forcing it on his guests. With young and old alike, with the ignorant and with the learned, he was ready to talk on the most intimate questions of the soul and of private conduct. Yet on the least hint of compulsion the old aristocratic pride would reassert itself. His brother Sergéy, quoted by Count Ilyá Tolstoy, describes him well:

"He is always preaching humility and non-resistance, but he is proud for all that. Máshenka's sister had a footman called Forna. When he got drunk he used to get under the staircase, tuck up his legs and lie down. One day they came and told him that the Countess was calling him. 'She can come here and look for me if she wants me,' he answered. Lévochka [pet name for Lev, Leo] is just the same. When Dolgoruky [Governor-General of Moscow] sent his chief secretary Istomin to ask him to come and have a talk with him about Syutayev the sectarian, do you know what he answered? 'Let him come here, if he wants me.' Isn't that just like Forna?

No, Lévochka is very proud; nothing would induce him to go; and he was quite right; but it's no good talking of humility."—[*Ibid.*, pp. 185, 186.]

When his new conception of life had been fully formed, Tolstoy recovered his former gaiety of spirits. Biryukóv writes of him:

Some people have made a great mistake in supposing that the new, religious frame of mind of Lev Nikoláyevich finds its expression in gloom and sorrow. Such were only moments of acute struggle with the temptations that surrounded him. But as soon as his spiritual equilibrium was reestablished, Lev Nikoláyevich would assume a kindly, gay, joyous tone that infected all those about him with irrepressible gaiety.—[Biryukóv: II, 435.]

The wholesome and kindly home life was not destroyed. An institution of the family was the letter-box, into which each member dropped compositions, jokes, and verses, which were read aloud on the following Sunday. Naturally the father's contributions were the best. The following is a portrait of himself, taken from a *Bulletin of the Patients at Yásnaya Polyána Lunatic Asylum:*

No. 1. Sanguine complexion. One of the harmless sort. The patient is subject to the mania known to German lunatic doctors as *Weltverbesserungswahn.* The patient's hallucination consists in thinking that you can change other people's lives by words. *General symptoms:* discontent with all the existing order of things; condemnation of every one except himself, and irritable garrulity quite irrespective of his audience; frequent transitions from fury and irritability to an unnatural tearful sentimentality. *Special symptoms:* busying himself with unsuitable occupations, such as cleaning and making boots, mowing hay, etc. *Treatment:* complete indifference of all surrounding the patient to what he says; occupations designed to use up all his energy.—[Count Ilyá Tolstoy: *Reminiscences of Tolstoy*, p. 162.]

Towards the end of 1891 Tolstoy was brought face to face with a great conflict between his principles and actual conditions. To his honor be it said, he neglected his principles in order to render more efficient service to humanity. In the summer of 1891 a severe famine broke out in central and eastern Russia, but it was ignored by the Russian government. Tolstoy, when from a personal visit to one of the suffering districts he had seen the destitution of the peasants, determined to do what he could to relieve them. In November he went to the estate of his friend Rayevsky, at Begíchevka, a village in the province of Ryazán, some hundred miles from his own home, and remained there at work, with some intervals, until July, 1893. Not only he himself but his wife and sons and daughters threw themselves into the work. He published articles setting forth the needs of the population and the inefficiency of the government's action, and the Countess inserted in the Moscow newspapers an appeal for money contributions. Funds began to flow in from Russia and from abroad, and soon Tolstoy, the anarchistic scorner of cooperation,

found himself at the head of a tolerably large philanthropic organization. His reports on the work done show
a shrewd practical sense and knowledge of peasant
ways in the precautions taken to prevent the giving of
aid to peasants able to help themselves. In the use
of charitable funds, as his son tells us, Tolstoy was
cautious and even parsimonious. His plan was to
make no house to house distribution of supplies, but
to establish eating-houses to which the needy must
come for relief. Only those in real want would resort
to these simple restaurants. In his report for July,
1892, he gives the number of eating-houses under his
charge as 246, at which from ten to thirteen thousand
persons were fed. Besides this he had established 124
"children's shelters," at which from two to three thousand children were fed with milk porridge. He also had
charge of the distribution of firewood, of flax and
bast for work, of horses for ruined farms, of potatoes,
oats, and other seed for sowing, of the sale of baked
bread at low prices, and of the feeding of the peasants'
horses. Visitors to the famine districts give accounts
of the unselfish personal service done by Tolstoy and
his family. The peasants venerated the Count, though
the priests were meanwhile denouncing him as Antichrist.

Tolstoy's success in this experiment at practical
philanthropy makes one wish that his energy had more
often taken this course, instead of being diverted into
whimsical by-paths. But each man must follow his
own genius. Tolstoy fretted at the part he was play-

ing. "I am living miserably," he wrote to Feinermann in December, 1891, when his work was just beginning. "I do not know myself how I was drawn into this work of feeding the hungry, which is oppressive to me. It is not for me, who am fed by them, to feed them. But I have been so drawn in that I have become a distributor of the vomit thrown up by the rich. I feel that this is miserable and disgusting, but I cannot withdraw; not that I regard this as necessary—I think that I ought to withdraw, but I have not the strength."* In the following February he wrote to another friend:

It is a surprising thing! If I still had any doubts whether or not it were possible to do good with money, then now, when I am buying grain with money and feeding some thousands of men, I have become perfectly convinced that nothing but evil can be done with money.

You will say: "Why then do you continue to do so?"

Because I cannot tear myself away, and because I feel nothing except the deepest oppression, and so think that I am not doing this for the satisfaction of my personality.

The oppression is not in the toil—the toil on the contrary is joyous and draws me on—and not in an occupation for which I feel no heart, but in a constant inward consciousness of being ashamed of myself.—[*Letters, collected by Sergéyenko and edited by Gruzinsky* (Moscow, 1912): pp. 109, 110.]

Love and asceticism were constantly struggling in Tolstoy's nature! Despite his principles Tolstoy was

Letters, collected by Sergéyenko (Moscow, 1910): I, 208.

again drawn into similar work of famine relief, on a smaller scale, in company with his son Ilyá, in the spring of 1899.*

Tolstoy's impatience with business details is amusing. On May 1, 1892, he wrote to his wife:

Yesterday I was again at work writing my report; reckoned up the accounts, got mixed, tried to straighten things out, and, it seems, did so. I was confused mainly by not knowing how to figure up accounts and keep books; and we have not only double but triple book-keeping, and not as an aid to order, but to disorder. Finally I decided to reckon up how much we really have left over, and then how much we have spent, and so to determine how much we received. It came out almost in agreement with the entries of receipts that we have here.—[*Letters to Wife*, p. 407.]

This is from the man who had written in 1862, in his article *On Popular Education:* "It seems that there is no need of proving that *tenue des livres, Buchhaltung*, which is taught in Germany and England, is a science that requires only a quarter of an hour's explanation for any pupil who knows the four rules of arithmetic."

Despite his intense aversion to the Russian Church, Tolstoy retained a certain admiration for the monastic life. This is illustrated by his repeated pilgrimages to the Optin Monastery in the province of Kaluga, some hundred miles from Yásnaya Polyána. The first of

* Count Ilyá Tolstoy: *Reminiscences of Tolstoy*, pp. 352–359.

these was in 1877, when he was still a member of the church; the second he made on foot, in 1881, dressed as a peasant pilgrim, and accompanied only by his servant Arbuzov. On this trip he was shocked to see a monk offering to a poor woman, who had asked for the Gospels, a description of the monastery in place of them; he forthwith bought a copy of the Gospels and gave it to the woman. When his identity was discovered the archimandrite insisted that he be lodged in the luxurious hotel instead of in the quarters of the common pilgrims; Tolstoy, after repeated refusals, consented. He passed four hours in conversation with Father Ambrose, the celebrated holy man of the monastery. Still a third journey was made in 1890, largely for a visit to his sister Marya, who had become a nun in the convent at Shámordino, some eight miles from the Optin Monastery.

Tolstoy's familiarity with monastic life is attested by his posthumous tale *Father Sergy*, written at intervals from 1890 to 1898. The hero of this story is a wealthy young aristocrat who, from religious conviction, has entered a monastery and become famous for his saintly life. Proud of his own fame, he succumbs to the temptation of a girl who is brought into his cell to be healed. Crushed in spirit, he wanders forth from the monastery, becomes a vagabond, and is sent to Siberia. "In Siberia he settled in a hut on the grounds of a rich peasant and is now living there. He works in his host's garden, teaches children, and tends the sick." The theme, that of the danger of pride in one's own moral progress, is one that runs through all Tolstoy's work.

Tolstoy's conversion, though it estranged him from his friend Fet, brought into his circle of intimates numbers of men who sympathized with his doctrines and who tried to realize them in practice. Freaks of all sorts sought his acquaintance, but among his new associates were a few persons of considerable force of character. Among these were Vladimir Chertkóv and Pavel Biryukóv, who became in a sense his literary agents, aiding in the publication abroad, mainly in Switzerland and England, of those of his works that were prohibited in Russia. (Biryukóv was one of his most zealous helpers in the famine relief.) They were instrumental in organizing in Russia a publishing firm, the Mediator, which aimed to furnish cheap literature of good quality for the peasants. Thanks largely to the cooperation of a Moscow publisher named Sytin, this undertaking was a practical success. For it Tolstoy wrote numerous tracts and stories, and other authors did the same. Biryukóv estimates the number of booklets distributed by the firm in the nineties as some 3,500,000 copies a year.* As none of these works were copyrighted, reprints of them were frequent.

No such success attended the efforts of Tolstoy's disciples to organize communities in which they should live according to the teachings of their master. The

*Life of Tolstoy (London and New York, 1911), p. 104.

associations all failed, generally through internal dissensions. Tolstoy himself, who was not a Tolstoyan (compare page 279), apparently never attached great importance to these projects, though they were directly inspired by his counsel in *What Shall We Do Then?*; he took no part in founding them. Indeed organization of any sort was abhorrent to Tolstoy's nature, which, as has already been repeatedly emphasized, was fundamentally individualistic. This may be illustrated by quotations from his *Journal* for December, 1897, and January and February, 1898:

I had a talk with Dushan [Dr. Makovitsky, later Tolstoy's companion in his flight from home]. He said that since he has become involuntarily my representative in Hungary, then how was he to act. I was glad for the opportunity to tell him and to clarify it to myself that to speak about Tolstoyanism, to seek my guidance, to ask my decision on problems, is a great and gross mistake. There is no Tolstoyanism and has never been, nor any teaching of mine; there is only one eternal, general, universal teaching of the truth, which for me, for us, is especially clearly expressed in the Gospels.—[*The Journal of Leo Tolstoy, 1895–1899*, translated by Strunsky: pp. 178, 179.]

Organization, every kind of organization, which frees from any kind of human, personal, moral duties. All the evil in the world comes from this.—[*Ibid.*, p. 195.]

Fáresov told me about Málikov's teaching. All this was beautiful, all this was Christian: be perfect like your Father; but it was not good that all this teaching had for its end

influence over people and not inner satisfaction, not an answer
to the problem of life.   Influence on others is the main Achilles'
heel.—[*Ibid.*, p. 210.]

Thus Tolstoy stoutly resisted every attempt of his
admirers to make him the leader of a sect.   In 1892 a
group of his disciples formed the idea of calling a congress
of Tolstoyans and giving some organization to their body.
But when they appealed for advice to Tolstoy himself,
he advised against any external union;   each man should
trust the promptings of his own spirit: "By what
signs am I to find out that I am destined to be united
with Iván and not with Peter, or not with a horse-
thief from Krapivo or with the Governor of Chernigov?"   But Feinermann, who tells of this incident,
adds:

It is interesting that a few years later . . . L. N. no longer
held these anti-communal views, but spoke of the necessity of
communal life, and two years ago [1910?] when in St. Petersburg a society of Free Christians was founded, and their
regulations were sent to L. N., he replied with full agreement
to the organization of the new community.   The spirit of L. N.
grew in deep sincerity, and what at the first glance seems a
contradiction is really a sign of life.—[Teneromo, *Living Words
of L. N. Tolstoy*, p. 255.]

In 1895 members of a Russian sectarian body, the
Dukhobors, under the influence of the Tolstoyan teaching, which they had received through their exiled
leader, Verigin, publicly burned the arms that they were

carrying as members of the Russian army. In return they were flogged by Cossacks and subjected to cruel persecution. They attracted the attention of Tolstoy and his followers, who found their beliefs remarkably consonant with their own, and who obtained from the Russian authorities permission for them to leave Russia. The Canadian government was willing to provide lands for them as immigrants, but funds were lacking for the expenses of the trip to Canada. To aid in securing these, Tolstoy took from his chest *Resurrection*, a novel begun some years before, completed it, and sold it to Marx, a prominent Russian publisher, who printed it in 1899. To do work for money involved Tolstoy in a compromise with his conscience, but in this instance he decided that the end justified the means. Marx offered 30,000 rubles for the right of copyright for a short time, and 12,000 rubles for the right merely of serial publication in his weekly paper. Tolstoy, after some hesitation, accepted the smaller sum. As soon as the weekly installments were printed, other publishers began to reissue them, and Marx made complaints to Tolstoy. Tolstoy then wrote an open letter, praying publishers to refrain from reprinting any part of the work until its completion, and so great was his moral authority in Russia that his request was heeded. Tolstoy, in revising the book, so greatly lengthened it that Marx voluntarily added an extra 10,000 rubles to his fee. But the profit for the Dukhobors, both from the publication in Russia, and from the translations, was less than if the work had been handled in the ordinary commercial fashion.

Once settled in northwest Canada, the Dukhobors at first through misunderstandings caused trouble to the Canadian authorities, but with the lapse of time nearly all of them have become industrious and inoffensive colonists.

The Dukhobor leader Verigin in his letters had argued against the use of books and railways, stating with truth that for the production of each hard labor underground and at furnaces is needful. This was a perfectly legitimate corollary of doctrine already preached by Tolstoy. But Tolstoy, instead of approving his too apt disciple, replied to him with a characteristic vein of opposition. For once he takes the sound position that one must try to ameliorate social conditions instead of merely to cancel work already done by man:

To tell you the truth, your obstinate attack on books has seemed to me a narrow-minded sectarian way of defending an opinion once accepted and expressed. And such narrow-mindedness is not in accord with the opinion that I have formed of your intelligence and above all of your frankness and sincerity. . . .

As for your argument that for books and railways men need to crawl underground for ore and into a blast-furnace, they need to do so just as much for a plowshare, a spade, or a scythe. And in crawling underground for ore or working at a blast-furnace there is nothing bad; and I myself when I was young would have gladly done so, and even now any fine young man will gladly crawl underground from mere high spirits and will work iron, provided only this is not com-

pulsory and does not last all his life and is accompanied by
all the conveniences that men will surely invent, in case all
men are to work and not merely hired slaves. . .

When I see an ant-hill in the meadow I can in no way
admit that the ants made a mistake in raising this hill and
in doing all that they are doing in it. Just so, looking at all
that men have done in a material way, I cannot admit that they
have done all this by mistake. As a man (and not an ant)
I see mistakes in the human hill and cannot help wishing
to correct them—that is my part in the general work—but I
do not wish to destroy the whole hill of human toil, but only
to arrange more regularly in it all that has been arranged irregularly in it. And in the human hill very much has been
arranged irregularly: of this I have written and still write;
because of this I have suffered and still suffer; and I am
trying, up to the measure of my strength, to change it. . . .

If men only knew that the aim of humanity is not material
progress, that this progress is an inevitable growth, but that
the only aim is the good of all men, that this aim is higher
than any material aim that men may set themselves—then all
would fall into its proper place. And to this the men of our
time should direct all their strength. [*Second Letter:* printed
in *Letters of Verigin* (Christchurch, 1901), pp. 215–219.]

Another and a very important instance of Tolstoy's
concessions to practicality is his enthusiastic adoption
and advocacy of Henry George's single-tax program,
with its object of freeing the land from private owner-
ship. The sufferings of the Russian peasants for lack
of land had weighed upon Tolstoy, and he caught at
this solution, which seemed to him just and practi-

cable; he supports it, among other places, in his paper
To the Working People (1902). He wrote to his wife
in 1897 that the death of Henry George affected him
as that of a very near friend.* In conversation he
likened the single-tax question in contemporary society
to that of the emancipation of the serfs in the days of
his own youth. The single-tax system of course implies
a strong government to collect the tax, and thus contradicts Tolstoy's ideal. His reply was, that so long
as government existed, men should try to secure good
laws, and that the single tax would be one of the best
possible.† Thus Tolstoy has adopted a practical point
of view such as one might expect from a Liberal or a
Socialist. But do not be too sure of his conversion; the
spirit of the loyal Russian noble was still alive in him.
"I think," he told a visitor in 1894, "that such a change
[as the single-tax system] may be carried out by the
absolute authority. As the freeing of the peasants was
realized by the will of the tsar, so the abolition of land
injustice may be realized by a similar authority. No
other authority will do it, because it will contradict the
interests of the classes who support that authority."‡

To the last Tolstoy never fully overcame his dislike
for the Liberals and the Socialists, against whom on
occasion he would fulmine out his scorn. And yet, now
that he himself was a prominent figure in the political

* *Letters to Wife*, p. 532.
† Maude: II, 629.
‡ Semenov, in *Messenger of Europe*, Sept., 1908, p. 37.

world, if only as a denier of politics, and now that his
acquaintance with men of all stripes of opinion was
broader than in his younger days, he at times uttered
views that were quite at variance with his fundamental
no-government attitude. He was stirred to indignation
in 1895, when the young tsar, Nicholas II, in reply to
a loyal petition of the Tver provincial council, praying
that the people might be given a voice in the government of the country, denounced their requests as "in-
sensate dreams."* He refers to this incident in a letter
to the tsar, written in 1902, in which he denounces
autocracy as "an outlived form of government, that
may answer to the demands of a people somewhere in
central Africa, distant from the whole world, but not
to the demands of the Russian people, which is becoming
more and more enlightened with the enlightenment
common to the whole world." Of the Socialists and
Revolutionists he gives a not unkindly picture in *Resurrection*. While he denounces their methods, he is stirred
by their heroism and finds among them admirable types
of character. The moral nature of his heroine Katyusha
is aroused by their unselfish enthusiasm.

It is striking that while Tolstoy's writings were
prohibited in Russia, and his followers often severely
persecuted, he himself was left in peace. Alone and
unaided, he was a man whom the government feared
to touch. He was acknowledged as beyond comparison
the chief man of letters in Russia, and as a good man,

* Maude: II, 500.

the glory of the nation.   He had repeatedly denounced
acts of violence committed against the government with
the same indignation that he had shown towards those
perpetrated by the government.   Force used against a
man whose creed was simple goodness would have
raised a tempest of indignation all through the empire.
Tolstoy's personality was stronger than the state.

At one time an attempt was made to have Tolstoy
confined in a monastery as a heretic.   This is said to
have been thwarted by the tsar Alexander III himself, who is reported to have said to the minister of the
interior: "I beg you not to touch Lev Tolstoy; I have
no intention of making a martyr of him and drawing on
myself the dislike of all Russia. If he is to blame, so
much the worse for him."*

The Russian Church, however, did not allow Tolstoy's
attacks on it to pass without notice.   On March 10,
1901, the Holy Synod, its governing body, published an
official notice stating that Tolstoy "with the zeal of a
fanatic" preached "the overthrow of all the dogmas
of the Orthodox Church and of the very essence of the
Christian faith," and that "therefore the church does
not regard him as a member and cannot so regard him
until he repents and renews his communion with it."
This was generally regarded as a decree of excommunica-
tion.   The effect of the document was to increase the

---

* The statement rests on the authority of the Countess A. A. Tolstoy
(*Correspondence with the Countess A. A. Tolstoy,* p. 60).   There are
difficulties in accepting it; see Maude: II, 448.

dislike and contempt for the church authorities felt by thinking Russians, and to deepen their reverence for Tolstoy; on the other hand it was the cause of considerable annoyance to him through the feeling that it stirred up among the less intelligent part of the population. It roused him to a burst of noble eloquence in defence of his own position. His summary of his own creed, with which he closes his reply, demands quotation:

Here is what is just and what is unjust in the Synod's decree in regard to me. I really do not believe in what they say that they believe in. But I believe in much in which they wish to convince people that I do not believe.

I believe in the following: I believe in God, whom I understand as Spirit, as Love, as the Beginning of All. I believe that He is in me and I in Him. I believe that the will of God is most clearly, most comprehensibly expressed in the teaching of the man Christ, to understand whom as God and to pray to whom I regard as the greatest blasphemy. I believe that the true good of man is in the fulfilling of the will of God, and that His will consists in that men should love one another and in consequence of this do unto others as they would have others do unto them, as it is said in the Gospel that in this is all the law and the prophets. I believe that the sense of life of every man is therefore only in the increasing of love within himself; that this increasing of love leads an individual man in this life to continually greater and greater good; and after death gives him greater good in proportion as love is greater within him; and at the same time contributes more than aught else to establishing in this world the Kingdom of God, that is, an order of life in which the discord, deceit, and violence at present reigning shall be replaced by free concord, truth, and brotherly love of men one to another. I believe that for progress in love there is only one means, prayer—not public prayer in temples, which is directly prohibited by Christ (Matt. vi, 5–13)—but prayer the model of which was given us by Christ, solitary prayer, consisting in the establishing and fixing in our own consciousness of the sense of our own life and of our dependence only on the will of God.

Whether or not these beliefs of mine offend, grieve, or seduce any man, hinder anything or anybody or are displeasing to him—I can change them just as little as my own body. I must live alone and die alone (and very soon), and therefore I cannot believe otherwise than I do believe, preparing to go to that God from whom I came. I do not believe that my faith is indubitably the one truth for all time, but I see none other that is simpler, clearer, and more correspondent to all the demands of my mind and heart; if I learn of such a faith, I shall at once accept it, because God needs naught but the truth. But I can in no way return to that from which I have just come forth with such sufferings, as a flying bird cannot return to the eggshell from which it has come forth.

"He who begins by loving Christianity better than Truth will proceed by loving his own Sect or Church better than Christianity, and end in loving himself [his own repose] better than all," said Coleridge.

I have proceeded by the opposite path. I began by loving my orthodox faith more than my repose, then I came to love Christianity more than my Church, and now I love Truth more than all else in the world. And for me Truth still coincides with Christianity, as I understand it. And I profess this Christianity, and in the measure in which I profess it I live

calmly and joyously, and calmly and joyously I approach
death.

Tolstoy was busy with writing on religious and social
questions almost to the day of his death. His longest
and most important work of this sort after *What Shall
We Do Then?* is *The Kingdom of God is Within You*,
which was composed in 1892–93, while he was busy with
the relief of the starving peasants. In form this book is a
defence of *My Religion* against attacks that had been
made on it; in substance it is mainly an eloquent
denunciation of war. In *My Religion* Tolstoy had
treated of the personal life, in *What Shall We Do Then?*
of the life of the community; he now broadened his
field to include international relations. The propaganda
of this work is the part of Tolstoy's teaching that has
rightly won most admiration and least ridicule throughout the world. Tolstoy became famous—and influential
—as the greatest living apostle of international peace.
His remedy, to be sure, was not that of other peace
advocates. They would end war by international agree-
ments, scraps of paper that in the past nations have
repeatedly violated for the sake of temporary advantage. Tolstoy would obtain peace by a transformation of the conscience of humanity, so that no man
would consent to serve in an army, whether in war or in
peace. Here, as always, Tolstoy is more powerful in
denouncing ills than in showing the way out from them.
But this time the ills are those felt by all humanity, so

that Tolstoy's voice was the clearest and most penetrating among those of a band of reformers rather than a cry from the wilderness. Despite the desolation that is now sweeping over Europe, he has been an influence of real power, a prophet of a better time to come.

Tolstoy resumed the same theme in numerous short pamphlets, such as *Christianity and Patriotism* (1894), *Patriotism or Peace* (1896), *Patriotism and Government* (1900), and *Bethink Yourselves!* (1904), the last of which was occasioned by the war between Russia and Japan. Here he denounced patriotism as "a crude, harmful, disgraceful, and bad, and above all, an immoral feeling."* Tolstoy's ideal was that of the saint. Patriotism, though it is a modified form of selfishness, is at least higher than the personal selfishness, the love of ease and quiet and the forgetfulness of all ideals, which is at present opposed to it more often than the saintliness of Tolstoy. The aim may sometimes justify the means, as Tolstoy often showed in his own practice. War for a high ideal, in the name of freedom and of peace, is a lesser evil than supine submission to the wrong done in the world. Pathetically enough, Tolstoy found that the spirit of the artillery officer was not dead within him; he "nearly wept at the news of the fall of Port Arthur."†

In general, Tolstoy's latest religious writings consist of a multitude of essays, letters, and notes, which of course cannot be considered separately. Some of their departures from the point of view of the works imme-

* *Patriotism and Government*, ch. 7.   † Maude: II, 618.

diately following his conversion have already been mentioned. His emphasis on non-resistance becomes more extreme than ever. In *My Religion* he had countenanced force used towards a child for a good aim;* now, in his letter to Rakhmanov (1891) he disapproves even of resistance to an animal.† He told Anuchin that one must not even kill a wolf that attacks him; "for if we may kill a wolf, we may also kill a dog, and a man, and there will be no limit!"‡

In his latest years Tolstoy made a collection of passages from great thinkers, from Lao-tsze and Plato to Emerson and Henry George, interspersed with passages of his own writing, arranged as a *Course of Reading* for every day in the year. To this he attached great importance. "I should like to have my readers experience in the daily reading of this book," he writes in his preface, "the same beneficent, elevating feeling which I have experienced in its compilation and now continue to experience in its perusal."

What impresses one in Tolstoy's old age is his constant mental and spiritual activity, his ever-youthful search for new truth, even if that truth, when found, be but the old expressed in different words. He fulfills the prophecy that he had written in *Youth:* "I am convinced that if I am fated to live to extreme old age, and my tale overtakes my years, as an old man of

---

*See p. 239, above.
† *Letters, collected by Sergéyenko* (Moscow, 1910): I, 200.
‡ Maude: II, 474.

seventy I shall indulge in the same impossible, childish dreams as now."* In Tolstoy there was no calm, whether of intellectual, self-confident repose, or of spiritual saintliness. "It is evil," he writes in a private letter, "when a man says to himself: 'I have become better than I was; thus I do not smoke, I do not commit adultery, I give away the tenth part of my property, and do not act as the publicans do.' God grant that you may always be dissatisfied and not see the road that you have traversed in drawing near Him!"† "The disagreement of life with what it should be, or, more exactly speaking, with what it will be, is just its characteristic mark, the sign of life. . . . In every man a movement takes place from an inferior state to a superior state, from the worse to the better, from the smaller to the larger: all this may be called life."‡

Yet this account of Tolstoy's last years may best close with a picture of him as a quiet, practical counsellor. In a letter to his wife, written in 1894, he tells of an interview with an eccentric vagrant who came to him for counsel:

I tried in every way to persuade him to settle with his father, and there, resting from the ascetic life that he is leading—he wears bast shoes and is covered with lice—to choose some work for himself, and above all to make people love him, instead of being afraid of him, as they are now; to try to be useful and pleasant to men.—[*Letters to Wife*, p. 482.]

* See page 33, above.
† *Correspondance inédite* (Paris, 1907), pp. 351, 352.
‡ *Ibid.*, p. 349.

CHAPTER IX

OLSTOY'S continued growth in a religious view of life had the effect of deepening his kindly feelings toward Turgenev. In 1881 he twice visited Turgenev on his estate. Upon the poet Polonsky, who was also visiting Turgenev at the time, he made the impression of a changed man, "as it were reborn, penetrated with another faith, another love." "On neither of us did he force his way of thinking, and he listened calmly to the objections of Turgenev. In a word, this was no longer the Count whom ·I had once known in his youth."*

In 1882 Turgenev wrote to a friend his impression of Tolstoy's *Confession:*

I recently received through a very charming Moscow lady Tolstoy's *Confession,* which the censorship has prohibited. I have read it with great interest; it is remarkable for its sincerity, truthfulness, and force of conviction. But it is all built on false premises and finally leads to the most gloomy negation of all human life. . . . This is a nihilism of its own sort. I wonder why Tolstoy, who among other things denies

* Biryukóv: II, 393, 394.

302

even art, surrounds himself with artists, and what they can derive from his conversation. And yet Tolstoy is almost the most remarkable man of contemporary Russia.—[Biryukóv: II, 435.]

Turgenev had been a constant admirer of Tolstoy's artistic genius and had never ceased to lament his friend's neglect of it. In 1879 he had written to Polonsky: "L. Tolstoy, as a great and living talent, will leap out of the mire in which he is stuck, and with benefit to literature." In 1883 he addressed to Tolstoy himself, from his death-bed, the following touching appeal:

DEAR AND BELOVÈD LEV NIKOLÁYEVICH!

I have not written to you for a long time, for I have been ill, and am, to speak frankly, on my death-bed. I cannot recover, and there is no use thinking of it. I am writing to you just to tell you how glad I have been to be your contemporary, and to express to you my last request. My friend, return to your literary work. That gift of yours comes from the same source as all else. Ah, how happy I should be if I could think that my request would have an effect upon you! . . . I am a doomed man; the doctors do not even know what to call my complaint, *nevralgie stomocale gouteuse.* I can neither walk, nor eat, nor sleep! It is tiresome even to mention all this. My friend, great writer of the Russian land, heed my request. Let me know whether you receive this paper, and permit me once more to embrace closely, closely yourself, your wife, and all yours. I can no more. I am weary.—[Biryukóv: II, 451, 452.]

This appeal had no direct effect on Tolstoy, who worked according to his own bent, quite independently of any urging from others. In 1884 he wrote to his wife, presumably in reference to one of his religious works: "I must write, I absolutely must, but I have not that passionate longing without which it is impossible."* As a matter of fact he disliked the title "great writer of the Russian land," which Turgenev had bestowed on him, and which clung to him ever afterwards.† But after Turgenev's death, despite his dislike for public speaking, he eagerly accepted an invitation from the Society of Lovers of Russian Literature in Moscow to give an address at a projected celebration in Turgenev's honor, and he applied himself with enthusiasm to the reading of his works. He was particularly charmed by *Enough*, of which he had written most contemptuously in 1865.‡ Unfortunately the Russian authorities forbade the projected public celebration; and, as Tolstoy would not write out his speech for publication, Russian literature was deprived of what would have been a most striking verdict on Turgenev's life and work.

For eight years after the completion of *Anna Karenin* Tolstoy entirely laid aside realistic fiction, the type of work in which he was supreme. During this interval the only works of the imagination that he produced were a few short stories, often containing supernatural elements, and some of them founded on popular legends,

* *Letters to Wife*, p. 229.
† Count Ilyá Tolstoy: *Reminiscences of Tolstoy*, p. 230.
‡ *Letters to Wife*, p. 202; and Biryukóv: II, 66.

of which *What Men Live By* (1881) is perhaps the best. This and succeeding tales of the same sort are not without power, but taken by themselves they would give no hint of Tolstoy's real genius. His religious and sociological writings, *My Religion* and *What Shall We Do Then?*, make their appeal, as has already been pointed out, by the illustrations drawn from daily life, by the same intimacy with the readers' daily lives that distinguishes *War and Peace*. These short tales have the same patent didactic purpose as the religious writings with which they are contemporary, but unfortunately they seem deprived of the truth of observation that is Tolstoy's distinguishing trait. In an article, *On the Truth in Art* (1887), Tolstoy strove to justify his methods in them by saying that the fundamental truth of moral ideas is the only thing that matters in art. Yet in *What is Art?* (1898) he characteristically did not class these stories as good art, but preferred to them *God Sees the Truth* and *The Prisoner of the Caucasus* (cf. p. 344), in which the supernatural machinery is absent and a plain, direct narrative enforces its own lesson. Tolstoy's genius, wonderful in its picturing of every-day reality, was not adapted to symbolism; he reached success in but few cases, among which one may mention particularly his late tale *Esarhaddon* (1903).

But Tolstoy's genius could not permanently be diverted from its native bent. In 1886 he suddenly produced *The Death of Iván Ilyich* (a story), and *The Power of Darkness* (a drama); three years later he wrote

The Kreutzer Sonata (a short novel) and *The Fruits of Enlightenment* (a comedy); in 1895 there followed a short story, *Master and Man;* then, in 1899, he completed, under circumstances that have been already described, a long novel, *Resurrection,* of which he had received the subject in 1888 from his friend Senator Koni. To these we may add *The Devil* (1889), *Father Sergy* (1890–98), *The Living Corpse* (1900), *Hadji Murad* (1896–1904), and a few other works which were left unfinished or without final revision, and which were not published until after his death. These writings show the novelist's genius undimmed by the lapse of years.

Undimmed, but not unchanged. Through this series of works there runs a somber, intense moral purpose that continually transforms them into Puritan tracts.

Not even the earliest of Tolstoy's works can be called gay. The author of *Childhood* was so wide awake to the seamy side of human character that his picture of the world at times appears pessimistic. In *War and Peace,* despite the fullness of happy life that pervades the book, there is a strain of intensity; life is serious and grim despite its joyous aspects. Now, in these works written after his religious conversion (if we except *The Fruits of Enlightenment* and *Hadji Murad*) the note of joy, of eager delight in the life of the flesh, has disappeared. No gracious, maidenly figures like Natasha dance through these later works; murder, moral torture, lust, adultery, lie at their foundation. The life of the body is shown to be wholly bad, while to it Tolstoy contrasts a spiritual bliss, a moral awakening, to which he vainly strives to give convincing human form.

The mildest of the somber series is the first, *The Death of Iván Ilyich*. A lawyer of fair talents, a Philistine worldling, an average man, neither bad nor good, neither rich nor poor, injures himself internally by a fall from a step-ladder. The injury, which at first caused only slight discomfort, becomes more and more painful; Iván Ilyich sees before him a slow, agonizing death. In his wife and children he finds no true sympathy; to them his helpless suffering is nothing but a nuisance. Only his peasant man-servant, healthy and with an uncorrupted natural unselfishness, treats him with genuine kindness. At last Iván Ilyich perceives that his years on earth have been wasted in ignorance of life's true meaning. He dies after three days that have been one yell of pain, from which his family have sheltered themselves behind closed doors. His wife is mainly concerned about receiving her pension; his colleagues, about the appointment of a successor.

This tale, of some eighty pages, is distinguished from Tolstoy's earlier writings by its unity, its concentration on one central theme. Tolstoy no longer strives to give the full, rounded presentation of life that he had achieved in *Anna Karenin*. Hence comes the overpowering intensity of the work. Rolland tells of finding enthusiasm for it among the French bourgeoisie, a class naturally impervious to art and literature. Amid its darkness there is a ray of hope; the new consciousness of life, of the unborn, untemporal life, awakens in Iván Ilyich just before his death. From the stark, grim reality that confronts the reader at every turn the only escape is in the spiritual life.

In *Master and Man* Tolstoy resumed the same theme, the kindling in a callous soul of a spark of spiritual truth. The setting is the same as in the youthful *Snow-storm* (1856), but what a difference in tone! A coarse, skinflint merchant, driving with his peasant workman, is overtaken by a snowstorm. He sees the peasant freezing to death, throws himself upon him, and warms him with the heat of his own body. Himself dying, he feels the bliss of self-sacrifice. The peasant survives while the merchant perishes.

The same theme of conversion occurs in *The Power of Darkness*, a ghastly drama of peasant life, founded on an incident that had actually come before a court in Tula. As a mere literary achievement, it is remarkable that Tolstoy at the age of fifty-eight should have been able to take up the dramatic form. In 1863, to be sure, he had written two comedies, neither of which has been published, and in 1870 he had a period of intense enthusiasm for the drama, reading eagerly Shakespeare, Molière, and Goethe. Nevertheless the dramatic form was essentially new to him. His novels are as little dramatic as any ever written; the attempts to recast *Anna Karenin* and *Resurrection* as acting plays have resulted in dismal parodies. Conversation in his stories is relatively insignificant and commonplace, while very much depends on the description of accessories, manner, and gesture, and on the analysis of the characters' thoughts. Tolstoy himself likened the difference between a novel and a drama to that between painting and sculpture. He told Feinermann of his difficulties:

The whole difference between the novel and the drama I came to understand when I set to work on my *Power of Darkness*. At first I attacked it with those novelist's methods to which I was more accustomed. But after the first pages I saw that here matters were different. Here it was impossible, for example, to prepare the crises of the heroes' experiences, impossible to make them think on the stage and remember things, to light up their characters by digressions into the past—all this is tiresome, wearisome, and unnatural. One needs crises already prepared. Before the public there must be states of the soul already formed, decisions that have been adopted. Only such reliefs of the soul, such chiseled forms in mutual collisions agitate and touch the spectator.

But monologues and various transitions with tableaux and tones of voice—all such things disgust the spectator, who begins to regret that the chairs were not set with their backs to the stage. To be sure, I did not restrain myself, and I inserted several monologues in *The Power of Darkness*, but, while inserting them, I felt that I was not acting properly. It is hard for an old novelist to refrain from that, as it is hard for a coachman to hold in his horses, when a heavy coach is pressing down on them from a slope.—[Teneromo: *Life and Conversations of L. N. Tolstoy*, p. 40.*]

* In general, information furnished by Feinermann must be received with caution, but this account smacks of the truth.

That Tolstoy could overcome these difficulties, change his whole technique, concentrate his action and make the conversation tell the story, and, finally, that he could produce a drama that is not only the most powerful in all Russian literature, but one which has been recognized as among the masterpieces of the modern realistic drama, influencing for example the development of the drama in Germany, is a new proof of his many-sided literary genius.

It is strange also that this grewsome play should be based on the life of the peasantry, the class from which Tolstoy drew his religious inspiration. The drama proves that Tolstoy had his eyes open to peasant conditions, seeing about him no sentimental "sweet Auburn." The sturdy industry and faith of certain peasant types had aided in his own conversion, but he had made no false artistic generalization from them.

In a peasant family a wife deserts her sickly husband and sins with a lusty young laborer, Nikita. Her confederate and helper is Nikita's mother. Nikita also intrigues with the woman's half-witted daughter, who bears a child. This child Nikita and the wife murder. The play ends with Nikita's confession of his sins; remorse of conscience has overwhelmed him. The influence towards righteousness in the play is Nikita's father, the old cesspool-cleaner Akím, the man of God. The play is a tragedy of darkness and degradation, a repulsive picture of village wickedness beside which *The Widow in the Bye Street* seems pale. The conversion in it is not a *tour de force*, brought in to teach a moral lesson; it follows naturally from what we have learned of Nikita's character. Tolstoy followed the advice that he himself gave to Feinermann: "Do not crush or bend to suit your own purposes the events of a tale, but follow it wherever it leads you."*

In this play the evil influences all come from women. One must admit that in his later works Tolstoy constantly expresses an unfavorable view of feminine character. Woman lacks the idealism of man; she can form no new philosophy of life, nor understand one when it is presented to her. (Tolstoy, despite his love and devotion for his wife, was doubtless affected by her failure to adopt his religious views.) Tolstoy's condemnation of women flows from the ascetic side of his ethical system, which constantly becomes more prominent. This aspect of his teaching reaches its utmost development in *The Kreutzer Sonata* (1889).

Tolstoy's greatest novels had been panegyrics upon family life. At the close of *What Shall We Do Then?* (1886) he had devoted to motherhood some of his most eloquent pages. Now, in *The Kreutzer Sonata*, written only three years later, he definitely reverses himself and adopts a position like that of St. Paul (in I Corinthians, vii, 1–11). Absolute celibacy is the ideal for every virtuous man, while promiscuity is the sin that must be shunned most of all. Marriage is a half-way

*Letter of December, 1886; in *Letters, collected by Sergéyenko* (Moscow, 1910): I, 153.

station, a compromise, not absolutely sinful, but full of danger and without inspiration. Such is the philosophy that underlies his new picture of family relations.

In a railway train a murderer, Pózdnyshev, pours out to a chance acquaintance the story of his life. In his youth he had acted like most young men, consorting freely with harlots and regarding the indulgence of his sexual desires in the same light as drinking or smoking. Then he had married. His life with his wife was based on sexual desire, not on any unselfish love, but still he counted himself a moral man because he was not outwardly unfaithful to her. Quarrels were continual; there was no mutual esteem. They had children, who, however, meant little to them. The wife, who was the feminine counterpart of her husband, found the care of children irksome, and with a doctor's aid took means to avoid having more. When she was freed from childbearing and nursing, her sexual impulses remained the same, while her attractiveness increased. Other men paid her attentions, notably a violinist. The husband became wildly jealous, particularly so one evening when his wife and the violinist were playing together the *Kreutzer Sonata* of Beethoven, music that in a drawing room, where there are women in décolleté, arouses, according to Tolstoy, the most sensual feelings. Pózdnyshev left home, and returned late at night, convinced of his wife's falsity; he seized a dagger, and, finding the woman with her lover, he stabbed her. He was ac-

quitted by the court on the ground of having been
justified in his vengeance.

Among all Tolstoy's works, *The Kreutzer Sonata* is
the most horrible in its plainness of speech—and this
despite a slight modification that the author introduced
at the urging of his wife. Tolstoy lays bare the crude
medical facts of life without the faintest gauzy covering
of romanticism. The book is a sermon on modern
tampering with the sex instinct. Its readers instinctively
denounce the whole sex impulse as vile and low.

The Kreutzer Sonata raised a fury of disgust in society, a fury that was more than half hypocrisy. In
America it was for a time forbidden the right of transmission through the mails, as an immoral work. To
explain his parable, Tolstoy added a postscript, in which
he details the Russian attitude to the sexual life, one
very different from the English Puritan tradition. Gratification of the sexual instinct is not regarded as a sin,
and parents teach their children how to indulge it
without risk of disease. Married men have intercourse
with their wives during pregnancy, thus violating the
laws of nature. Women sterilize themselves that they
may indulge their lusts and aid men in lust without
the bringing forth of children, the only thing that can
justify the yielding to sexual feeling. All this Tolstoy
denounces as bad. The way out is not to compromise
with the sex feeling, as is likely to be the case in marriage, but to strive for the ideal of absolute chastity.
This will, he admits, lead to the extinction of the human

race. But no one has proved that the perpetuation of a lustful race is in itself a good. As the race advances in self-control it may well die out.

We have seen (page 259) how Tolstoy had written in his diary in 1881: "The family is flesh. To abandon one's family is the second temptation—to kill oneself. The family is one body. But do not yield to the third temptation: serve not the family, but God alone." Then he was still on the sane ground of compromise, of regulating natural impulses rather than extinguishing them. Now asceticism has led him into a more consistent position, of mortification of the flesh. He writes in his *Epilogue to The Kreutzer Sonata:*

I was horrified at my own conclusions and wished not to believe them, but it was impossible not to believe them. And however much these conclusions contradict the whole order of our life, however much they contradict what I previously thought and even expressed, I was obliged to accept them.

Passages in Tolstoy's Journal for 1897 and 1898 show his altered point of view:

All calamities which are born from sex relations, from being in love, come from this, that we confuse fleshly lust with spiritual life, with—terrible to say—love; we use our reason not to condemn and limit this passion, but to adorn it with the peacock feathers of spirituality. Here is where *les extrèmes se touchent.* To attribute every attraction between the sexes to sex desire seems very materialistic, but, on the contrary, it is the most spiritual point of view: to distinguish from the realm of the spiritual everything which does not belong to it, in order to be able to value it highly.—[*The Journal of Leo Tolstoi, 1895–1899*, translated by Strunsky: p. 154.]

Yesterday there was a conversation about the same thing: Is exclusive love [love of one woman] good? The résumé is this: a moral man will look on exclusive love—it is all the same whether he be married or single—as on evil and will fight it; the man who is little moral will consider it good and will encourage it. An entirely unmoral man does not even understand it and makes fun of it.—[*Ibid.*, p. 222.]

No student of the religious life, or, more concretely, no admirer of St. Paul, no respecter of a chaste, celibate, duty-loving priest, can throw a stone at Tolstoy for the conclusion he has reached. The ascetic impulse created monasticism in Buddhism and in Christianity. Tolstoy after his religious conversion rejected monasticism, maintaining that he would remain in the world and still serve God.* But now he advocates an ideal that is essentially monastic; his aspirations at this stage of his progress might be summed up as poverty, chastity, and *dis*obedience. What the medieval church enjoined as an ideal on a few men Tolstoy announces as a universal human duty; his now democratic soul will make no distinction between monk and worldling, priest and layman. The church, following St. Paul and other teachers, separated its clergy from the worldly life by depriving them of wives, not to speak of promiscuous

My Religion, ch. 10: cf. p. 250.

intercourse; Tolstoy will prescribe the same remedy for
all men, and he gives reasons for his doctrine founded on
the modern conditions that he sees about him. But he
still is inconsistent: suicide would be the next logical
step in self-abnegation, and that Tolstoy continues to
abhor. Buddhists and Christians may be withheld
from suicide by its futility; men cannot hope to escape a
temporal life after death. Tolstoy, not yet restrained
by any such belief, should logically have accepted
suicide as a release from the ills of the flesh. Suicide by
violence, to be sure, would have contradicted his cardinal
principle of non-resistance to evil by violence: for this
same reason he rejects self-mutilation as a means of
attaining chastity, and condemns the Russian sect of
Eunuchs for their practice of it. By violence they
hinder the production of future generations who might
attain an ideal of voluntary chastity unknown to them.*
But suicide by self-starvation would hardly be open to
this objection; it would be only the extreme development of Tolstoy's doctrine of self-denial. Asceticism
and the passion for renunciation of the life of the body,
however, never led Tolstoy to this abyss. Worthy of
admiration are his clear perception that any ethical
ideal, to be sound, must be valid for all men and women,
and his attempt, however inadequate, to justify his
position on that basis. Here, as has been noted (page
253), he is a follower of Kant, a rationalist. Illogical

* *On the Sex Question* (*Thoughts of L. N. Tolstoy, collected by Vladimir Chertkóv*).

though his doctrine may be, it is at least more consistent than the temporizing systems developed under Buddhism and Christianity, with their prescription of varying ideals for priest and layman. For Tolstoy the moralist, with his doctrine that the body is the source of all human ills, the sexual impulse must ultimately prove wholly repulsive.

Father Sergy and *The Devil* are kindred in spirit to *The Kreutzer Sonata*. The former has been already mentioned (page 286). It represents woman as the great temptress of man, the chief obstacle to a righteous life. Father Sergy resists the seduction of a beautiful courtesan only to submit later to that of a merchant's daughter. Yielding, his phrase is: "Marya, you are a devil."

The devil of the second story is the same. A young landowner in his bachelor days has an intrigue with a peasant woman. After his marriage to a woman of his own class temptation from his former mistress returns upon him. Unable to resist, he kills himself. One thinks of Tolstoy's confession to Maude, that his desire for women was the hardest to overcome of all his animal passions, and of his entry in his diary for 1903: "I am now experiencing the torments of hell: I remember all the abominations of my former life. Those recollections do not leave me, and they poison my life."* He notes characteristically at the close of his story that none could comprehend the cause of the suicide. Sin such as

* Maude: I. 52; II, 402.

that with which the man struggled seemed the most
commonplace act to those about him.

With the tone of these works one may compare entries
in Tolstoy's diary for August, 1898:

> Woman—and the legends say it also—is the tool of the
> devil. She is generally stupid, but the devil lends her his
> brain when she works for him. Here you see, she has done
> miracles of thinking, far-sightedness, constancy, in order to
> do something nasty; but as soon as something not nasty is
> needed, she cannot understand the simplest thing; she can-
> not see further than the present moment and there is no self-
> control and no patience (except child-birth and the care of
> children).
>
> All this concerns women, un-Christians, unchaste women,
> as are all the women of our Christian world. Oh, how I would
> like to show to women all the significance of a chaste woman!
> A chaste woman (not in vain is the legend of Mary) will save
> the world.—[*The Journal of Leo Tolstoi, 1895–1899*, translated
> by Strunsky: pp. 251, 252.]

Strangely enough, while Tolstoy was at work on his
acrid denunciation of family life in *The Kreutzer Sonata*
he was also writing a genial comedy, for his children
to present at private theatricals, *The Fruits of Enlightenment*. The zealot had not absorbed the jocose and merry
father.

The Fruits of Enlightenment presents to us a well-to-do
Russian family, in which the father is a spiritualist,
and the mother a fanatic on the germ theory. In
seventeenth-century England it would have been called

a comedy of "humors," of eccentric types. The thread
of action is supplied by some peasants, who have come
to town wishing to buy land. A clever chambermaid,
Tanya, at a spiritualistic séance contrives to trick
her master Zvezdintsev (Star-gazer) into signing the
deed. The character of Tanya is the mainspring of the
comedy. Her natural good sense overcomes the pom-
pous folly of the master and mistress and their learned
friend Professor Krugosvetlov (Round-the-world-boy).
The play is full of deliciously humorous situations and
excellent comic dialogue. Tolstoy's moral enthusiasm
is here tempered by fun; he pours out copious ridicule
on aristocratic gluttony and credulity. Here we see the
Tolstoy of the home circle, the merry contributor to the
letter-box.

In the earlier portions of *Resurrection*, which were
probably written about 1888, there are pages that by
their impartial, slightly satirical picture of Russian high
society suggest Tolstoy's earlier work. But the book as a
whole is a controversial pamphlet, attacking fiercely both
church and state.

A rich young Russian of gentle birth, Prince Dmitry
Nekhlyudov—the name is the same as that of one of the
main characters in *Youth* and in some others of Tolstoy's
early works—meets at his aunts' house a young girl of
the humblest origin, Katyusha, who lives with his aunts
half as protégée, half as chambermaid. Her freshness
and girlish charm tempt him, and he seduces her. The
scene depicting the seduction, while wholly free from

sensual details, is written in Tolstoy's most vivid style. Nekhlyudov deserts Katyusha, leaving money as payment for his crime. The girl, he is told, bears a child, and is expelled from the house, but he learns nothing further of her. In reality she sinks into misery and becomes a common prostitute, living in a house of ill-fame. To this place comes a merchant, bent on enjoying himself in a strange city. He is murdered at a hotel, and suspicion falls on Katyusha, who has been his companion. She is arraigned for the crime, and Nekhlyudov is drawn as a juror for the trial of the case. Seated in the box, he recognizes the accused as the girl whom he had corrupted years before. A wave of repentance and contrition sweeps over him. At the trial, through a misunderstanding on the part of the jurors, the girl is condemned for the murder, of which she is innocent, and is sentenced to life exile in Siberia. Nekhlyudov seeks in vain to have the sentence reversed. Overcome by remorse, he gives up his position in society, breaks his engagement with a rich young woman, and follows Katyusha into Siberia. She refuses persistently his offer of marriage. At last a pardon comes for her from the tsar. She marries one of her fellow exiles. Nekhlyudov finds that a new life has dawned for him in the spirit of Christ's five commandments, which are naturally those expounded by Tolstoy in *My Religion*. A conversion such as for Tolstoy was the work of years takes place in Nekhlyudov in a few weeks.

Into *Resurrection* Tolstoy pours out all his contempt

for government institutions, above all for courts of law and for prisons. He pictures judges and advocates, who condemn men for crimes for which they themselves are spiritually responsible. He describes the types of criminals met by Katyusha on her journey, men and women who, if guilty, have been led astray by the hard circumstances of life rather than by badness of heart. Meanwhile a priest is performing a mummery called a sacrament, which does no good and merely extorts hard-earned money from peasants; and a fashionable English preacher—the reflection of a real missionary, Lord Radstock—tells idle aristocrats that they may be saved by faith in the merits of Christ rather than by their own good lives.

In technique, *Resurrection*, with its digressions and its discussions of social questions, reverts to Tolstoy's earlier manner. Though it lacks the comprehensive sympathy of *War and Peace* and *Anna Karenin*, it has pages of wonderful beauty and strength. In the prison scenes the author's insight sheds human kindliness over the most wretched surroundings. His frankness of speech, however, gave offence, though to a less degree than in *The Kreutzer Sonata*. A letter of the English Quaker John Bellows refers to the matter:

One thing I had to get through at our last Committee was the question of the novel Tolstoy wrote to help the Doukhobor migration expenses—*Resurrection*. Our people received £150 of the proceeds; but the work is an objectionable one in its giving far too full details of "smutty" things; and my wife and I felt we had better sacrifice this sum ourselves rather than let the Society of Friends be in complicity with its publication. So I paid the sum back out of my own pocket, and then wrote Tolstoy a long and earnest letter on the subject, to which he has as yet not sent a reply; but his friend who helped the translation, etc., came to the Committee to defend it against my charges. The Committee, however, took my view, and unanimously condemned the work as unfit for our homes; and ordered the £150 to be refunded to me.

Tolstoy's delayed reply to Bellows was as follows:

7th of December, 1901.

DEAR FRIEND,

I received your letter and meant to answer it; but the last two months I have been so weak that I could not do it, so you must excuse me my long silence.

I read your letter twice and considered the matter as well as I could, and could not arrive at a definite solution of the question. You may be right, but I think not for every person which [*sic*] will read the book. It can have a bad influence over persons who will read not the whole book and not take in the sense of it. It might also have quite the opposite influence so as it was intended to. All that I can say in my defence is, that when I read a book, the chief interest for me is the *Weltanschauung des Autors:* what he likes and what he hates. And I hope that the reader which will read my book with the same view will find out what the author likes or dislikes and will be influenced with the sentiments of the author, and I can say that when I wrote the book I abhorred with all my heart the lust, and to express this abhorrence was one of the chief aims of the book.

If I have failed in it I am very sorry, and I am pleading guilty if I was so inconsiderate in the scene of which you write that I could have produced such a bad impression on your mind.

I think that we will be judged by our conscience and by God, not for the results of our deeds which we cannot know, but for our intentions, and I hope that my intentions were not bad.   Yours truly,

LEO TOLSTOY.*

As to matters of this sort there may be a legitimate difference of opinion. One may note that in 1893 Tolstoy wrote to his wife that it was "of course too early" for their fourteen-year-old son Mikhaíl to read *Anna Karenin*.† And when *The Kreutzer Sonata* was read aloud in his home he admitted that it was "better for the young ladies to leave." ‡

In *The Living Corpse*, an unfinished drama, a drunken, worthless fellow disappears from sight in order to spare his family the disgrace of his presence. Tolstoy presents him as morally superior to the self-satisfied followers of convention who remain respected and honored members of society. For once Tolstoy seems to have adopted the manner of Dostoyevsky.

There is rare charm in *Hadji Murad*, a tale which by its subject matter takes us back to the days of Tolstoy's youthful service in the Caucasus. Hadji Murad was a

---

* *John Bellows: Letters and Memoir* (London, 1905): pp. 361, 362.
† *Letters to Wife*, p. 445.
‡ Tsinger, in *On Tolstoy*, p. 380.

Mohammedan warrior, second only to Shamil himself in his tenacious resistance to the Russians. Tolstoy tells his story in a simple, matter-of-fact way, with full delight in his physical strength and bravery. The old hunter and warrior was never quite lost in Tolstoy the saint. Tolstoy loved adventure even in books; he wrote to his wife (1897) that the death of Alexander Dumas had affected him in the same way as that of Henry George.* The opening paragraphs of Tolstoy's tale are especially delightful:

I was returning home through the fields. It was midsummer. They had already mowed the meadows and were just beginning to reap the rye.

There is a delightful choice of flowers at that time of year: red, white, and pink fragrant, fluffy clover; milk-white daisies with their bright yellow centers and pleasant spicy smell; yellow rape, with its scent of honey; towering, purple and white, tulip-like campanulas; creeping vetch; yellow, red, and pink scabiosa; regular, purple plantain, with a faintly pinkish down and a barely perceptible pleasant scent; corn flowers, bright blue in the sun and in their youth, but light blue and reddening in the evening and as they grow old; and tender, almond-scented, quickly withering convolvulus.

I had gathered a large bouquet of various flowers and was walking home, when I noticed in the ditch a marvelous purple thistle in full bloom, of the sort that we call "Tatar," and which the mowers carefully avoid, and, when it is accidentally mown, cast out from the hay, in order not to prick

*Letters to Wife, p. 532.

their hands on it. The thought came to me of plucking this thistle and putting it in the middle of my bouquet. I stepped down into the ditch, and, after driving away a bumble-bee that had nestled down into the center of the flower and had there gone sweetly and idly to sleep, I set to plucking the blossom. But this was very hard: the stem not only pricked me from all sides, even through the handkerchief that I had wrapped around my hand, but was so terribly tough that I struggled with it for some five minutes, breaking one fiber after another. When at last I had torn off the flower, the stem was all in shreds, and the flower no longer seemed so fresh and beautiful. Besides this, with its coarseness and roughness it did not go with the delicate flowers of the bouquet. I felt sorry that I had uselessly ruined the flower, which had been good in its own place, and I cast it aside. "Yet what energy and force of life," I thought, remembering the efforts with which I had torn off the flower. "With what vigor it defended itself and how dear it sold its life." . . .

And I remembered a story of the Caucasus of long ago, part of which I had seen, part heard from eye-witnesses, and part imagined.

This joy in flowers appears repeatedly in Tolstoy's letters. In truth, the love of beauty was always one of Tolstoy's passions. And yet, when he came to write a treatise on esthetics, in *What is Art?* (1898), he won fame, or shall we say notoriety, by denying that beauty is a necessary or important element in works of art.

What is Art? is on the one hand an expansion of the idea as to the popular, infectious character of great art that Tolstoy had expressed twenty-six years earlier in his article on *Yásnaya Polyána School* (see pp. 119–121), and on the other an obvious corollary to his ethical system. His fundamental thought, and fundamental error, is that beauty has nothing to do with true art. To the demolition of this view he devotes an introduction in which he reviews the theories of preceding writers on esthetics. He likewise disapproves of the attempt to construct a definition of art by scientific induction from objects of art:

All existing systems of esthetics are constructed on this plan. Instead of giving a definition of true art, and then deciding what is and what is not art by judging whether a given production suits or does not suit that definition, a certain class of productions that for some reason please people of a certain set are recognized as art, and a definition of art is devised that will cover all these productions.—[*What is Art?*, ch. 4.]

Yet Tolstoy's own definition is itself founded on induction, though on an induction so swift and simple that he does not recognize it as such; and it is a definition that in no way excludes beauty from the province of art or even prevents it from being an essential feature of art. His definition is, briefly, that art consists in the conscious transfer of emotion:

To call forth in oneself a feeling that has been once experienced, and, after calling it forth in oneself, to transfer that feeling by means of movements, lines, colors, sounds, or images expressed in words, so that others may experience the same feeling—in this consists the activity of art. Art is an activity of man which consists in this, that one man consciously, by certain external signs, transfers to others feelings experienced by him, and other men are infected with these feelings and live through them.—[Ch. 5.]

This definition belongs to the emotionalist school of esthetics. Tolstoy has taken a definition by Véron, which he cites (ch. 3) as: "Art is the manifestation of feeling, transferred externally, by means of a grouping of lines, forms, or colors, or by a succession of gestures, sounds, or words, subjected to certain rhythms,"* and has added to it the self-evident supplement that the artist must so express his emotion that it will be felt by other men who come in contact with his production.

Obviously this definition, if accepted, does not prevent beauty from being an important, or even conceivably an essential element in art. For surely the sense of pleasure in the harmony of line, color, or sound is an emotion that an artist may experience and wish to convey to others. Tolstoy sees the danger and vainly tries to escape it. He has admitted that ornaments may be objects of good art. He then adds:

I fear that here I shall be reproached that, while denying that the concept of beauty constitutes an object of art, I here once more recognize beauty as an object of art. This reproach is unjust, because the artistic content of ornaments of all sorts consists not in their beauty, but in the feeling of

* See Véron: *Æsthetics*, translated by Armstrong (London, 1879), p. 89.

delight and admiration for a combination of lines or colors which the artist experiences and with which he infects the spectator. Art has been, is, and can be nothing else than the infection by one man of another or others with the feeling which the infecter has experienced. Among these feelings is the feeling of delight in what pleases the sight. And objects that please the sight may be such as please a small number of men, or a larger number, or such as please all men. And peculiarly such are all ornaments. A landscape of a very exceptional locality, a very special *genre*, may not please all, but ornaments, from those of the Yakuts to those of the Greeks, are accessible to all and arouse the same feeling of admiration in all, and therefore in a Christian community this species of neglected art should be prized much more highly than exclusive, pretentious paintings and sculptures.— [*What Is Art?*, ch. 16.]

But what is "the feeling of delight and admiration for a combination of lines or colors" except the sense of beauty, the feeling of *pleasure* in an artistic production, which Tolstoy affects so to despise?

Leaving then the soundness of Tolstoy's definition of art as something over which estheticians may wrangle, let us merely point out that the definition is not a consequence of his ethical theory, is not moralistic; and that it does not exclude from art the element of beauty: that it might be used, by critics of other temperament than his own, to justify works of art that he condemns, and to condemn those that he praises. Tolstoy's peculiarity, his originality, lies not in his definition of art, but in his use of that definition; and namely, in his

instant connection with it of his whole ascetico-al-
truistic ethical system. This connection he makes
very simply.

Primarily, all purposed communication of feeling is
art; a boy meets a wolf in the woods, and later, telling
of the incident to his companions, imparts to them the
feeling of fear that he has himself experienced. But—

we call art in the narrow sense of the word not all human
activity that communicates feelings, but only such activity
as we for some reason separate from all this activity and to
which we assign special significance. Such special significance
all men have always assigned to that part of this activity
which communicated feelings flowing from the religious
consciousness of men; and this small part of all art they have
called art in the full sense of this word.—[Ch. 5.]

Hence at all times art that has expressed the ideas of
the reigning religion has been regarded as good art,
that which contradicted it as bad art:

If religion places the sense of life in earthly happiness,
in beauty and strength, then the joy and vigor of life communicated by art will be regarded as good art; but art which
communicates a feeling of effeminacy or dejection will be
bad art, as it was recognized among the Greeks. . . .

Christianity of the earliest times recognized as good productions of art only legends, lives of saints, sermons, prayers,
and hymn-singing that evoked in men feelings of love for
Christ, tender reverence for his life, desire to follow his example, renunciation of the life of the world, humility and

love of men; but all productions that communicated feelings of personal enjoyment it regarded as bad, and therefore it rejected all heathen plastic art, admitting only symbolic plastic representations.—[*What Is Art?*, ch. 6.]

Ecclesiastic Christianity, though a corruption of Christ's teaching, was nevertheless a higher conception than paganism. It gave birth to true art, in architecture, painting, sculpture, music, and literature. But after the Renaissance men lost faith in the church and did not return to the religion of primitive Christianity, which was retained or attained only by a few men such as Francis of Assisi and Chelčický. The upper classes, left without religion, went back to the base pagan conception of the Greeks, which made the meaning of life consist in beauty and enjoyment, a conception that Plato had already condemned. On this conception modern art is based; it is therefore nothing but an imitation of pagan art. To justify this pagan art men have invented esthetic theories, of which the most typical is that of Baumgarten, with his triad of the Good, the Beautiful, and the True, "from which it appears that the best that can be done by the art of nations who have lived the Christian life for 1800 years consists in choosing as the ideal of their life the one held 2000 years ago by a half-savage, slave-holding little people, which imitated very well the nakedness of the human body and erected buildings pleasant to look at."*

* *What is Art?*, ch. 7. Tolstoy himself had once believed in this triad: see p. 102, above.

But the members of this triad are in no way coordinate:

The good is the eternal, highest aim of our life. However we may understand the good, our life is nothing else than a striving towards the good, that is, towards God. . . .

But beauty, if we do not content ourselves with words, but speak of what we understand, beauty is nothing else than what pleases us.

The concept of beauty not only does not coincide with the good, but rather is opposed to it, since the good generally coincides with victory over our inclinations, while beauty is the foundation of all our inclinations. The more we give ourselves up to beauty, the more we withdraw from the good. . . .

By truth we mean only the correspondence of the expression or definition of an object with its essence, or with the general understanding of an object common to all men. What is there in common between the concepts of beauty and truth on the one hand and that of good on the other ? . . . Truth . . . is one of the means for the attainment of the good, but in itself truth is neither the good, nor beauty, and does not even coincide with them.—[Ch. 7.]

In these pages Tolstoy reiterates the aversion to modern tendencies in science and art that he had already expressed in *What Shall We Do Then?* Science and art in themselves he never rejected, exclaiming fervently:

I not only do not deny science, that is, the rational activity of man, and art, the expression of that rational activity; but only in the name of that rational activity and its expressions do I say what I say; only in order that there may be a possibility for humanity to emerge from the savage condition into which it is swiftly falling, thanks to the false teaching of our time—only for this do I say what I say.

Science and art are as necessary for men as food and drink and clothing, even more necessary. . . .

[True] science has always had as its subject the knowledge of what is the mission, and therefore the true good, of each man and of all men. . . .

Ever since men have existed, true art, that which has been highly prized by men, has had no other meaning than the expression of the mission and the good of man.

Always and up to the latest times art has served the teaching of life, what was later termed religion, and only then was it what men prized so highly. But at the same time that into the place of the science of the mission and the good of men there stepped a science about anything one happens to think of—from the time that science lost its sense and meaning, and men began contemptuously to give the name religion to genuine science—from that time on art also vanished as an important activity of man.—[*What Shall We Do Then?*, ch. 36.]

That is to say, science has abandoned the care of man's spiritual welfare in order to devote itself to his bodily comfort. Hence the useless truth of modern science is even detrimental to right living. This rejection has been already discussed (pp. 276, 277). Now Tolstoy states with equal fervor his rejection of modern art: he who in his earlier life had been in raptures over the beauty of Greek literature, above all of the pagan Homer (see pp. 68, 140; cf. p. 353); he who so loved flowers, which are

the natural emblems of something else than Christian
asceticism! Since the later pages of his book are in
part deductions from the principles that have been set
forth, we may pause for a moment to examine those
principles.

In his connection of art with religion, Tolstoy is
absolutely sound, if one accepts his definition of religion.
For him religion is not a system of dogmas, promulgated
from a supernatural source and upheld by a hieratic
organization; it is the life conception of each individual
man, the complex of fundamental ideas which each
man, whether consciously or unconsciously, holds as to
himself and his relations to his fellow men and to the
general world order, and by which he regulates his
conduct. When Tolstoy says that a man lacks religion,
he means that he has no true religion; that he is a
pagan, guided by the lusts of the flesh, that his religion is that of the animal personality, not that of the
rational personality, to adopt the language of his book,
On Life. Now, since each man's art, or enjoyment of
other men's art, expresses his personality, it must be religious in this broad sense of the term. All art is religious
in embodying a certain life conception, true or false,
high or low. Hence no man can possibly condemn art
in itself; he condemns merely the art of men who hold
another life conception than his own. Plato, when he
banished poets from his ideal republic, did not likewise banish philosophers, who were, in his day at least,
equally artists; he banished merely a degraded form of

art, a lower beauty in order to preserve a higher. A truly consistent Puritan would find the rigid lines and the aspiring wooden steeple of a Massachusetts meeting-house more lovely than the gorgeous mundane beauty of the Doges' Palace; if he does not do so, he shows that a spark of the fleshly Adam remains within him. So Tolstoy, when he says that all modern art is irreligious, means that it does not express his own type of ascetic Christian altruism. He condemns modern art, in general, on exactly the same grounds on which he condemns modern society. If, though we reject Tolstoy's ethics, we find much inspiration in his criticism of modern society, so we may find much that is admirable in his critique of modern art. He is on the other side of the golden mean (a term that he would despise) from most modern tendencies. But his departure from that mean is more strident in his criticism of art than in his social criticism. For a man's art, more frequently than his social activity—and with good reason—tends to be an expression of his unascetic, unaltruistic enjoyment of life, and to appeal to the same instincts in other men.

The first consequence of the irreligious quality of modern art, Tolstoy continues, is that it has become exclusive, the property of a small circle of men, the irreligious, idle upper classes, and is incomprehensible to the masses of toiling humanity. One may at once query whether the Sunday newspapers and cheap magazines that furnish reading matter to the toiling masses of the United States are more religious in any sense of the term than literature of a more exclusive type; whether the moving-picture shows are more religious than the Metropolitan Art Museum—but we must let Tolstoy state his case without interrupting him at every turn. This exclusive art, he proceeds to say, has become (1) impoverished in content, (2) artificial and obscure, without beauty of form, which is synonymous with clearness, and (3) insincere and affected.

The classes for whom modern art is created crave only enjoyment. Their feelings may be reduced to three: (a) pride, (b) sexual impulse, and (c) the weariness of life. To these, and above all to the second, modern art must pander. It has become affected with an erotic mania.

The life of a laboring man with his endlessly various forms of toil and the dangers connected with them on the sea and under the earth, with his journeys, with his association with employers, bosses, comrades, with men of other faiths and nationalities; with his struggle with nature and wild animals, with his relations to domestic animals; with his labors in the forest, on the prairie, in the field, orchard, and garden; with his relations to his wife and children, not only as near and dear persons, but as co-workers, aiders and substitutes in toil; with his relations to all economic questions, not as subjects for ratiocination or vanity, but as questions of life for himself and his family; with his pride of self-contentment and service to men; with his joys of repose; with all these interests penetrated by a religious relation to these phenomena— to us, who have not these interests and have no religious understanding, to us this life seems monotonous in comparison with those little pleasures and insignificant cares of our life, not of toil and not of creation, but of employment and destruction of what others have done for us.—[*What is Art?*, ch. 9.]

In the second place, art destined only for a class strives to develop a peculiar means of expression, comprehensible only to the initiated. It becomes obscure, hazy, mystical, symbolic, expressing itself only by hints. The most striking examples of this are the French decadent poets, Verlaine and his school. Their works are incomprehensible to Tolstoy and his fellows, trained in the habits of the first half of the nineteenth century. But similarly, Tolstoy continues, the artists whom his own contemporaries have learned to prize are unintelligible to the mass of humanity. Laborers and many who are not laborers can make nothing of Goethe, Schiller, Hugo, Dickens, Beethoven, Chopin, Raphael, Michelangelo, or Leonardo da Vinci.

Becoming constantly poorer in content and more obscure in form, modern art has finally ceased even to be sincere; it has ceased to be real art and has become only the imitation of art:

Universal art arises only when some man of the people, having experienced a strong feeling, has the need of communicating it to men. But the art of the rich arises not because of the artist's need for it, but mainly because men of the higher classes require amusements, for which they give large rewards. The men of the rich classes require from art the transfer of feelings pleasant to them, and the artists try to satisfy these requirements. But to satisfy these requirements is very hard, since men of the rich classes, passing their lives in idleness and luxury, require unceasing amusements from art; but art even of the very lowest order cannot be produced at will: it must be born in the artist of its own accord. And therefore artists, in order to satisfy the demands of men of the higher classes, have been obliged to develop methods by means of which they might produce objects similar to art. And these methods have been developed. They are the following: (1) borrowing, (2) imitation, (3) strikingness, (4) entertainingness.

The first method consists in borrowing from former productions of art either whole subjects or only separate traits of former poetic productions that are known to every one, and in working them over in such a way that with some additions they present something new. . . . Thus in our circle legends, sagas, old traditions of all sorts are regarded as poetic subjects. Maidens, warriors, shepherds, hermits, angels, devils in all forms, moonlight, thunderstorms, mountains, the sea, precipices, flowers, long hair, lions, a lamb, a dove, a nightingale, are regarded as poetic persons and objects. . . .

The essence of the second method consists in reproducing the details that accompany what is described or represented. In the literary art this method consists in describing to the smallest details the external form, the faces, the clothes, the gestures, the sounds, the habitations of the actors, with all the accidental circumstances that are met with in life. . . .

The third method is an action on the external feelings, an action often of a quite physical sort—what is called strikingness or effectiveness.   These effects in all the arts consist mainly in contrasts: in the juxtaposition of the awful and the tender, the beautiful and the ugly, the loud and the soft, the dark and the bright, the most ordinary and the most unusual. . . .

The fourth method is entertainingness, that is, an intellectual interest joined to a production of art. Entertainingness may consist in a complicated plot, a method which no long time ago was much employed in English novels and in French comedies and dramas, but has now begun to go out of fashion, and has been replaced by documentality, that is, by a cir- cumstantial description either of some historic period or of some separate branch of contemporary life. Thus for instance entertainingness consists in describing in a novel Egyptian or Roman life, or the life of miners, or of clerks in a large shop; and the reader is interested and takes this interest for an artistic impression.—[*What Is Art?*, ch. 11.]

Of all these methods Tolstoy gives copious examples, condemning in the process most of modern art, such as that of Ibsen, Maeterlinck, Puvis de Chavannes, Brahms, and above all Wagner, to whom he devotes a most entertaining tirade.

Leaving out of account the question of the subject matter of art, true art is distinguished from false art by its infectiousness, by the degree to which it affects the feelings of all men:

The stronger the infection, the better is the art as art, leaving out of account the subject matter—that is, independ- ently of the worth of the feelings that the art transfers.

Art becomes more or less infectious in consequence of three conditions: (1) in consequence of the greater or less individuality of the feeling that is transferred; (2) in consequence of the greater or less clearness of the transfer of that feeling; (3) in consequence of the sincerity of the artist, that is, the greater or less force with which the artist himself experiences the feeling that he transfers.—[Ch. 15.]

Quite aside from these universal artistic conditions, the subject matter of art changes as mankind advances in spiritual vision. At present all true art must transfer not pagan feelings, but Christian feelings, the love of God and the love of one's neighbor:

Christian art either arouses in men those feelings that through love of God and of one's neighbor draw them to ever greater and greater unity, and so makes them ready and capable of that unity; or else it arouses in them those feelings that show them that they are already united by a unity of life's joys and sorrows. And therefore, the Christian art of our time may be and is of two sorts: (1) art that transfers feelings that flow from the religious consciousness of the position of man in the world, in relation to God and to his neighbor—religious art, and (2) art transferring the most simple feelings of life, but such as are accessible to all men of all the world—the art of common life, of a whole nation, of all the world. Only these two species of art may be regarded as good art in our time.—[Ch. 16.]

As examples of the first type of art, religious art, in modern times, Tolstoy cites Hugo's *Les Misérables*, Dickens' novels, especially *A Tale of Two Cities* and *The*

Chimes, *Uncle Tom's Cabin*, *Adam Bede*, and Dostoyevsky's works, especially his *House of the Dead*.
He cannot cite modern literary works of the second
type, universal art. Even Molière's comedies, *Don
Quixote*, *David Copperfield*, and some works of Maupassant, which approach this type, are spoiled by the exclusiveness of the feelings transferred, by an excess of
special details of time and place, and by poverty of
content. The great model of this type of art is the
biblical story of Joseph and his Brethren.

Such, in brief, is the content of Tolstoy's book on art,
which, despite its shortcomings, may be pronounced
the most stimulating critical work of our time, perhaps
of all modern times. Tolstoy's *definition* of art is emotionalistic, and, quite properly, has nothing to do with
morals. In *estimating* works of art, however, he has two
criteria, the first emotionalistic, relating to the infectious
quality of the work considered; the second moralistic,
relating to its subject matter. It is obvious that he is
still actuated by the same impulses that in 1862 made
him condemn Beethoven and Pushkin because they are
unintelligible to Russian peasants.* Now, however, he
has added to his demand for universal art a demand for
an art that shall express the Christian doctrines of self-
sacrifice and love.

Tolstoy's different criteria cannot be applied separately; the emotionalistic and the moralistic must be
mingled. Infectiousness is not an adequate test of art;

* Compare p. 119, above.

a well-simulated laugh or shout of pain will convey emotion to a baby or an idiot for whom the tale of Joseph and his Brethren will be unintelligible. Again, a clever smutty story, a tavern jest passed about by vulgar boys, unfortunately appeals to as universal human emotions as the story of Joseph. Thus the two classes of good art may be at times opposed to each other. *Adam Bede* and *A Tale of Two Cities*, Tolstoy must admit, are clogged with an excess of transient details that make them exclusive rather than universal art. One is amazed that Tolstoy has not cited the parable of the Prodigal Son, which belongs to both his classes of good art.

Finally, if Tolstoy's ethical system is narrow and limited, as we have tried to show, then the art criticism based on it may be equally narrow and limited. Works of art conveying the emotions of power and beauty, the *Iliad* and the *Song of the Nibelungs*, *Macbeth* and *Paradise Lost*, may be as worthy of admiration as *Uncle Tom's Cabin*. They may even become universal art in Tolstoy's sense of the term; the story of the *Iliad* has appealed to successive generations of American boys, and *Paradise Lost* in a prose translation is one of the favorite books of the Russian common people. If modern society must be fundamentally transformed, as Tolstoy argues in *What Shall We Do Then?*, then its art must be similarly uprooted. But if society is capable of reform without change in its inmost characteristics, then its art may be similarly lopped and pruned rather than cut out root and branch. In his crusade against art that is really immoral Tolstoy has attacked art that merely fails to conform to his own special type of ascetic and altruistic morality. Power and beauty may retain a place in the world along with self-sacrifice and love of one's neighbor.

Then what value remains in Tolstoy's doctrine? One may reply at once that, just as his teaching of the moral purpose of art contains a fundamental truth, though his conception of morality is limited, so his theory of the universality of true art contains a kernel, or more than a kernel, of truth. China dolls, which Tolstoy correctly classes as objects of universal art, are not so lovely as the Venus of Milo, but only fanatics would care to have all dolls destroyed forever and the beautiful Venus preserved at that price. Folk songs may not be on the same esthetic plane as Beethoven's symphonies, but we should have no hesitation which to sacrifice. We may go still further and say that one would gladly part with all artistic fiction, from *Daphnis and Chloe* to Anatole France, if that were the sole condition on which folk tales like that of Joseph and his Brethren might be preserved. But fortunately no such alternatives will ever be presented to mankind; china dolls and the Venus of Milo live at peace together.

Furthermore, we recognize in the songs of Burns, with their universal appeal, a higher artistic quality than in the lyrics of Swinburne. The general human interest of the first adds to their artistic value. *Robinson Crusoe, The Pilgrim's Progress,* and *Tom Sawyer* won popular success before their merits were admitted by professional critics.

Still further, all eccentric, extravagant writers, such as Lyly, Marini or Góngora, who through certain affectations appealed to a small literary set, have become mere objects of historic study, while Chaucer, Molière, and Cervantes give delight to successive generations. Shakespeare lives by his appeal to fundamental human emotions, not by his whimsicality of style in *Love's Labor's Lost.*

Yet, despite Tolstoy, we must admit that a certain cultivation, a training of the taste, is required for the appreciation of some really great authors, such, notably, as Dante, whom Tolstoy condemns as "exclusive" (ch. 16), or even classes among writers of productions that are "coarse, savage, and for us almost senseless" (ch. 12). But that cultivation must be such as does not stifle fundamental human feelings. The qualities that make Dante's thought valuable are those of our common humanity; he is a man whole and well-proportioned. To understand him we have to take pains in order to overcome certain external obstacles, but we are rewarded. Only a special student will make similar efforts to comprehend the whimsicalities of Donne and Cowley. An admirer of Swinburne is obliged to acknowledge his shortcomings; he rightly admires his beauty of line, but confesses that to appreciate him one must lay aside for the moment intellectual and moral criteria and give himself up to purely sensuous enjoyment.

In discussing critical principles in *What is Art?* Tolstoy as a rule does not generalize from his own practice. Tolstoy the moralist is now speaking, not Tolstoy the master of realistic fiction. By his attack on *imitation* he condemns the very method of which he was the unrivaled master. His passion for simplicity now makes him worship the unadorned narrative of the folk tale. Work approaching this type he had done himself, and from his own labors—most of which he classes as bad art—he singles out for praise the stories *God Sees the Truth* and *The Prisoner of the Caucasus.** Fine as those stories are in their own kind, one may rejoice that he rescued and completed the manuscript of *Resurrection.* One should add, in his justification, that he himself always used *imitation* as an aid in the transfer of emotion. A bit of his conversation on this point is more enlightening than his drastic condemnation of imitation in *What is Art?*

No trifle can be neglected in art, because sometimes a half-torn-off button may light up a certain side of the life of a given person. And the button must be pictured without fail. But all one's efforts, and even the half-torn-off button, must be directed exclusively to the inner essence of the matter, and not distract the attention from what is central and important to details and trifles, as continually happens. Some contemporary writer, describing the adventure of Joseph with Potiphar's wife, would be sure to seize the chance of showing

* Included in his *Third* and *Fourth Readers* (see p. 88); the second must not be confused with Pushkin's poem of the same title (see p. 50)

off his knowledge of life, and would write: " ' Come unto me,' languidly uttered the wife of Potiphar, stretching out to Joseph her hand, tender from aromatic ointments, with such and such accessories," and so forth. And all these details would not only not light up more brightly the essence of the matter, but would inevitably make it dim.—[Sergéyenko: *How Count Tolstoy Lives and Works* (Moscow, 1898), p. 65.]

On the other hand, in his condemnation of *borrowing*, *strikingness*, and *entertainingness*, Tolstoy utters principles that relate more to his own practice than to his moral system. For it is hard to see any discrepancy between "borrowing" such as Tolstoy censures and either universality or the Christian ideal of love expressed in art, such as he advocates. It is in his own moral tales, which are really those least congenial to his creative impulse, that Tolstoy is most apt to borrow. Here he uses "hermits, angels, and devils," borrowed from previous stories and "regarded as poetic persons." In his novels he had depended on life itself, not on such conventional accessories. Similarly he had scorned to decorate *War and Peace* with "entertaining" details of a by-gone time such as furnish half the charm of *Ivanhoe*. Accepting Tolstoy's own definition of art, why should not a writer who feels the picturesqueness of a medieval tournament seek to infect others with that feeling? In reply Tolstoy might assert that such trifles have no meaning for a man with the Christian ideal of life. But as a matter of fact he had scorned such ornaments long before his moral ideal became fixed. So it is with *strikingness*, obvious rhetorical devices of antithesis and exaggeration. These the young Tolstoy had disliked so much that Turgenev had written of him in 1862: "The fear of phrases has driven Tolstoy into the most desperate phrases."

The inmost convictions of Tolstoy the artist appear when he pronounces the central qualities of truly infectious art to be *individuality*, *clearness*, and *sincerity*. What he means by these terms he makes more plain in his notable *Preface to the Works of Guy de Maupassant* (1894).

Maupassant, Tolstoy tells us, "possessed that special gift called talent, which consists in the capacity of intense, concentrated attention directed on some object or other, according to the tastes of the author, whereby a man gifted with that capacity sees in the objects on which he directs his attention something new, something that others do not see." This is obviously artistic individuality. Clearness also Maupassant possessed, and clearness, Tolstoy here tells us, is synonymous with beauty of form.

In this dictum an essential characteristic, and an essential weakness, of Tolstoy the artist is made plain. To refute the statement that beauty is synonymous with clearness is hardly worth while; the matter is a commonplace of our rhetorics. "Your father lies in water five fathoms deep; his bones have turned

into coral and his eyes into pearls," is no less clear
than:

> Full fathom five thy father lies;
>   Of his bones are coral made;
> Those are pearls that were his eyes.

But there is a decided difference in the beauty of form of
the two passages! Tolstoy might reply with justice that,
though the first passage conveys information even more
clearly than the second, the second is clearer in the
transference of emotion. But there is nothing in his
writings to hint at such a retort, and much that points
in the contrary direction. Tolstoy once expressed regret,
for example, that Matthew Arnold had not written in
prose such poems as *Rugby Chapel* and *Self-dependence.*[*]
He himself made almost no attempts at the writing of
serious verse. More than this, though he revised his
works of fiction with the minutest care, he seems never
to have striven for music of style, for beauty of language
as distinguished from beauty of substance. He strives
to render clearly the joy of Levin or of Nikoláy Rostóv in
the sunlight and the fresh air, but, like the men whom
he is describing, he never drops into poetic phrases.
Hence Tolstoy, of all the greatest literary masters,
suffers least in translation. To render him well an exact
knowledge of Russian is required, and a vigorous, supple
command of English, but no exceptional power of suggestive expression.

* Maude: *Tolstoy and his Problems*, p. 193; compare pp. 21, 22, above.

Tolstoy's passion for clearness of expression is the key to his attitude towards music. Of music he was passionately fond; yet in his later years, as he makes plain in *The Kreutzer Sonata*, he seems to have absolutely feared its influence. For music arouses the emotions without giving them a definite direction towards either good or evil.

Sincerity also Maupassant possessed, "an unfeigned feeling of love or hatred to what the artist represents." But Maupassant lacked any firm moral point of view, so that much of his work, despite the talent shown in it, is vicious and untrue to life's real meaning. He was apt to regard men and women as animals, controlled only by greed and sex impulse. His work, admirable on the side of artistic method, transfers feelings that are base and ignoble. No bit of criticism is more impressive than Tolstoy's lecture to Maupassant on this theme; the greatest of realists rebukes a craftsman who hid his lack of soul by his mastery of technique.

Of another sort is Tolstoy's celebrated attack on Shakespeare, in his essay, *On Shakespeare and the Drama* (1906), in which he stigmatizes Shakespeare as "an insignificant, inartistic author, not only not moral, but directly immoral" (ch. 8). In judging this essay one must allow for Tolstoy's vein of contradiction; he once confessed to his wife: "I should involuntarily loathe a man of whom they talked so much rubbish [as myself]."* The essay is, further, an old man's work, lacking the vigor

* *Letters to Wife*, p. 560.

and cogency of his earlier pieces, and it was written without adequate knowledge of the subject, with some misstatements of fact. And yet, after making all these allowances, it is a critical utterance worthy of great respect. Tolstoy points out real defects in Shakespeare and admits real excellences; his divergence from sounder critics is in his comparative estimate of those defects and excellences.

Tolstoy's primary charge against Shakespeare is that he lacked any religious view of life. This is true and just; we admire Shakespeare for his "cloudless, boundless human view," not for any underlying unity of view as to man and his problems such as is found in many lesser authors, let us say in Milton and in Bunyan. Shakespeare, in Emerson's phrase, was "master of the revels to mankind"; he suggests queries as to all manner of human relations, but on the fundamental problem of human destiny, as to man's mission here on earth and his relation to the infinite, the question that would not let Tolstoy rest, he is silent. This radical difference in temperament blinds Tolstoy as to the glory of Shakespeare's unreligious art. One may remark, and Tolstoy might sadly admit the justice of the charge, that it would be possible to make a cento of passages from *War and Peace* that would give a Shakespearian impression of unthinking delight in the world of men here on earth. Shakespeare had but one side, that of contemplation of the world as it is, while to this Tolstoy added spiritual enthusiasm for making it a better world. The creator of Stiva Oblonsky is repelled by Falstaff, but then on occasion he would be repelled by his own creation as well.

Tolstoy also denies Shakespeare "external beauty, attained by a technique proper to a certain type of art. Thus, in dramatic art the technique will be: a truthful style, corresponding to the characters of the persons; a natural and at the same time touching plot; a regular conduct of the scenes; manifestation and development of feeling; and a feeling of measure in all that is represented" (ch. 6). On the other hand he grants to Shakespeare the ability to express the play of emotions in individual scenes:

That a great mastery in the representation of characters is ascribed to Shakespeare proceeds from the fact that Shakespeare really has a peculiarity that on superficial observation, taken in connection with the play of good actors, may appear an ability to represent characters. This peculiarity consists in the ability to conduct scenes in which the movement of feelings is expressed. However unnatural are the positions in which he places his persons, however unsuited to them is the language which he makes them speak, however characterless they are, the very movement of feeling, the increase in it, the change of it, the combination of many contradictory feelings are often expressed truly and strongly in some scenes of Shakespeare. And in the play of good actors this arouses at least for a certain time sympathy with the persons taking part in them.

Shakespeare, himself an actor and a clever man, knew how to represent, not only by speeches, but by exclamations, gestures, repetitions of words, the spiritual states and the changes of feeling that occur in the persons taking part. Thus in many places the persons of Shakespeare, instead of using words, merely exclaim or weep, or in the midst of a monologue often show by gestures the sadness of their condition (thus Lear asks to have his button undone), or in a moment of strong agitation ask the same question several times over and make persons repeat the word that particularly strikes them, as Othello, Macduff, Cleopatra, and others. Such clever methods of representing the movement of feelings, by giving good actors an opportunity to show their strength, have often been mistaken and are still mistaken by many critics for the representation of character. But however strongly the movement of feeling may be represented in one scene, one scene cannot give the character of a person, when that person after a truthful exclamation or gesture begins at great length, not in his own language, but according to the caprice of the author, to utter speeches that are totally useless and do not correspond to his character.—[*On Shakespeare*, ch. 4.]

Tolstoy seems further to admit that many of the speeches and aphorisms in Shakespeare, though not deep or original, and though inappropriate to the persons uttering them, are in themselves impressive.

In all this Tolstoy is condemning Shakespeare because he is not a realist and psychologist of Tolstoy's own school, because he is a romantic writer who used technical methods which were popular in his own time, and which, if general experience be of any weight, have not lost their appeal today. Tolstoy is in accord with some modern critics who, whether we agree with them or not, cannot be stigmatized as ignorant and superficial;

who, in fact, condemn with perfect justice the effort to discover in Shakespeare all the technical qualities that we prize in dramatists of our own time.* Shakespeare often neglected consistency of character, not to speak of realistic truth of diction, in his search for poetic ornament or for immediate dramatic effect. Goethe, whom Tolstoy incorrectly terms the founder of Shakespeare's present fame, makes a remark that is exactly in Tolstoy's own tone: "He regarded his plays as a lively and changing scene which should pass rapidly before eye and ear, and his only interest was to be effective and significant for the moment."†

Finally, Tolstoy denies to Shakespeare *sincerity*, a vivid sympathy by the author with that which he represents. "In all his works one sees calculated artificiality; it is evident that he is not 'in earnest,' that he is playing with words" (ch. 6). Here, despite the conceits of *Love's Labor's Lost* and *Romeo and Juliet*, one must definitely part company with Tolstoy. This is a personal opinion, founded partly on minor defects in Shakespeare's style, but more on Tolstoy's own repugnance for his lack of the religious point of view.

Tolstoy further repeats the old denunciations of

---

* One may cite, for example, Professor E. E. Stoll, particularly his *Othello, an Historical and Comparative Study* (Minneapolis, *Bulletin of the University of Minnesota*, 1915). From a thorough study of Elizabethan dramatic art he draws conclusions as to Shakespeare's technical methods, though not as to his general worth as a poet and an artist, strikingly similar to those of Tolstoy. Mr. Shaw's attacks on Shakespeare also offer parallels to Tolstoy.

† *Conversations with Eckermann*, quoted by Stoll, *Othello*, p. 57.

Shakespeare for his anachronisms, for his coarseness and exaggeration, and for the conventionality of his borrowed plots. He denies that these demerits of Shakespeare were due merely to the age in which he lived:

However far Homer may be from us, we transfer ourselves without the slightest effort into the life that he describes. And we transfer ourselves, mainly, because, however strange to us are the events that Homer describes, he believes in what he is saying, and speaks seriously about what he is saying, and therefore never exaggerates, and the feeling of measure never deserts him. Hence it comes that, not to speak of the marvelously clear, living, and beautiful characters of Achilles, Hector, Priam, and Odysseus, and the forever touching scenes of the farewell of Hector, the embassy of Priam, the return of Odysseus and others, the whole *Iliad*, and still more the *Odyssey*, are as naturally near to us as though we ourselves had lived and were living amid gods and heroes. It is not so with Shakespeare. From his very first words one sees exaggeration: exaggeration of events, exaggeration of feelings, and exaggeration of expressions. One sees at once that he does not believe in what he is saying, that he does not care for it, that he is thinking up the events that he is describing, and is indifferent to his own persons; that he has devised them only for the stage, and therefore makes them act and speak only what may impress his public; and therefore we do not believe either in the events, or in the acts or in the miseries of his characters. Nothing shows so clearly the complete absence of esthetic feeling in Shakespeare as the comparison of him with Homer. The works that we call the works of Homer are artistic, poetic, original works that were lived through by the author or authors.

But the works of Shakespeare, being borrowed compositions, thought up for an occasion, glued together externally and artificially, out of little pieces, like a mosaic, have nothing in common with art and poetry.—[*On Shakespeare*, ch. 5.]

Here speaks the apostle of simplicity as well as the master of modern realism. On both sides of his genius, the artistic and the religious, Tolstoy was temperamentally alien to Shakespeare. His essay is valuable as a stimulus to thought, but not as a guide to a just estimate of Shakespeare.

CHAPTER X

CONCLUSION

EARLY in the morning of November **10, 1910,** Tolstoy left his home forever, accompanied by his friend and physician Dr. Makovitsky. His departure was caused by his gnawing dissatisfaction with the conflict between his faith and surroundings, and in particular by the clash of his own ideals with those of his wife. For his future life he apparently had no definite plan; he wished merely to get away. To his wife he wrote a last message:

My departure will grieve you. I am sorry for this, but pray understand and believe that I could not act otherwise. My position in the house is becoming unbearable. I can no longer live amid those conditions of luxury in which I have been living; and I am doing what old men of my age usually do. They retire from the life of the world in order to live in solitude and quiet the last days of their lives. Please understand this and do not follow me if you learn where I am. Your coming will not change my resolution. I thank you for your honorable life of forty-eight years with me, and I beg you to forgive me for all the wrong that I may have done you, just as I with my whole soul pardon you for whatever wrong you may have done me. I counsel you to be reconciled to the new position in which my departure places you, and not to have any unkind feelings for me.—[Ksyunin: *The Departure of Tolstoy*, pp. 22, 23.]

Tolstoy's first night away from home was spent at the Optin Monastery, a place with which he was familiar from his previous visits there (see pages 285, 286); on the next day he visited his sister in the convent at Shámordino, where he was joined on November 12 by his daughter Alexandra, to whom he had confided his intention of flight. The next day he left for a further journey, with his daughter and Dr. Makovitsky, but he was taken ill on the train, and was forced to stop at Astápovo, a little wayside station, where the kindly station-master lodged him in his own quarters. Here he was soon joined by Chertkóv and other friends and by various members of his family. His wife came at once to Astápovo, but respected his desire not to see her; she did not enter his room until after his death. "If she comes here," Tolstoy told Chertkóv with tears, "I shall be unable to refuse her; but if I see her, it will be ruinous for me"—evidently meaning that he should not have the strength to resist her plea that he return to the old home surroundings. The sick man's strength rapidly failed. His preoccupation with religious questions continued to the last; to his daughter Alexandra he dictated, for his diary, some last *Thoughts on God*. A few days before he died he charged his daughter Tatyana to think of all humanity rather than of her father alone. "I have but one bit of counsel for you," he said, "to remember that in this world there are many men besides Leo Tolstoy; but you look at none but Leo."* He died early on the morning of November 20. His body was taken home, and was buried, according to his wishes, without religious ceremonies or addresses, on the spot in his estate where he had requested that it should rest. The heartfelt emotion of the throng assembled by the grave and their singing of "Eternal Memory" were the best tributes that could have been rendered to the departed prophet.

Tolstoy has been given a place in this series of volumes beside Homer, Virgil, Dante, Shakespeare, Cervantes, Molière, and Goethe, as a Master Spirit of Literature. Whether his name will remain permanently associated with that great company it is impossible to be sure. But of two things at least one may feel perfectly certain: that he is the master spirit among all writers whom Russia has yet produced, and that he is the master spirit among all the writers of the world since the time of Goethe.

In Russia Tolstoy's position is secure, despite voices that nowadays tend to depreciate him in favor of the morbid Dostoyevsky. Such eccentric opinions seem mere whining protests against the almost crushing fame of Tolstoy. Moreover, Tolstoy is not only the greatest writer of Russia, but the writer most typical of Russian society as it had shaped itself in the three

* Chertkóv: *The Last Days of L. N. Tolstoy*, pp. 12–14.

hundred years between the establishment of serfdom at
the end of the sixteenth century and the beginnings of
the industrial and political revolution in our own time.
Tolstoy is, to borrow a phrase that Dostoyevsky applied
with some tinge of scorn to him and to Turgenev,*
a writer of "landed-proprietor's literature"—though his
scope is far wider than the term at first suggests. He
draws the life of Russian aristocrats in their fields, in
their country manors, in their city homes, in the army;
he draws with equal insight the life of the peasants
on whom they depended for their support. He knew
the hidden souls of both aristocrat and peasant as well
as their outer lives. He is the embodiment of the
kindliness and the loyalty, the emotional honesty of
the Russian nature, and at the same time of its passionate
individuality, its revolutionary boldness. With the
pride of the aristocrat he united the moral fervor of the
peasant sectarian. Through his work Russia of the
nineteenth century received lasting artistic expression of
its external forms of life and of its spiritual yearnings.

And among other great writers of our time what man
can compare with Tolstoy in universal fame? If a
Frenchman exalts Victor Hugo or a Pole Sienkiewicz,
the world feels that they are prompted by patriotic
affection rather than by sober reason. Yet we are perhaps so close to Tolstoy, so much under the immediate
appeal of his artistic genius, his moral fervor, and his
brotherly personality, that we cannot judge with perfect

* Letter to Strakhov, May 18 [30], 1871.

impartiality whether three hundred years hence he will
occupy a place like that of Shakespeare or Cervantes in
our own day.

Certainly if realistic fiction retains its hold upon men's
minds Tolstoy's glory will not soon fade away. For his
fiction has already triumphed over place, if not over
time, as has none other before it. Writing in a language
scarcely known outside his own country, he has created
men and women who have become brothers and sisters
to all humanity. Reading *War and Peace* and *Anna
Karenin*, we forget the bounds of nationality in our
sympathetic understanding of the human beings whose
lives we share. These novels, critics tell us, are lacking
in form; "he wanted art," as men said of Shakespeare.
But the genius of the author triumphed over his neglect
of formal rules, which are at best but general statements
of literary method, useful in many cases but not binding
on a man who can gain his effects without them. In
Tolstoy the interpretation of our daily life reached new
heights. In his works men and women are lovely without ceasing to be commonplace, and they are commonplace without ceasing to be lovely. They are lovely because their creator, to use his own beautiful phrase,
"saw through with love" (page 159). His art had none
of the esthetic aloofness that parts an artist from his kind;
it was an art that made the proud aristocrat a brother to
the whole world.

Nor does mere artistic sympathy exhaust Tolstoy's
power as a student of character. He has also the *saeva*

indignatio, the burning indignation of a Swift. *The Kreutzer Sonata*, *The Death of Iván Ilyich*, and *The Power of Darkness* will ever retain a place in the literature of rebuke and scorn.

When we turn from Tolstoy the master of realistic fiction to Tolstoy the moralist and the preacher, we are on ground where prophecy may be more hazardous. His writings on ethical and social questions will live, we may be sure, if they do live, not as a rounded presentation of ultimate truth, but as the revelation of a powerful personality and of a unified and noble view of human conduct. Great religious classics do not derive their value solely from the ethical truth that they contain, but from the fervor with which they present certain aspects of human conduct, and from the artistic, poetic form in which they may be clothed. Bunyan's *Grace Abounding* has become a classic of religious autobiography, read by men who have no sympathy whatever with the theory of salvation on which it is based. So Tolstoy's *Confession*, that cry of a soul in agony, that voice of a searcher after God, with its concentrated, ardent expression of human experience, may outlast *War and Peace* in the memory of mankind. Plato's *Republic* embodies a philosophy in which few men now believe, but it has more readers and is perhaps a more potent influence than Aristotle's *Ethics*, the doctrine of which is never likely to be superseded. *The Imitation of Christ* and the *Meditations* of Marcus Aurelius appeal to men who are not likely ever to become monks or

Stoics. The Christian Gospels have never lost their inspiration for generations of men who, consciously or unconsciously, reject them as a guide of life. So *My Religion* and *What Shall We Do Then?* may continue to have readers and admirers, may continue to stimulate thought in men for whom Tolstoy's gospel of Christian anarchy, founded on non-resistance to evil by violence, is an absurdity.

An objector may say that Tolstoy's religious works would be far less read were it not for his fame as a novelist. In this charge, owing to the frailty of human nature, which loves to be amused rather than instructed or made to think, there is some truth, but truth that is of small importance. It is more important to remember that Tolstoy's artistic genius filled with life his religious works, lending force to doctrine that otherwise expressed might seem either "staled by frequence, shrunk by usage," or else so extravagant as to be merely curious. And on the other hand his novels owe their greatness in no small degree to the moral insight and the moral fervor of their author. Tolstoy's work, changing in its form and complex in its subject matter, is animated by one rich and varied personality.

In a famous passage at the close of his essay on Shakespeare Emerson laments the failure of the great poet of England to draw from his marvelous insight into the world of men and from his appreciation of its beauty, some measure of wisdom for the guidance of his own conduct: "It must even go into the world's history that the best poet led an obscure and profane life, using his genius for the public amusement." Even so, we may add, the great poet of Germany, though he shaped his conduct by a conscious philosophy, led a life that was anything but inspiring from a moral point of view; Goethe's marvelous self-cultivation, concentrated on the development of his own powers and on his own enjoyment, was selfish and in a sense narrow. Yet in the next breath Emerson denounces the opposite failure of "priest and prophet, Israelite, German, and Swede," who "beheld the same objects" and "also saw through them that which was contained. And to what purpose? The beauty straightway vanished; they read commandments, all-excluding mountainous duty; an obligation, a sadness, as of piled mountains, fell on them, and life became ghastly, joyless, a pilgrim's progress, . . . and the heart of the seer and the heart of the listener sank in them." "It must be conceded that these are half-views of half-men," Emerson concludes—"the world still wants its poet-priest, a reconciler, who shall not trifle with Shakespeare the player, nor shall grope in graves with Swedenborg the mourner; but who shall see, speak, and act, with equal inspiration. For knowledge will brighten the sunshine; right is more beautiful than private affection; and love is compatible with universal wisdom."

Perhaps Tolstoy has done more than any other writer to unite these two views of life, the esthetic and the moralistic, although even he was far from blending them in perfect harmony. The "great writer of the Russian land" was an interpreter of conduct as well as a portrayer of it; he saw the comedy and the tragedy of human life with a marvelous impartiality approaching that of Shakespeare, but he drew them as an earnest actor in them, not as a spectator or a showman. Unlike both Shakespeare and Goethe, he became a servant of his fellow men, filled with a spirit of Christian love. To the spirit of Shakespeare he added that of Milton and of Bunyan, endeavoring to "justify the ways of God to man." He showed all men Russia as it was in his own time, he made clear to all men the spiritual realities that lay hidden behind the passing show mirrored in his writings, and he strove to shape his own life in accord with those realities.

And finally, the personality of Tolstoy may remain significant, independently of the work that he achieved. The writings of some great authors are finer than the lives of the men who produced them: so it is with Shakespeare, with Molière, with Goethe, with Rousseau. On the other hand one feels that Dante was a personality even more powerful than his writings, though unluckily we know almost nothing of his daily life. But of Tolstoy, as of Milton, we know everything; and with him, as with Milton, the human personality is of even more inspiration than the literary genius. Tolstoy was the great type of the prophet in an age that was materialistic and occupied with worldly prosperity. His shortcomings and failures, one must admit, were pathetic; his compromises with his doctrine, a doctrine that was itself the antithesis of compromise, at times verged on the ludicrous. Yet, when all this is granted, he still differs from most modern religious teachers in being more eager to adapt his life to his message than are they; his imperfect strivings are nobler than their acquiescence in social conventions. Tolstoy was of the stuff of which heroes are made. Had he not lived in an age when the burning of heretics (though unfortunately not of all our fellow men) has passed out of fashion, he would have died at the stake. Under real persecution he would have been the most constant of martyrs. To the day of his death he was ever searching for new truth. He realized his own ideal of the man seeking and striving for righteousness.

And the ideal of righteousness that Tolstoy sought and found was that of a little child. When he himself was over seventy he wrote thus of his brother Nikoláy, who was six years older than himself:

He was a marvelous boy and later a marvelous man. . . . He it was who, when I was five, Mítenka six, and Serezha seven years old, announced to us that he had a secret through which, when it should be disclosed, all men. should be made happy, there should be no disease and no disagreements; no one should be angry with any one, and all people should love one another, all should become ant (*muravéynyye*) brothers—probably these were the Moravian Brethren, of whom he had heard or read, but in our language they were the ant brothers. And I remember that the term *ant brothers* was specially pleasing to me, reminding me of ants in a hill. We even devised a game of ant brothers, which consisted in seating ourselves under chairs, which we fenced about with boxes and hung with handkerchiefs, and in sitting there in the dark, snuggling close to one another. I remember that I then experienced a peculiar feeling of love and tenderness and was very fond of this game.

The ant brothers were revealed to us, but the main secret, how to cause all men to be free from any misfortune, never to quarrel or be angry, and to be continually happy—this secret, as he told us, he had written on a green stick; and he had buried this stick by the road, on the edge of a certain ravine on our estate, at the spot where, since my body must be buried somewhere, I have asked to be interred in memory of Nikólenka. . . .

The ideal of ant brothers, cleaving lovingly to one another, only not under two armchairs hung with handkerchiefs, but of all men of the world under the whole vault of heaven, has remained the same for me. And as I then believed that there existed a green stick on which was written what should destroy all evil in men and give them a great blessing, so I believe even now that this truth exists and that it will be disclosed to men and will give them what it promises.—[Biryukóv: I, 84–87, quoting from Tolstoy's manuscript reminiscences of his childhood.]

Tolstoy lies at rest in the spot where he had believed the green stick was buried that should cause all men to cease from quarreling and from anger, and should give them continued happiness.

BIBLIOGRAPHY

The first three of the following lists include such English works as seem most useful for students of Tolstoy. A few books in French are added. The fourth list is of various books in Russian that have been used in the preparation of the present volume.

1. TRANSLATIONS

WIENER.—*The Complete Works of Count Tolstoy.* Translated from the original Russian and edited by Leo Wiener. 24 vols. Boston, Estes, 1904-5. [This set includes practically all of Tolstoy's writings through the year 1902. Volumes may be obtained separately. It is the most complete translation in English, and is very accurate, but its literary style is sometimes not all that could be desired. It is invaluable for any careful study of Tolstoy. The translator's indexes, chronological table, bibliography, and account of the life and writings of Tolstoy add greatly to its usefulness.]

GARNETT.—*Anna Karenin,* translated from the Russian by Constance Garnett. London, Heinemann, 1911.—*War and Peace. Ibid.,* 1911. [For general use these are the most satisfactory translations of Tolstoy's two chief novels.]—*The Death of Iván Ilyich and Other Stories. Ibid.,* 1915.—*The Kingdom of God Is Within You. Ibid.,* 1894.

MAUDE, AYLMER.—*Hadji Murad,* translated by Aylmer Maude. New York, Dodd, 1912.—*What is Art?* New York, Crowell, 1899.

MAUDE, LOUISE.—*Resurrection,* translated by Mrs. Louise Maude. New York, Dodd, 1900.

MAUDE, LOUISE and AYLMER.—*The Cossacks and Other Tales of the Caucasus,* translated by Louise and Aylmer Maude. Oxford University Press, 1917.—*Plays: The Power of Darkness, The*

First Distiller, Fruits of Culture. New York, Funk, 1904.—*Sevastopol and Other Military Tales. Ibid.,* 1903.

HAPGOOD.—*Childhood, Boyhood, Youth,* translated from the Russian by Isabel F. Hapgood. New York, Crowell, 1911.

CHERTKÓV [TCHERTKOFF].—*Tolstoy on Shakespeare,* translated by V. Tchertkoff and I. F. M. New York, Funk, 1906.

WRIGHT (editor).—*Father Sergius and Other Stories,* edited by Dr. Hagberg Wright. New York, Dodd, 1912.—*The Forged Coupon and Other Stories. Ibid.,* 1912.—*The Light that Shines in Darkness. Ibid.,* 1912.—*The Man Who Was Dead; The Cause of It All. Ibid.,* 1912.

————*My Confession; My Religion; The Gospel in Brief.* New York, Crowell, 1911.

HOGARTH and SIRNIS.—*The Diaries of Leo Tolstoy,* translated from the Russian by C. J. Hogarth and A. Sirnis. [Vol. I.] *Youth, 1847 to 1852.* New York, Dutton, 1917. [This was received when the present work was already in type—too late to be of service. The writer has been unable to consult the Russian text of this work.]

STRUNSKY.—*The Journal of Leo Tolstoi (first volume—1895-1899),* translated from the Russian by Rose Strunsky. New York, Knopf, 1917. [The writer has been unable to consult the Russian text of this work.]

BIENSTOCK.—*Léon Tolstoï: Correspondance inédite, réunie, annotée et traduite par J. W. Bienstock.* Paris, Charpentier, 1907.

Cheap editions of *What I Believe ("My Religion"), What Shall We Do?, On Life, The Kingdom of God Is Within You,* and others of Tolstoy's religious writings have been issued by the Free Age Press, London.

2. BIOGRAPHY

PAVEL BIRYUKÓV [PAUL BIRUKOFF]: *Lev Nikoláyevich Tolstoy, a Biography.* [In Russian], 2 vols. Moscow, 1906-8; ed. 2, 1911-13. [This is the authority on Tolstoy's life up to 1884; it has not been completed. Though invaluable as a collection of materials, it is poorly digested and ill written. References in this volume are to the first Russian edition; reference is made to Biryukóv even when his sources were accessible to the writer and used by him.—

The first volume has appeared in an English translation: *Leo Tolstoy, his Life and Work;* New York, Scribner, 1906. Both volumes are accessible in French: *Léon Tolstoï; vie et œuvre, mémoires;* Paris, Mercure de France, 1906-9.]

———*The Life of Tolstoy,* translated from the Russian. New York, Cassell, 1911. [Not to be confused with the preceding. A short sketch of Tolstoy's life, mainly from the point of view of his religious teaching. The writer has been unable to consult the Russian text of this work.]

AYLMER MAUDE: *The Life of Tolstoy.* 2 vols. New York, Dodd, 1910. [This is the best English work on Tolstoy's life. The first volume is mainly a rehandling of Biryukóv's materials; the second is to a considerable degree based on personal reminiscences of Tolstoy. Cited in foot-notes as *Maude.*]

NATHAN HASKELL DOLE: *The Life of Count Lyof N. Tolstoï.* New York, Crowell, 1911. [This gives the facts as to Tolstoy's life in shorter compass than the work of Maude.]

COUNT ILYÁ TOLSTOY: *Reminiscences of Tolstoy,* by his son, Count Ilyá Tolstoy; translated by George Calderon. New York, Century, 1914. [The writer has been unable to consult the Russian text of this work.]

S. A. BEHRS: *Reminiscences of Count L. N. Tolstoy.* [In Russian], Smolensk, 1893. [Behrs was the brother of the Countess Tolstoy. There is an English translation by Charles Edward Turner, *Recollections of Count Leo Tolstoy:* London, Heinemann, 1893.]

P. SERGÉYENKO [SERGYEENKO]: *How Count L. N. Tolstoy Lives and Works.* [In Russian.] Moscow, 1898. [Accessible in an English translation by Isabel F. Hapgood: New York, Crowell, 1899.]

Accounts of Tolstoy's work during the famine of 1891-93 are given in *In the Land of Tolstoi,* by Jonas Stadling and Will Reason (London, Clarke, 1897), and in *In the Track of the Russian Famine,* by E. A. Brayley Hodgetts (London, Unwin, 1892).

Accounts of the Dukhobors and of Tolstoy's connection with them are given in *A Peculiar People, the Doukhobors,* by Aylmer Maude (New York, Funk, 1904), and *The Doukhobors,* by Joseph Elkinton (Philadelphia, Ferris, 1903).

3. CRITICISM

ROMAIN ROLLAND: *Vie de Tolstoï.* Paris, Hachette, 1911. [A wonderfully sympathetic, penetrating, and many-sided appreciation
of Tolstoy as artist and thinker. It is accessible in an English
translation by Bernard Miall: New York, Dutton, 1911.]

WILLIAM DEAN HOWELLS: *My Literary Passions.* New York, Harper,
1895. [The last chapter is a fine tribute to Tolstoy.]

D. S. MEREZHKOVSKY [MEREJKOWSKI]: *L. Tolstoy and Dostoyevsky;
Life, Work, and Religion.* [In Russian.] St. Petersburg, 1912.
(Vols. VII–IX of Merezhkovsky's *Works.*) [The first two parts
of this work are translated under the title *Tolstoi as Man and
Artist, with an Essay on Dostoïevski:* New York, Putnam, 1902.
The work, though written from an eccentric point of view, contains
brilliant criticism.]

AYLMER MAUDE: *Tolstoy and his Problems.* Ed. 2. London, Grant
Richards, 1902.

OSSIP-LOURIÉ: *La Philosophie de Tolstoï.* Paris, Alcan, 1899.

General accounts of Tolstoy's work may of course be found in all
books on modern Russian literature. Attention may be called to the
following:

E. M. DE VOGÜÉ: *Le roman russe.* Paris, Plon, 1886. [English translation by Colonel H. A. Sawyer: *The Russian Novel;* London,
Chapman, 1913.]

ERNEST DUPUY: *Les grands maîtres de la littérature russe au dix-
neuvième siècle.* Paris, Legène, 1885. [English translation by
Nathan Haskell Dole: *The Great Masters of Russian Literature in
the Nineteenth Century;* New York, Crowell, 1886.]

A. BRÜCKNER: *A Literary History of Russia,* translated [from the
German] by H. Havelock. New York, Scribner, 1908.

P. KROPOTKIN: *Russian Literature.* New York, McClure, 1905.

WILLIAM LYON PHELPS: *Essays on Russian Novelists.* New York,
Macmillan, 1911.

4. RUSSIAN SOURCES

The following titles are translated from the Russian.

Letters of Count L. N. Tolstoy to his Wife, 1862-1910. Edited by A. E.
Gruzinsky. Moscow, 1913.

Correspondence of L. N. Tolstoy with the Countess A. A. Tolstoy, 1857-1903. Published by the Society of the Tolstoy Museum. St. Petersburg, 1911.

Tolstoy Almanach. Letters of L. N. Tolstoy, 1848-1910. Collected and edited by P. A. Sergéyenko. 2 vols. Moscow, 1910-11.

A New Collection of Letters of L. N. Tolstoy. Collected by P. A. Sergéyenko, edited by A. E. Gruzinsky. Moscow, 1912.

Correspondence of L. N. Tolstoy with N. N. Strakhov. Published in *The Contemporary World*, January to December, 1913.

E. BOGOSLOVSKY: *Turgenev on Lev Tolstoy.* Tiflis, 1894.

V. F. BULGAKOV: *With L. N. Tolstoy during the Last Year of his Life.* Moscow, 1911.

V. CHERTKÓV: *On the Last Days of L. N. Tolstoy.* Moscow, 1911.

M. DRAGOMIROV: *Sketches.* Kiev, 1898. [Contains a critique on *Count Tolstoy's "War and Peace" from a Military Point of View.*]

N. KAREYEV: *The Historical Philosophy of Count L. N. Tolstoy in "War and Peace."* St. Petersburg, 1888. [Reprinted from *The Messenger of Europe*, July, 1887.]

A. KSYUNIN: *The Departure of Tolstoy.* St. Petersburg, 1911.

SERGEYÉNKO (compiler): *International Tolstoy Almanach: On Tolstoy.* Moscow, 1909. [A collection of articles by various writers.]

I. TENEROMO [FEINERMANN]: *Life and Discourses of L. N. Tolstoy.* St. Petersburg, n. d.

———*Living Words of L. N. Tolstoy.* Moscow, 1912.

INDEX

NOTE:—Specific references to Tolstoy's life, personality, literary characteristics, and teachings are grouped under the heading *Tolstoy, Count Leo (Lev Nikoláyevich)*; but references to his individual writings will be found under their titles (*Anna Karenin, War and Peace*, etc.). References to *characters in Tolstoy's novels* are gouped under that heading.

The following abbreviations are used:

An. Kar.—*Anna Karenin.*
C. B. Y.—*Childhood, Boyhood, and Youth.*
W. and P.—*War and Peace.*

A CATALOGUE OF SELECTED DOVER BOOKS
IN ALL FIELDS OF INTEREST

A CATALOGUE OF SELECTED DOVER BOOKS
IN ALL FIELDS OF INTEREST

WHAT IS SCIENCE?, *N. Campbell*
The role of experiment and measurement, the function of mathematics, the nature of scientific laws, the difference between laws and theories, the limitations of science, and many similarly provocative topics are treated clearly and without technicalities by an eminent scientist. "Still an excellent introduction to scientific philosophy," H. Margenau in *Physics Today*. "A first-rate primer . . . deserves a wide audience," *Scientific American*. 192pp. 5⅜ x 8.
Paperbound $1.25

THE NATURE OF LIGHT AND COLOUR IN THE OPEN AIR, *M. Minnaert*
Why are shadows sometimes blue, sometimes green, or other colors depending on the light and surroundings? What causes mirages? Why do multiple suns and moons appear in the sky? Professor Minnaert explains these unusual phenomena and hundreds of others in simple, easy-to-understand terms based on optical laws and the properties of light and color. No mathematics is required but artists, scientists, students, and everyone fascinated by these "tricks" of nature will find thousands of useful and amazing pieces of information. Hundreds of observational experiments are suggested which require no special equipment. 200 illustrations; 42 photos. xvi + 362pp. 5⅜ x 8.
Paperbound $2.00

THE STRANGE STORY OF THE QUANTUM, AN ACCOUNT FOR THE GENERAL READER OF THE GROWTH OF IDEAS UNDERLYING OUR PRESENT ATOMIC KNOWLEDGE, *B. Hoffmann*
Presents lucidly and expertly, with barest amount of mathematics, the problems and theories which led to modern quantum physics. Dr. Hoffmann begins with the closing years of the 19th century, when certain trifling discrepancies were noticed, and with illuminating analogies and examples takes you through the brilliant concepts of Planck, Einstein, Pauli, Broglie, Bohr, Schroedinger, Heisenberg, Dirac, Sommerfeld, Feynman, etc. This edition includes a new, long postscript carrying the story through 1958. "Of the books attempting an account of the history and contents of our modern atomic physics which have come to my attention, this is the best," H. Margenau, Yale University, in *American Journal of Physics*. 32 tables and line illustrations. Index. 275pp. 5⅜ x 8.
Paperbound $1.75

GREAT IDEAS OF MODERN MATHEMATICS: THEIR NATURE AND USE, *Jagjit Singh*
Reader with only high school math will understand main mathematical ideas of modern physics, astronomy, genetics, psychology, evolution, etc. better than many who use them as tools, but comprehend little of their basic structure. Author uses his wide knowledge of non-mathematical fields in brilliant exposition of differential equations, matrices, group theory, logic, statistics, problems of mathematical foundations, imaginary numbers, vectors, etc. Original publication. 2 appendixes. 2 indexes. 65 ills. 322pp. 5⅜ x 8.
Paperbound $2.00

THE MUSIC OF THE SPHERES: THE MATERIAL UNIVERSE — FROM ATOM TO QUASAR, SIMPLY EXPLAINED, *Guy Murchie*
Vast compendium of fact, modern concept and theory, observed and calculated data, historical background guides intelligent layman through the material universe. Brilliant exposition of earth's construction, explanations for moon's craters, atmospheric components of Venus and Mars (with data from recent fly-by's), sun spots, sequences of star birth and death, neighboring galaxies, contributions of Galileo, Tycho Brahe, Kepler, etc.; and (Vol. 2) construction of the atom (describing newly discovered sigma and xi subatomic particles), theories of sound, color and light, space and time, including relativity theory, quantum theory, wave theory, probability theory, work of Newton, Maxwell, Faraday, Einstein, de Broglie, etc. "Best presentation yet offered to the intelligent general reader," *Saturday Review*. Revised (1967). Index. 319 illustrations by the author. Total of xx + 644pp. 5⅜ x 8½.
Vol. 1 Paperbound $2.00, Vol. 2 Paperbound $2.00,
The set $4.00

FOUR LECTURES ON RELATIVITY AND SPACE, *Charles Proteus Steinmetz*
Lecture series, given by great mathematician and electrical engineer, generally considered one of the best popular-level expositions of special and general relativity theories and related questions. Steinmetz translates complex mathematical reasoning into language accessible to laymen through analogy, example and comparison. Among topics covered are relativity of motion, location, time; of mass; acceleration; 4-dimensional time-space; geometry of the gravitational field; curvature and bending of space; non-Euclidean geometry. Index. 40 illustrations. x + 142pp. 5⅜ x 8½.   Paperbound $1.35

HOW TO KNOW THE WILD FLOWERS, *Mrs. William Starr Dana*
Classic nature book that has introduced thousands to wonders of American wild flowers. Color-season principle of organization is easy to use, even by those with no botanical training, and the genial, refreshing discussions of history, folklore, uses of over 1,000 native and escape flowers, foliage plants are informative as well as fun to read. Over 170 full-page plates, collected from several editions, may be colored in to make permanent records of finds. Revised to conform with 1950 edition of Gray's Manual of Botany. xlii + 438pp. 5⅜ x 8½.   Paperbound $2.00

MANUAL OF THE TREES OF NORTH AMERICA, *Charles Sprague Sargent*
Still unsurpassed as most comprehensive, reliable study of North American tree characteristics, precise locations and distribution. By dean of American dendrologists. Every tree native to U.S., Canada, Alaska; 185 genera, 717 species, described in detail—leaves, flowers, fruit, winterbuds, bark, wood, growth habits, etc. plus discussion of varieties and local variants, immaturity variations. Over 100 keys, including unusual 11-page analytical key to genera, aid in identification. 783 clear illustrations of flowers, fruit, leaves. An unmatched permanent reference work for all nature lovers. Second enlarged (1926) edition. Synopsis of families. Analytical key to genera. Glossary of technical terms. Index. 783 illustrations, 1 map. Total of 982pp. 5⅜ x 8.
Vol. 1 Paperbound $2.25, Vol. 2 Paperbound $2.25,
The set $4.50

It's Fun to Make Things From Scrap Materials,
Evelyn Glantz Hershoff

What use are empty spools, tin cans, bottle tops? What can be made from rubber bands, clothes pins, paper clips, and buttons? This book provides simply worded instructions and large diagrams showing you how to make cookie cutters, toy trucks, paper turkeys, Halloween masks, telephone sets, aprons, linoleum block- and spatter prints — in all 399 projects! Many are easy enough for young children to figure out for themselves; some challenging enough to entertain adults; all are remarkably ingenious ways to make things from materials that cost pennies or less! Formerly "Scrap Fun for Everyone." Index. 214 illustrations. 373pp. 5⅜ x 8½. Paperbound $1.50

Symbolic Logic and The Game of Logic, *Lewis Carroll*

"Symbolic Logic" is not concerned with modern symbolic logic, but is instead a collection of over 380 problems posed with charm and imagination, using the syllogism and a fascinating diagrammatic method of drawing conclusions. In "The Game of Logic" Carroll's whimsical imagination devises a logical game played with 2 diagrams and counters (included) to manipulate hundreds of tricky syllogisms. The final section, "Hit or Miss" is a lagniappe of 101 additional puzzles in the delightful Carroll manner. Until this reprint edition, both of these books were rarities costing up to $15 each. Symbolic Logic: Index. xxxi + 199pp. The Game of Logic: 96pp. 2 vols. bound as one. 5⅜ x 8. Paperbound $2.00

Mathematical Puzzles of Sam Loyd, Part i
selected and edited by M. Gardner

Choice puzzles by the greatest American puzzle creator and innovator. Selected from his famous collection, "Cyclopedia of Puzzles," they retain the unique style and historical flavor of the originals. There are posers based on arithmetic, algebra, probability, game theory, route tracing, topology, counter and sliding block, operations research, geometrical dissection. Includes the famous "14-15" puzzle which was a national craze, and his "Horse of a Different Color" which sold millions of copies. 117 of his most ingenious puzzles in all. 120 line drawings and diagrams. Solutions. Selected references. xx + 167pp. 5⅜ x 8. Paperbound $1.00

String Figures and How to Make Them, *Caroline Furness Jayne*

107 string figures plus variations selected from the best primitive and modern examples developed by Navajo, Apache, pygmies of Africa, Eskimo, in Europe, Australia, China, etc. The most readily understandable, easy-to-follow book in English on perennially popular recreation. Crystal-clear exposition; step-by-step diagrams. Everyone from kindergarten children to adults looking for unusual diversion will be endlessly amused. Index. Bibliography. Introduction by A. C. Haddon. 17 full-page plates, 960 illustrations. xxiii + 401pp. 5⅜ x 8½. Paperbound $2.00

Paper Folding for Beginners, *W. D. Murray and F. J. Rigney*

A delightful introduction to the varied and entertaining Japanese art of origami (paper folding), with a full, crystal-clear text that anticipates every difficulty; over 275 clearly labeled diagrams of all important stages in creation. You get results at each stage, since complex figures are logically developed from simpler ones. 43 different pieces are explained: sailboats, frogs, roosters, etc. 6 photographic plates. 279 diagrams. 95pp. 5⅜ x 8⅜. Paperbound $1.00

PRINCIPLES OF ART HISTORY,
H. Wölfflin

Analyzing such terms as "baroque," "classic," "neoclassic," "primitive," "picturesque," and 164 different works by artists like Botticelli, van Cleve, Dürer, Hobbema, Holbein, Hals, Rembrandt, Titian, Brueghel, Vermeer, and many others, the author establishes the classifications of art history and style on a firm, concrete basis. This classic of art criticism shows what really occurred between the 14th-century primitives and the sophistication of the 18th century in terms of basic attitudes and philosophies. "A remarkable lesson in the art of seeing," *Sat. Rev. of Literature.* Translated from the 7th German edition. 150 illustrations. 254pp. 6⅛ x 9¼.   Paperbound $2.00

PRIMITIVE ART,
Franz Boas

This authoritative and exhaustive work by a great American anthropologist covers the entire gamut of primitive art. Pottery, leatherwork, metal work, stone work, wood, basketry, are treated in detail. Theories of primitive art, historical depth in art history, technical virtuosity, unconscious levels of patterning, symbolism, styles, literature, music, dance, etc. A must book for the interested layman, the anthropologist, artist, handicrafter (hundreds of unusual motifs), and the historian. Over 900 illustrations (50 ceramic vessels, 12 totem poles, etc.). 376pp. 5⅜ x 8.   Paperbound $2.25

THE GENTLEMAN AND CABINET MAKER'S DIRECTOR,
Thomas Chippendale

A reprint of the 1762 catalogue of furniture designs that went on to influence generations of English and Colonial and Early Republic American furniture makers. The 200 plates, most of them full-page sized, show Chippendale's designs for French (Louis XV), Gothic, and Chinese-manner chairs, sofas, canopy and dome beds, cornices, chamber organs, cabinets, shaving tables, commodes, picture frames, frets, candle stands, chimney pieces, decorations, etc. The drawings are all elegant and highly detailed; many include construction diagrams and elevations. A supplement of 24 photographs shows surviving pieces of original and Chippendale-style pieces of furniture. Brief biography of Chippendale by N. I. Bienenstock, editor of *Furniture World.* Reproduced from the 1762 edition. 200 plates, plus 19 photographic plates. vi + 249pp. 9⅛ x 12¼.   Paperbound $3.50

AMERICAN ANTIQUE FURNITURE: A BOOK FOR AMATEURS,
Edgar G. Miller, Jr.

Standard introduction and practical guide to identification of valuable American antique furniture. 2115 illustrations, mostly photographs taken by the author in 148 private homes, are arranged in chronological order in extensive chapters on chairs, sofas, chests, desks, bedsteads, mirrors, tables, clocks, and other articles. Focus is on furniture accessible to the collector, including simpler pieces and a larger than usual coverage of Empire style. Introductory chapters identify structural elements, characteristics of various styles, how to avoid fakes, etc. "We are frequently asked to name some book on American furniture that will meet the requirements of the novice collector, the beginning dealer, and . . . the general public. . . . We believe Mr. Miller's two volumes more completely satisfy this specification than any other work," *Antiques.* Appendix. Index. Total of vi + 1106pp. 7⅞ x 10¾.

Two volume set, paperbound $7.50

THE BAD CHILD'S BOOK OF BEASTS, MORE BEASTS FOR WORSE CHILDREN, and A MORAL ALPHABET, *H. Belloc*

Hardly and anthology of humorous verse has appeared in the last 50 years without at least a couple of these famous nonsense verses. But one must see the entire volumes — with all the delightful original illustrations by Sir Basil Blackwood — to appreciate fully Belloc's charming and witty verses that play so subacidly on the platitudes of life and morals that beset his day — and ours. A great humor classic. Three books in one. Total of 157pp. 5⅜ x 8.

Paperbound $1.00

THE DEVIL'S DICTIONARY, *Ambrose Bierce*

Sardonic and irreverent barbs puncturing the pomposities and absurdities of American politics, business, religion, literature, and arts, by the country's greatest satirist in the classic tradition. Epigrammatic as Shaw, piercing as Swift, American as Mark Twain, Will Rogers, and Fred Allen, Bierce will always remain the favorite of a small coterie of enthusiasts, and of writers and speakers whom he supplies with "some of the most gorgeous witticisms of the English language" (H. L. Mencken). Over 1000 entries in alphabetical order. 144pp. 5⅜ x 8. Paperbound $1.00

THE COMPLETE NONSENSE OF EDWARD LEAR.

This is the only complete edition of this master of gentle madness available at a popular price. *A Book of Nonsense, Nonsense Songs, More Nonsense Songs and Stories* in their entirety with all the old favorites that have delighted children and adults for years. The Dong With A Luminous Nose, The Jumblies, The Owl and the Pussycat, and hundreds of other bits of wonderful nonsense. 214 limericks, 3 sets of Nonsense Botany, 5 Nonsense Alphabets, 546 drawings by Lear himself, and much more. 320pp. 5⅜ x 8. Paperbound $1.00

THE WIT AND HUMOR OF OSCAR WILDE, *ed. by Alvin Redman*

Wilde at his most brilliant, in 1000 epigrams exposing weaknesses and hypocrisies of "civilized" society. Divided into 49 categories—sin, wealth, women, America, etc.—to aid writers, speakers. Includes excerpts from his trials, books, plays, criticism. Formerly "The Epigrams of Oscar Wilde." Introduction by Vyvyan Holland, Wilde's only living son. Introductory essay by editor. 260pp. 5⅜ x 8. Paperbound $1.00

A CHILD'S PRIMER OF NATURAL HISTORY, *Oliver Herford*

Scarcely an anthology of whimsy and humor has appeared in the last 50 years without a contribution from Oliver Herford. Yet the works from which these examples are drawn have been almost impossible to obtain! Here at last are Herford's improbable definitions of a menagerie of familiar and weird animals, each verse illustrated by the author's own drawings. 24 drawings in 2 colors; 24 additional drawings. vii + 95pp. 6½ x 6. Paperbound $1.00

THE BROWNIES: THEIR BOOK, *Palmer Cox*

The book that made the Brownies a household word. Generations of readers have enjoyed the antics, predicaments and adventures of these jovial sprites, who emerge from the forest at night to play or to come to the aid of a deserving human. Delightful illustrations by the author decorate nearly every page. 24 short verse tales with 266 illustrations. 155pp. 6⅝ x 9¼.

Paperbound $1.50

THE PRINCIPLES OF PSYCHOLOGY,
William James
The full long-course, unabridged, of one of the great classics of Western literature and science. Wonderfully lucid descriptions of human mental activity, the stream of thought, consciousness, time perception, memory, imagination, emotions, reason, abnormal phenomena, and similar topics. Original contributions are integrated with the work of such men as Berkeley, Binet, Mills, Darwin, Hume, Kant, Royce, Schopenhauer, Spinoza, Locke, Descartes, Galton, Wundt, Lotze, Herbart, Fechner, and scores of others. All contrasting interpretations of mental phenomena are examined in detail—introspective analysis, philosophical interpretation, and experimental research. "A classic," *Journal of Consulting Psychology.* "The main lines are as valid as ever," *Psychoanalytical Quarterly.* "Standard reading . . . a classic of interpretation," *Psychiatric Quarterly.* 94 illustrations. 1408pp. 5⅜ x 8.
Vol. 1 Paperbound $2.50, Vol. 2 Paperbound $2.50,
The set $5.00

VISUAL ILLUSIONS: THEIR CAUSES, CHARACTERISTICS AND APPLICATIONS,
M. Luckiesh
"Seeing is deceiving," asserts the author of this introduction to virtually every type of optical illusion known. The text both describes and explains the principles involved in color illusions, figure-ground, distance illusions, etc. 100 photographs, drawings and diagrams prove how easy it is to fool the sense: circles that aren't round, parallel lines that seem to bend, stationary figures that seem to move as you stare at them — illustration after illustration strains our credulity at what we see. Fascinating book from many points of view, from applications for artists, in camouflage, etc. to the psychology of vision. New introduction by William Ittleson, Dept. of Psychology, Queens College. Index. Bibliography. xxi + 252pp. 5⅜ x 8½. Paperbound $1.50

FADS AND FALLACIES IN THE NAME OF SCIENCE,
Martin Gardner
This is the standard account of various cults, quack systems, and delusions which have masqueraded as science: hollow earth fanatics. Reich and orgone sex energy, dianetics, Atlantis, multiple moons, Forteanism, flying saucers, medical fallacies like iridiagnosis, zone therapy, etc. A new chapter has been added on Bridey Murphy, psionics, and other recent manifestations in this field. This is a fair, reasoned appraisal of eccentric theory which provides excellent inoculation against cleverly masked nonsense. "Should be read by everyone, scientist and non-scientist alike," R. T. Birge, Prof. Emeritus of Physics, Univ. of California; Former President, American Physical Society. Index. x + 365pp. 5⅜ x 8. Paperbound $1.85

ILLUSIONS AND DELUSIONS OF THE SUPERNATURAL AND THE OCCULT,
D. H. Rawcliffe
Holds up to rational examination hundreds of persistent delusions including crystal gazing, automatic writing, table turning, mediumistic trances, mental healing, stigmata, lycanthropy, live burial, the Indian Rope Trick, spiritualism, dowsing, telepathy, clairvoyance, ghosts, ESP, etc. The author explains and exposes the mental and physical deceptions involved, making this not only an exposé of supernatural phenomena, but a valuable exposition of characteristic types of abnormal psychology. Originally titled "The Psychology of the Occult." 14 illustrations. Index. 551pp. 5⅜ x 8. Paperbound $2.25

FAIRY TALE COLLECTIONS, *edited by Andrew Lang*
Andrew Lang's fairy tale collections make up the richest shelf-full of traditional children's stories anywhere available. Lang supervised the translation of stories from all over the world—familiar European tales collected by Grimm, animal stories from Negro Africa, myths of primitive Australia, stories from Russia, Hungary, Iceland, Japan, and many other countries. Lang's selection of translations are unusually high; many authorities consider that the most familiar tales find their best versions in these volumes. All collections are richly decorated and illustrated by H. J. Ford and other artists.

THE BLUE FAIRY BOOK. 37 stories. 138 illustrations. ix + 390pp. 5⅜ x 8½.
Paperbound $1.50

THE GREEN FAIRY BOOK. 42 stories. 100 illustrations. xiii + 366pp. 5⅜ x 8½.
Paperbound $1.50

THE BROWN FAIRY BOOK. 32 stories. 50 illustrations, 8 in color. xii + 350pp. 5⅜ x 8½.
Paperbound $1.50

THE BEST TALES OF HOFFMANN, *edited by E. F. Bleiler*
10 stories by E. T. A. Hoffmann, one of the greatest of all writers of fantasy. The tales include "The Golden Flower Pot," "Automata," "A New Year's Eve Adventure," "Nutcracker and the King of Mice," "Sand-Man," and others. Vigorous characterizations of highly eccentric personalities, remarkably imaginative situations, and intensely fast pacing has made these tales popular all over the world for 150 years. Editor's introduction. 7 drawings by Hoffmann. xxxiii + 419pp. 5⅜ x 8½.
Paperbound $2.00

GHOST AND HORROR STORIES OF AMBROSE BIERCE, *edited by E. F. Bleiler*
Morbid, eerie, horrifying tales of possessed poets, shabby aristocrats, revived corpses, and haunted malefactors. Widely acknowledged as the best of their kind between Poe and the moderns, reflecting their author's inner torment and bitter view of life. Includes "Damned Thing," "The Middle Toe of the Right Foot," "The Eyes of the Panther," "Visions of the Night," "Moxon's Master," and over a dozen others. Editor's introduction. xxii + 199pp. 5⅜ x 8½.
Paperbound $1.25

THREE GOTHIC NOVELS, *edited by E. F. Bleiler*
Originators of the still popular Gothic novel form, influential in ushering in early 19th-century Romanticism. Horace Walpole's *Castle of Otranto*, William Beckford's *Vathek*, John Polidori's *The Vampyre*, and a *Fragment* by Lord Byron are enjoyable as exciting reading or as documents in the history of English literature. Editor's introduction. xi + 291pp. 5⅜ x 8½.
Paperbound $2.00

BEST GHOST STORIES OF LEFANU, *edited by E. F. Bleiler*
Though admired by such critics as V. S. Pritchett, Charles Dickens and Henry James, ghost stories by the Irish novelist Joseph Sheridan LeFanu have never become as widely known as his detective fiction. About half of the 16 stories in this collection have never before been available in America. Collection includes "Carmilla" (perhaps the best vampire story ever written), "The Haunted Baronet," "The Fortunes of Sir Robert Ardagh," and the classic "Green Tea." Editor's introduction. 7 contemporary illustrations. Portrait of LeFanu. xii + 467pp. 5⅜ x 8.
Paperbound $2.00

EASY-TO-DO ENTERTAINMENTS AND DIVERSIONS WITH COINS, CARDS, STRING, PAPER AND MATCHES, *R. M. Abraham*
Over 300 tricks, games and puzzles will provide young readers with absorbing fun. Sections on card games; paper-folding; tricks with coins, matches and pieces of string; games for the agile; toy-making from common household objects; mathematical recreations; and 50 miscellaneous pastimes. Anyone in charge of groups of youngsters, including hard-pressed parents, and in need of suggestions on how to keep children sensibly amused and quietly content will find this book indispensable. Clear, simple text, copious number of delightful line drawings and illustrative diagrams. Originally titled "Winter Nights' Entertainments." Introduction by Lord Bader Powell. 329 illustrations. v + 186pp. 5⅜ x 8½.   Paperbound $1.00

AN INTRODUCTION TO CHESS MOVES AND TACTICS SIMPLY EXPLAINED, *Leonard Barden*
Beginner's introduction to the royal game. Names, possible moves of the pieces, definitions of essential terms, how games are won, etc. explained in 30-odd pages. With this background you'll be able to sit right down and play. Balance of book teaches strategy — openings, middle game, typical endgame play, and suggestions for improving your game. A sample game is fully analyzed. True middle-level introduction, teaching you all the essentials without oversimplifying or losing you in a maze of detail. 58 figures. 102pp. 5⅜ x 8½.   Paperbound $1.00

LASKER'S MANUAL OF CHESS, *Dr. Emanuel Lasker*
Probably the greatest chess player of modern times, Dr. Emanuel Lasker held the world championship 28 years, independent of passing schools or fashions. This unmatched study of the game, chiefly for intermediate to skilled players, analyzes basic methods, combinations, position play, the aesthetics of chess, dozens of different openings, etc., with constant reference to great modern games. Contains a brilliant exposition of Steinitz's important theories. Introduction by Fred Reinfeld. Tables of Lasker's tournament record. 3 indices. 308 diagrams. 1 photograph. xxx + 349pp. 5⅜ x 8.   Paperbound $2.25

COMBINATIONS: THE HEART OF CHESS, *Irving Chernev*
Step-by-step from simple combinations to complex, this book, by a well-known chess writer, shows you the intricacies of pins, counter-pins, knight forks, and smothered mates. Other chapters show alternate lines of play to those taken in actual championship games; boomerang combinations; classic examples of brilliant combination play by Nimzovich, Rubinstein, Tarrasch, Botvinnik, Alekhine and Capablanca. Index. 356 diagrams. ix + 245pp. 5⅜ x 8½.   Paperbound $1.85

HOW TO SOLVE CHESS PROBLEMS, *K. S. Howard*
Full of practical suggestions for the fan or the beginner — who knows only the moves of the chessmen. Contains preliminary section and 58 two-move, 46 three-move, and 8 four-move problems composed by 27 outstanding American problem creators in the last 30 years. Explanation of all terms and exhaustive index. "Just what is wanted for the student," Brian Harley. 112 problems, solutions. vi + 171pp. 5⅜ x 8.   Paperbound $1.35

SOCIAL THOUGHT FROM LORE TO SCIENCE,
H. E. Barnes and H. Becker
An immense survey of sociological thought and ways of viewing, studying, planning, and reforming society from earliest times to the present. Includes thought on society of preliterate peoples, ancient non-Western cultures, and every great movement in Europe, America, and modern Japan. Analyzes hundreds of great thinkers: Plato, Augustine, Bodin, Vico, Montesquieu, Herder, Comte, Marx, etc. Weighs the contributions of utopians, sophists, fascists and communists; economists, jurists, philosophers, ecclesiastics, and every 19th and 20th century school of scientific sociology, anthropology, and social psychology throughout the world. Combines topical, chronological, and regional approaches, treating the evolution of social thought as a process rather than as a series of mere topics. "Impressive accuracy, competence, and discrimination . . . easily the best single survey," *Nation.* Thoroughly revised, with new material up to 1960. 2 indexes. Over 2200 bibliographical notes. Three volume set. Total of 1586pp. 5⅜ x 8.
Vol. 1 Paperbound $2.75, Vol. 2 Paperbound $2.75, Vol. 3 Paperbound $2.50
The set $8.00

A HISTORY OF HISTORICAL WRITING, *Harry Elmer Barnes*
Virtually the only adequate survey of the whole course of historical writing in a single volume. Surveys developments from the beginnings of historiography in the ancient Near East and the Classical World, up through the Cold War. Covers major historians in detail, shows interrelationship with cultural background, makes clear individual contributions, evaluates and estimates importance; also enormously rich upon minor authors and thinkers who are usually passed over. Packed with scholarship and learning, clear, easily written. Indispensable to every student of history. Revised and enlarged up to 1961. Index and bibliography. xv + 442pp. 5⅜ x 8½.   Paperbound $2.50

JOHANN SEBASTIAN BACH, *Philipp Spitta*
The complete and unabridged text of the definitive study of Bach. Written some 70 years ago, it is still unsurpassed for its coverage of nearly all aspects of Bach's life and work. There could hardly be a finer non-technical introduction to Bach's music than the detailed, lucid analyses which Spitta provides for hundreds of individual pieces. 26 solid pages are devoted to the B minor mass, for example, and 30 pages to the glorious St. Matthew Passion. This monumental set also includes a major analysis of the music of the 18th century: Buxtehude, Pachelbel, etc. "Unchallenged as the last word on one of the supreme geniuses of music," John Barkham, *Saturday Review Syndicate.* Total of 1819pp. Heavy cloth binding. 5⅜ x 8.
Two volume set, clothbound $13.50

BEETHOVEN AND HIS NINE SYMPHONIES, *George Grove*
In this modern middle-level classic of musicology Grove not only analyzes all nine of Beethoven's symphonies very thoroughly in terms of their musical structure, but also discusses the circumstances under which they were written, Beethoven's stylistic development, and much other background material. This is an extremely rich book, yet very easily followed; it is highly recommended to anyone seriously interested in music. Over 250 musical passages. Index. viii + 407pp. 5⅜ x 8.   Paperbound $2.00

THREE SCIENCE FICTION NOVELS,
John Taine

Acknowledged by many as the best SF writer of the 1920's, Taine (under the name Eric Temple Bell) was also a Professor of Mathematics of considerable renown. Reprinted here are *The Time Stream*, generally considered Taine's best, *The Greatest Game*, a biological-fiction novel, and *The Purple Sapphire*, involving a supercivilization of the past. Taine's stories tie fantastic narratives to frameworks of original and logical scientific concepts. Speculation is often profound on such questions as the nature of time, concept of entropy, cyclical universes, etc. 4 contemporary illustrations. v + 532pp. 5⅜ x 8⅜.

Paperbound $2.00

SEVEN SCIENCE FICTION NOVELS,
H. G. Wells

Full unabridged texts of 7 science-fiction novels of the master. Ranging from biology, physics, chemistry, astronomy, to sociology and other studies, Mr. Wells extrapolates whole worlds of strange and intriguing character. "One will have to go far to match this for entertainment, excitement, and sheer pleasure . . ."*New York Times*. Contents: The Time Machine, The Island of Dr. Moreau, The First Men in the Moon, The Invisible Man, The War of the Worlds, The Food of the Gods, In The Days of the Comet. 1015pp. 5⅜ x 8.

Clothbound $5.00

28 SCIENCE FICTION STORIES OF H. G. WELLS.

Two full, unabridged novels, *Men Like Gods* and *Star Begotten*, plus 26 short stories by the master science-fiction writer of all time! Stories of space, time, invention, exploration, futuristic adventure. Partial contents: *The Country of the Blind, In the Abyss, The Crystal Egg, The Man Who Could Work Miracles, A Story of Days to Come, The Empire of the Ants, The Magic Shop, The Valley of the Spiders, A Story of the Stone Age, Under the Knife, Sea Raiders*, etc. An indispensable collection for the library of anyone interested in science fiction adventure. 928pp. 5⅜ x 8.

Clothbound $4.50

THREE MARTIAN NOVELS,
Edgar Rice Burroughs

Complete, unabridged reprinting, in one volume, of Thuvia, Maid of Mars; Chessmen of Mars; The Master Mind of Mars. Hours of science-fiction adventure by a modern master storyteller. Reset in large clear type for easy reading. 16 illustrations by J. Allen St. John. vi + 490pp. 5⅜ x 8½.

Paperbound $1.85

AN INTELLECTUAL AND CULTURAL HISTORY OF THE WESTERN WORLD,
Harry Elmer Barnes

Monumental 3-volume survey of intellectual development of Europe from primitive cultures to the present day. Every significant product of human intellect traced through history: art, literature, mathematics, physical sciences, medicine, music, technology, social sciences, religions, jurisprudence, education, etc. Presentation is lucid and specific, analyzing in detail specific discoveries, theories, literary works, and so on. Revised (1965) by recognized scholars in specialized fields under the direction of Prof. Barnes. Revised bibliography. Indexes. 24 illustrations. Total of xxix + 1318pp.

Vol. 1 Paperbound $2.00, Vol. 2 Paperbound $2.00, Vol. 3 Paperbound $2.00,

The set $6.00

HEAR ME TALKIN' TO YA, *edited by Nat Shapiro and Nat Hentoff*
In their own words, Louis Armstrong, King Oliver, Fletcher Henderson, Bunk Johnson, Bix Beiderbecke, Billy Holiday, Fats Waller, Jelly Roll Morton, Duke Ellington, and many others comment on the origins of jazz in New Orleans and its growth in Chicago's South Side, Kansas City's jam sessions, Depression Harlem, and the modernism of the West Coast schools. Taken from taped conversations, letters, magazine articles, other first-hand sources. Editors' introduction. xvi + 429pp. 5⅜ x 8½. Paperbound $2.00

THE JOURNAL OF HENRY D. THOREAU
A 25-year record by the great American observer and critic, as complete a record of a great man's inner life as is anywhere available. Thoreau's Journals served him as raw material for his formal pieces, as a place where he could develop his ideas, as an outlet for his interests in wild life and plants, in writing as an art, in classics of literature, Walt Whitman and other contemporaries, in politics, slavery, individual's relation to the State, etc. The Journals present a portrait of a remarkable man, and are an observant social history. Unabridged republication of 1906 edition, Bradford Torrey and Francis H. Allen, editors. Illustrations. Total of 1888pp. 8⅜ x 12¼.
Two volume set, clothbound $25.00

A SHAKESPEARIAN GRAMMAR, *E. A. Abbott*
Basic reference to Shakespeare and his contemporaries, explaining through thousands of quotations from Shakespeare, Jonson, Beaumont and Fletcher, North's *Plutarch* and other sources the grammatical usage differing from the modern. First published in 1870 and written by a scholar who spent much of his life isolating principles of Elizabethan language, the book is unlikely ever to be superseded. Indexes. xxiv + 511pp. 5⅜ x 8½. Paperbound $2.75

FOLK-LORE OF SHAKESPEARE, *T. F. Thistelton Dyer*
Classic study, drawing from Shakespeare a large body of references to supernatural beliefs, terminology of falconry and hunting, games and sports, good luck charms, marriage customs, folk medicines, superstitions about plants, animals, birds, argot of the underworld, sexual slang of London, proverbs, drinking customs, weather lore, and much else. From full compilation comes a mirror of the 17th-century popular mind. Index. ix + 526pp. 5⅜ x 8½.
Paperbound $2.50

THE NEW VARIORUM SHAKESPEARE, *edited by H. H. Furness*
By far the richest editions of the plays ever produced in any country or language. Each volume contains complete text (usually First Folio) of the play, all variants in Quarto and other Folio texts, editorial changes by every major editor to Furness's own time (1900), footnotes to obscure references or language, extensive quotes from literature of Shakespearian criticism, essays on plot sources (often reprinting sources in full), and much more.

HAMLET, *edited by H. H. Furness*
Total of xxvi + 905pp. 5⅜ x 8½. Two volume set, paperbound $4.75

TWELFTH NIGHT, *edited by H. H. Furness*
Index. xxii + 434pp. 5⅜ x 8½. Paperbound $2.25

LA BOHEME BY GIACOMO PUCCINI,
translated and introduced by Ellen H. Bleiler
Complete handbook for the operagoer, with everything needed for full enjoy-ment except the musical score itself. Complete Italian libretto, with new, modern English line-by-line translation—the only libretto printing all repeats; biography of Puccini; the librettists; background to the opera, Murger's La Boheme, etc.; circumstances of composition and performances; plot summary; and pictorial section of 73 illustrations showing Puccini, famous singers and performances, etc. Large clear type for easy reading. 124pp. 5⅜ x 8½.
Paperbound $1.00

ANTONIO STRADIVARI: HIS LIFE AND WORK (1644-1737),
W. Henry Hill, Arthur F. Hill, and Alfred E. Hill
Still the only book that really delves into life and art of the incomparable Italian craftsman, maker of the finest musical instruments in the world today. The authors, expert violin-makers themselves, discuss Stradivari's ancestry, his construction and finishing techniques, distinguished characteristics of many of his instruments and their locations. Included, too, is story of introduction of his instruments into France, England, first revelation of their supreme merit, and information on his labels, number of instruments made, prices, mystery of ingredients of his varnish, tone of pre-1684 Stradivari violin and changes between 1684 and 1690. An extremely interesting, informative account for all music lovers, from craftsman to concert-goer. Republication of original (1902) edition. New introduction by Sydney Beck, Head of Rare Book and Manuscript Collections, Music Division, New York Public Library. Analytical index by Rembert Wurlitzer. Appendixes. 68 illustrations. 30 full-page plates. 4 in color. xxvi + 315pp. 5⅜ x 8½.
Paperbound $2.25

MUSICAL AUTOGRAPHS FROM MONTEVERDI TO HINDEMITH,
Emanuel Winternitz
For beauty, for intrinsic interest, for perspective on the composer's personality, for subtleties of phrasing, shading, emphasis indicated in the autograph but suppressed in the printed score, the mss. of musical composition are fascinating documents which repay close study in many different ways. This 2-volume work reprints facsimiles of mss. by virtually every major composer, and many minor figures—196 examples in all. A full text points out what can be learned from mss., analyzes each sample. Index. Bibliography. 18 figures. 196 plates. Total of 170pp. of text. 7⅞ x 10¾.
Vol. 1 Paperbound $2.00, Vol. 2 Paperbound $2.00,
The set $4.00

J. S. BACH,
Albert Schweitzer
One of the few great full-length studies of Bach's life and work, and the study upon which Schweitzer's renown as a musicologist rests. On first appear-ance (1911), revolutionized Bach performance. The only writer on Bach to be musicologist, performing musician, and student of history, theology and philosophy, Schweitzer contributes particularly full sections on history of Ger-man Protestant church music, theories on motivic pictorial representations in vocal music, and practical suggestions for performance. Translated by Ernest Newman. Indexes. 5 illustrations. 650 musical examples. Total of xix + 928pp. 5⅜ x 8½.
Vol. 1 Paperbound $2.00, Vol. 2 Paperbound $2.00,
The set $4.00

THE METHODS OF ETHICS, *Henry Sidgwick*
Propounding no organized system of its own, study subjects every major methodological approach to ethics to rigorous, objective analysis. Study discusses and relates ethical thought of Plato, Aristotle, Bentham, Clarke, Butler, Hobbes, Hume, Mill, Spencer, Kant, and dozens of others. Sidgwick retains conclusions from each system which follow from ethical premises, rejecting the faulty. Considered by many in the field to be among the most important treatises on ethical philosophy. Appendix. Index. xlvii + 528pp. 5⅜ x 8½.
Paperbound $2.50

TEUTONIC MYTHOLOGY, *Jakob Grimm*
A milestone in Western culture; the work which established on a modern basis the study of history of religions and comparative religions. 4-volume work assembles and interprets everything available on religious and folkloristic beliefs of Germanic people (including Scandinavians, Anglo-Saxons, etc.). Assembling material from such sources as Tacitus, surviving Old Norse and Icelandic texts, archeological remains, folktales, surviving superstitions, comparative traditions, linguistic analysis, etc. Grimm explores pagan deities, heroes, folklore of nature, religious practices, and every other area of pagan German belief. To this day, the unrivaled, definitive, exhaustive study. Translated by J. S. Stallybrass from 4th (1883) German edition. Indexes. Total of lxxvii + 1887pp. 5⅜ x 8½.   Four volume set, paperbound $10.00

THE I CHING, *translated by James Legge*
Called "The Book of Changes" in English, this is one of the Five Classics edited by Confucius, basic and central to Chinese thought. Explains perhaps the most complex system of divination known, founded on the theory that all things happening at any one time have characteristic features which can be isolated and related. Significant in Oriental studies, in history of religions and philosophy, and also to Jungian psychoanalysis and other areas of modern European thought. Index. Appendixes. 6 plates. xxi + 448pp. 5⅜ x 8½.
Paperbound $2.75

HISTORY OF ANCIENT PHILOSOPHY, *W. Windelband*
One of the clearest, most accurate comprehensive surveys of Greek and Roman philosophy. Discusses ancient philosophy in general, intellectual life in Greece in the 7th and 6th centuries B.C., Thales, Anaximander, Anaximenes, Heraclitus, the Eleatics, Empedocles, Anaxagoras, Leucippus, the Pythagoreans, the Sophists, Socrates, Democritus (20 pages), Plato (50 pages), Aristotle (70 pages), the Peripatetics, Stoics, Epicureans, Sceptics, Neo-platonists, Christian Apologists, etc. 2nd German edition translated by H. E. Cushman. xv + 393pp. 5⅜ x 8.
Paperbound $2.25

THE PALACE OF PLEASURE, *William Painter*
Elizabethan versions of Italian and French novels from *The Decameron*, Cinthio, Straparola, Queen Margaret of Navarre, and other continental sources — the very work that provided Shakespeare and dozens of his contemporaries with many of their plots and sub-plots and, therefore, justly considered one of the most influential books in all English literature. It is also a book that any reader will still enjoy. Total of cviii + 1,224pp.
Three volume set, Paperbound $6.75

The Wonderful Wizard of Oz, *L. F. Baum*
All the original W. W. Denslow illustrations in full color—as much a part of "The Wizard" as Tenniel's drawings are of "Alice in Wonderland." "The Wizard" is still America's best-loved fairy tale, in which, as the author expresses it, "The wonderment and joy are retained and the heartaches and nightmares left out." Now today's young readers can enjoy every word and wonderful picture of the original book. New introduction by Martin Gardner. A Baum bibliography. 23 full-page color plates. viii + 268pp. 5⅜ x 8.
Paperbound $1.50

The Marvelous Land of Oz, *L. F. Baum*
This is the equally enchanting sequel to the "Wizard," continuing the adventures of the Scarecrow and the Tin Woodman. The hero this time is a little boy named Tip, and all the delightful Oz magic is still present. This is the Oz book with the Animated Saw-Horse, the Woggle-Bug, and Jack Pumpkinhead. All the original John R. Neill illustrations, 10 in full color. 287pp. 5⅜ x 8.
Paperbound $1.50

Alice's Adventures Under Ground, *Lewis Carroll*
The original *Alice in Wonderland*, hand-lettered and illustrated by Carroll himself, and originally presented as a Christmas gift to a child-friend. Adults as well as children will enjoy this charming volume, reproduced faithfully in this Dover edition. While the story is essentially the same, there are slight changes, and Carroll's spritely drawings present an intriguing alternative to the famous Tenniel illustrations. One of the most popular books in Dover's catalogue. Introduction by Martin Gardner. 38 illustrations. 128pp. 5⅜ x 8½.
Paperbound $1.00

The Nursery "Alice," *Lewis Carroll*
While most of us consider *Alice in Wonderland* a story for children of all ages, Carroll himself felt it was beyond younger children. He therefore provided this simplified version, illustrated with the famous Tenniel drawings enlarged and colored in delicate tints, for children aged "from Nought to Five." Dover's edition of this now rare classic is a faithful copy of the 1889 printing, including 20 illustrations by Tenniel, and front and back covers reproduced in full color. Introduction by Martin Gardner. xxiii + 67pp. 6⅛ x 9¼.
Paperbound $1.50

The Story of King Arthur and His Knights, *Howard Pyle*
A fast-paced, exciting retelling of the best known Arthurian legends for young readers by one of America's best story tellers and illustrators. The sword Excalibur, wooing of Guinevere, Merlin and his downfall, adventures of Sir Pellias and Gawaine, and others. The pen and ink illustrations are vividly imagined and wonderfully drawn. 41 illustrations. xviii + 313pp. 6⅛ x 9¼.
Paperbound $1.50

Prices subject to change without notice.

Available at your book dealer or write for free catalogue to Dept. Adsci, Dover Publications, Inc., 180 Varick St., N.Y., N.Y. 10014. Dover publishes more than 150 books each year on science, elementary and advanced mathematics, biology, music, art, literary history, social sciences and other areas.